The Heart of Play

— Games Manual —

Over 200 Activities for Connection & Joy

Howard Moody

Copyright, 2018
ISBN: 9781717700865
Heart of Play Publishing

www.howardmoody.com

Dedicated to all the children of the world, and to those who care for them.

The Heart of Play

Howard Moody

Acknowledgments

I want to thank the wonderful play teachers who have inspired me, and continue to inspire, me on this path. John O'connell, Bill Michealis, Pam Clelland, Joe Killian, Karl Rohnke and Steve Butler with Project Adventure, Gail Straub, The New Games Foundation, Frank Aycox, Jeanne Basis, Matt Weinstein with Playfair, David Darling, Artie Kamiya with Great Activities Publishing Company, Steve Gross with Life is Good Playmakers, and Martin Demaat of Second City Theater.

Joseph Chilton Pearce, for his pioneering research and his playful manner.

O. Fred Donaldson for his pioneering work on Original Play, and teaching me to get down on the ground and be in touch with children and thus knowing what is the Heart of Play.

All of the people that were a part of the Adventure Game Theater family.

To all of my Omega community, both guests and staff who have played with me, shared their energy, and supported my work.

To all the students I taught at the Woodstock Day School.

To all my colleagues and friends at ECRS for supporting my work and believing in my mission to bring more play into the world

To Jenn, Ann, Marcy, Jaye & Chris, Trisha, and Brian who gave me homes to stay in while I was doing my best to be a writer.

To Julia, Jane, John, Emily T., Emily D., Teddie, Chris, Hannah, Sara, Corey, Z, and all my other friends from Retribe. You are the best.

To Howard Glasser for pushing, prodding, guiding, and inspiring me to write.

And to Brian Allison, book editor and best friend—enough said.

The Heart of Play

Table of Contents

Acknowledgments vii

The Heart Of Play 3

How I became a Play Specialist 7

The Importance of Play 10

Play Leadership 15

Name Games 36

Ice Breakers & Energizers 45

Circle Games 82

Games for Younger Kids 106

Active Games 125

Tag Games 143

Games of Wildness 157

Trust Games & Activities 169

Games of Mindfulness 184

Team-Building Exercises 200

Communication & Sharing Exercises 218

The Art of Saying Yes 230

Improv Warm-Up Games 233

Improv Partner (or Small Group) Exercises 251

Improv Performance Structures 264

Resources 289

Index of Games 293

The Heart of Play

Howard Moody

The Heart of Play

Introduction

The Heart Of Play

Educating the mind without educating the heart is no education at all.
                                                                Aristotle

Over all the years that I have facilitated play experiences for thousands of children and adults, people have often asked me to write a book. I am glad to finally say, here it is. This is a comprehensive collection of over 200 games and exercises that foster playful connection and deep engagement. I hope my contribution to the world of playfulness will inspire you to bring more play into the lives of children.

Play is all about connection and joy, like an outward expression of what is in our hearts when we are most alive. Innately, we all love to play together, to laugh, and to experience joy, all from a place of safety, physically and emotionally. In essence, everyone wants to be seen and heard, to feel connected, and to have a sense of belonging. The games in this play manual, when led skillfully, work on all those levels, which is especially important for children, since play is the way they experience, discover, and engage with the world around them. Play is, most wonderfully, their primary mode of being.

Studies show the unequivocal importance of play in the healthy development of children. Especially the kind of play that involves social interaction. The games in this book are in a category I call, Integrative Social Play (ISP), and are all very effective in producing these kind of benefits. This book teaches you how to get the most out of these play experiences, and it also gives me the chance to describe the games and offer you key teaching points, as well as game variations, and highlighting educational elements, for teachers, counselors, parents, youth group workers, or really anyone who works with children. I also wanted to write something that would inspire the reader to delve more deeply into the study of why play is important for any child—and, for that matter, the child within all of us that still loves, and needs, to play.

Another motivation for me in writing this, is to help people who might

The Heart of Play

suffer from a bit of a "play deficit" to reconnect with the simple magic that is light-hearted play.

The problem is that play is still often misunderstood, underutilized, and undervalued in our society, and even in our educational systems. I hope to leave you with a newfound commitment to bring more and more play back into your life. The bulk of this book is simply games that work, games that I have used in over thirty years of leading play, with both children and adults. So, if you are an experienced leader of games, feel free to just jump in and use them. Bring them to life, maybe find some new favorites.

A primary focus of this book is on games that integrate easily within any curriculum and learning environment for school aged children that will help to build the social emotional competencies so important for the development of the whole child. As I encountered many other modalities of education, including from the fields of Social Emotional Learning (SEL), positive psychology, and mindfulness in education, I knew that Integrative Social Play touched into each of these bodies of knowledge. At a conference where I heard Linda Lantierri, a leader in the field of SEL, speaking brilliantly on the subject, I said to myself, Wow, I have been essentially teaching these skills in my play-shops and theater camps for over twenty years.

This collection is also meant as a follow up to the book, *Nurtured Heart Play*, which is the collaborative project I recently completed with Howard Glasser, the founder of the Nurtured Heart Approach (NHA®), and his master editor Melissa Lowenstein. NHA is a process that touches deeply on the importance of the social-emotional needs of children. In that book, I had the honor of taking the amazing process of the NHA and blending it with the Integrative Social Play model that I have been developing. In that book, I included 25 of my favorite heart-of-play games and activities, to be used in conjunction with the NHA—thus the title. While working on that book, as I was writing down the hundreds of great games I have used in my work, I thought, why not also create a companion resource for anyone who reads *Nurtured Heart Play*, and wants more activities to use. Or for anyone who just wants lots of great games.

To facilitate play effectively, there are techniques and perspectives that help to create the environment which fosters social-emotional learning and interpersonal connection. It is a vital responsibility on the part of the adult to inspire healthy physical movement, creative expression, and playfulness that will truly enhance the social-emotional intelligence of children.

Since play is so varied, so full of possibilities, and continually changing, all

Introduction

I can give you are some easy entry points with games that work well, as I have seen over and over again. This collection, with am emphasis on cooperation, creativity, fun, social engagement, and inclusiveness, will help people to experience feelings of connection and joy. Hopefully, this games manual, while reminding us all of the importance of play, will also inspire the acknowledgment of greatness in each other.

It is a responsibility on the part of the adult to inspire and model healthy physical movement, creative expression, and enthusiasm, and to offer as many play experiences that meet the social emotional needs of children. I hope this games manual will be a resource that inspires you to that—and more. To the very Heart of Play.

> From what I understand, games cannot be copy written, but rather exist in a public domain of play. Games that are shared and spread organically throughout society in a kind of folk tradition, orally or otherwise. The exception would be the reproduction of printed material. Most of the games in this book I've learned from various play teachers and organizations over my many years of training and facilitating. I will do my best to note those, however, I am sure I will forget where I learned some of them. I apologize to anyone that I have forgotten. I believe all my fellow teachers would want these games being played more, and in whatever way we get them out into the world is great. I have written them in my own words, and done my best to keep them concise, clear, usable, and—most importantly of all—fun.

The Heart of Play

Introduction

How I became a Play Specialist

"Play is the royal road to childhood happiness and adult brilliance."
—Joseph Chilton Pearce

I have been fascinated by play all my life. I have always been prone to making up games as a kid, even in college. I also loved playing sports. After college I came back to my hometown and coached high school wrestling. While coaching, I became passionate about peak performance. I read *The Ultimate Athlete*, by George Leonard. Though it was a book about athletic performance, he also wrote about something called the New Games festival, which he started with Stuart Brand out in California. The event was designed to get everyone playing together in ways that were different than in traditional sports, with an emphasis on lightheartedness and not on keeping score. Their motto was, "Play Hard. Play Fair. Nobody Hurt."

I could already see the need in our society for more of this kind of interaction and connection. I attended trainings from the New Games Foundation with inspiring instructors like Joe Killian and Bill Michaelis, which really lit the fire of love for play facilitation in me. During one training, we took a field trip to visit The Games Barn, in Pennsylvania. This was a big rustic structure that Bernie DeKoven had outfitted with—you guessed it—games of all kinds: ping pong, foosball, darts, board games, pinball, frisbees, etc. (Best field trip ever.)

I mention that because Bernie wrote a book called, *A Well Played Game*, in which he introduced me to the work of Mihaly Csikszentmihalyi, author of the now-classic book called, *Flow, the Psychology of Optimal Experience*. The Flow state is the experience that athletes describe when they are "in the zone." Bernie talked about how we can create those kinds of experiences in a well-played game, where everyone is in the moment, having fun, feeling included, feeling safe. And maybe feeling challenged enough physically and mentally to produce full-on engagement. I loved this concept of everyone playing for the purpose of joyous, peak experience, and creating interpersonal dynamics rich in learning opportunities.

The Heart of Play

After attending three New Game trainings, I began offering workshops to teachers and mental health care professionals, thus launching my career as a play facilitator. The rest, as they say, is history—a very playful history.

Ever since I took that first New Games training in 1978, I have been interested in the fields of recreation, alternative education, and play. I studied at Goddard College where I created my own curriculum and focused on adventure playgrounds and cooperative play. I also studied the work of Joseph Chilton Pearce, a pioneer in brain development though play and imagination, and other leaders in the field of childhood development. I went on to train with Project Adventure and its founder, Karl Rhonke, a true innovator in the field of progressive recreation.

Eventually, my love of play inspired me to co-create, with Brian Allison, an experimental theater process called the Adventure Game Theater (AGT), which we adapted for teens in 1987. AGT was featured on NPR and PBS in the mid 90s for the unique way in which it created community for teens. This innovative process continues to be played today, now run by the staff that grew up playing in our stories. The creation of this process for teens led me to a more serious study in improvisational theater. I was fortunate to have had the opportunity to train with Martin De Maat, the creative director of the renowned Second City Theater.

One of the other most influential experiences for me was discovering the work of O. Fred Donaldson, the international play specialist who coined the term "original play". Fred's work deepened my understanding of how important play is in the healthy development of a human being. A child needs that complete sense of healthy loving attachment to their parents, and then to others. Fred's work left a profound impact on me about the fullness and essence of what I know about play, because it clearly demonstrates how all mammals have a desire for belonging, connection, and a feeling of being loved—all of which occur through natural childhood play. Much of which being lost.

We need to run and chase and flee. We need to jump on the back of our mom and dad, to roll around on the ground, to be chased around the house. We want to play in the dirt with our brothers and sisters, and friends. This rough and tumble play, as some call it, is really not rough at all. It is full-on engagement with our mind-body essence. It is so simple and yet so profound in its impact.

Play is a uniquely developmental process, and mysterious, sometimes elusive—yet it can be brought forth. And that is the work of the Play Specialist.

Introduction

This Games Manual is primarily focused on group play, and games that can be played with school-aged children. I call the games in this collection an example of Integrative Social Play, or Integral Play, because they embody so many of the principles in social-emotional learning as well as the traditional benefits of play for children.

At each stage of their lives, kids grow and change in their preferences of play activities. The phenomenon of children playing begins as soon as they start exploring the world around them soon after they are born. The beginnings of which are simple play experiences with their immediate environment and care givers, the gentle touch of squeezing a hand, peek-a-boo, crawling, exploring toys with their mouth and hands, mirroring what they see from those around them. It's all developmental, and it's all play. Those first few years, fully immersed in loving touch and play, are crucial for the development of the healthy child, and continues throughout life. We are all still social playmates.

In the Resources section, you will find, *Hand in Hand Parenting*, and *Playful Parenting*, by Lawrence Cohen, as well as the work of Peter Gray, who advocates more Free Play. I'll leave those areas of expertise to their wisdom, as you go on to learn as much as you can about play. The world may be slow to grasp the significance of Original Play, but the games and exercises in this book should fit easily into any curriculum or group setting where people are looking for connection, engagement, and fun.

Over these years of leading hundreds of play-shops, immersive Adventure Game Theatre weeks, and humor workshops, I see that my life has been filled with play, and people have come to regard me as an expert on the topic. And yet sometimes I feel like I am only a beginner, following the lead of the child who is so much the embodiment of playfulness. Kids have the raw energy of play, and adults can provide the direction and structure, each benefiting from the other. But it is our job to provide the proper environment and guidance. Whether you are a teacher, parent, counselor or caretaker, Integrative Social Play will open up your connection with children, and requires only a willingness to get down and engage with them wholeheartedly. Play gives us the chance to enter into the world that is natural for children, which is sometimes difficult for adults, but very much worth the effort.

The Heart of Play

The Importance of Play

In my early days of leading play I found myself at the Omega Institute for Holistic Studies, where I had the great opportunity to work with Omega's Community leader, Stephen Pague. It was there that I began to see how deeply play can be used to help people of all ages connect to their hearts. Since Omega was becoming the leading holistic retreat center in the world, during the next number of years I also had the opportunity to be exposed to other great teachers, experts in mindfulness, holistic health, alternative education, and the healing arts. As I learned from these many other modalities, including the fields of social-emotional learning and positive psychology, I knew that play has the potential to touch on each of these.

At the same time, I was becoming more and more aware that play was largely misunderstood and painfully undervalued in our society, and that a kind of crisis was emerging. I saw kids with less and less access to the natural world than those in my generation had when growing up—less freedom to explore their neighborhoods and create their own games, less playtime at school, more time spent viewing screens and less time engaged with others. I sensed, with some degree of severity, that the well-being of children was going to suffer as a result. Could it be that this lack of play, and this change in the way kids were playing, was producing a generation of youngsters who struggled with self-regulation and feelings of alienation? Was a simple play-deficit part of the reason that more and more children were being diagnosed with ADD, ADHD, and other mental health issues?

Leaders in the field of Social-Emotional Learning and of Mindfulness in Education seem to be suggesting as much, and I knew my work was on the right track. I wanted to tell a story that threaded all of these modalities together, to try and write a book about how Integrative Social Play touches the heart and brings us together in ways that are uniquely beneficial. Then I met Howard Glasser at Omega, and collaborated with him on the book, *Nurtured Heart Play*, which took this whole process of teaching New Games, cooperative play and theater games to another level.

As Karl Rohnke, the founder of Project Adventure, said in one of his trainings, a collection of games like this can help you, "To have your best bag of tricks."

Introduction

And so, *The Heart of Play Games Manual* will give you bags-full. Whether for classroom teachers, parents, counselors, youth group leaders, facilitators, or anyone who wants to create greater engagement and connection, fun and laughter within your community, this book is meant to provide you with a fairly broad range of activities. I also give you guidelines on play leadership, ways to debrief games, ways to focus on the lessons being learned, the social-emotional needs being met.

The stakes are high in the modern world, and the challenge of raising healthy kids growing up into this society is enormous. We have to get back to some basics. Our kids need to move and play, to be in nature, and to receive the kind of modeling that teaches empathetic social interaction. From the non-verbal quality of connection that comes from Original Play, to the transformational neurolinguistics of the Nurtured Heart Approach, play can help us do that in so many ways.

I also know that teachers, administrators and parents will still be hesitant to really make a commitment to add more play into their curriculum. In our society we have a belief that play is frivolous, an extra to be added but not as a core value. For that reason I want to state far and wide that play offers so many answers to what plagues our culture at this point in time. Prioritize play!

As I was writing the book, *Nurtured Heart Play* and now this, *Heart of Play Games Manual*, I came upon two books that deepened my knowledge around what it is that children need to succeed in life.

One book is, *How Children Succeed,* by Paul Tough. The other is, *Creative Schools,* by Sir Ken Robinson. Both verified for me how controversial it is to create dynamic learning environments for children where they can truly receive what it is they need to go on to live happy, fulfilled and successful lives. There are many deeply held belief systems and indoctrination rather than methods based on good research. The educational models that are often used today are based on an industrial age assembly-line mentality that has been around for so many decades. In today's high-tech world with things changing so fast, what is it that children truly need to be successful learners and citizens? There are also many political, societal and cultural held views that limit adults from truly looking at what makes dynamic and successful learning environments.

The essential message in these two books that I would like to synthesize here can be boiled down to two basic principals. One is we need more play, more creativity, art, music dance, and theater in our schools—not less. The second is that the social-emotional needs of children are of utmost importance. I urge you

The Heart of Play

to read these two books because in there is credible scientific research which will verify what I am saying. Also there are numerous stories and examples of teachers, psychologists, school administrators, researchers, parents etc., who have created successful learning environments and comprehensive culture-wide programming that truly makes a difference.

We need a collective outcry from parents, teachers, administrators, mental health professionals, and youth workers that will be based on strong evidence-based research—and common sense—about what children need. The dissonance comes from what Paul Tough calls the cognitive dilemma. Many educators, parents, administrators, policy makers and politicians strongly believe that with more emphasis on the development of cognitive skills that children will be more successful. This has been driving educational policy for quite some time, resulting in a movement toward more academics at younger and younger ages. Work-sheets in preschool and kindergarten. More homework for elementary students. Read at a younger age. No child left behind? The research says otherwise. Any early gains in academic achievement disappear by third or fourth grade. The kids who played more did better.

> For students to thrive in school and classroom settings they need that deep connection to their teachers, mentors, aides counselors and fellow students. Creating an environment of safety, engagement and trust is vital for students to feel ready, willing and able to learn. It's all about building relational trust. The games, exercises and concepts in this Heart Of Play Manual are ideal for doing just that."

Introduction

What the research bears out is that SEL-based programming, play-based programming, character-education programming, and mindfulness initiatives all help in developing healthy learners. Paul Tough brought awareness to the benefits of character education. Developed from the positive psychology movement, the educational world has identified 20+ character qualities that a human needs to develop fully to be successful, empowered and happy as an adult. He refers to the work by the researchers David Levin and Dominic Randolph, who break it down to the most important seven character traits of Grit, Self Control, Zest, Social Intelligence, Gratitude, Optimism, and Curiosity.

The studies show that what truly creates success in adult life is having fully developed these character traits. And when educational institutions focus on highlighting and teaching these social-emotionally-learned behaviors and character qualities children flourish.

I decided to be bold and change these seven character traits just a bit and highlight eight, as you can see in the logo inside this book. I chose to use Mindfulness in place of Social Intelligence, just as a means to underscore this important new movement in education. I also chose to add Empathy, because of its key role in social well-being. It is central to effective communication. Really, social intelligence, as Paul Tough describes it, is really just a combination of mindfulness and empathy. And then I chose to use Playfulness in place of Zest as a more encompassing term. It seems to me that of all the character qualities, playfulness actually contains or inspires all the other traits. And that is why these games are so effective.

This is barely an introduction to these multifaceted and complex arenas of Social Emotional Learning, character development and mindfulness. All I want is that This *Heart of Play Manual*, along with *Nurtured Heart Play* to serve as a guide, a tool, a resource, and an inspiration to add more play into a child's life. In playing more and then focusing on what has been learned during play, reflecting on the positive character traits being expressed and using play of course for fun, connection and engagement there is an opportunity to learn together: learning how to be caring, strong, kind, resourceful, imaginative, creative and positive.

I feel eternally grateful to have learned from these great teachers, all of them fueling the fire of my love and respect for the art of play. The scope of my work feels rather complete these days, like something worth sharing, and with the societal need urging me on, it more and more feels like something that must be shared. May these contents fill your heart with the spirit of play!

The Heart of Play

Introduction

Play Leadership

"We must become the people we want our children to be."

—Joseph Chilton Pearce

Play has a magical quality. Play helps people connect to each other and to the joy that lies authentically inside them. Whenever a group gathers for class meetings or events, play can be used to break the ice, to help bring down barriers, to learn names, and to convey that although there will be other work or learning that will happen, there will also be lots of time for fun and connection. Part of the magic is knowing what game to choose for that particular group, what goals you have for them, how to lead the game effectively with enthusiasm, and how to make smooth transitions between games or activities. These are just some of the skills of being a good "play leader".

These games are some of the best that I have found in helping to create a safe play space and bring the participants into feeling they are part of a fun and supportive community. These activities work with most groups, and many are perfect for mixed ages. If you will be working with a particular age group, often it is just a matter of changing or adapting an activity to meet the needs of your group. The main thing in these games is an, "everyone wins when everyone-participates" philosophy.

From sports to board games, we have been deeply ingrained in games that emphasize competitive, win/lose scenarios. This often leads to a lack of connection, and even hurt feelings—particularly for younger children. Unfortunately, this zero-sum mentality carries over to the way many of us view life, as well. It is of utmost importance that you communicate, in the first few minutes of your play session, that the games you will be leading are primarily cooperative, not competitive. Everyone is working together to make if fun for everyone.

The games in this manual, for the most part, do not have winners and losers. However, when there is some competition it is not the primary emphasis. The more we, as play leaders and teachers, can embody the fun and cooperative

The Heart of Play

possibilities even within competitive games the more effective these games can be at fostering connection.

These games generally fall into several overlapping categories:

- ⌘ Games for creating and deepening connection
- ⌘ Games for creating laughter and lifting spirits
- ⌘ Games for awareness of being a cooperative member of a group
- ⌘ Activities that focus on awareness, trust, and relationship building
- ⌘ Active games that inspire and elicit vigorous movement
- ⌘ Team-building games that foster problem solving and creativity
- ⌘ Games of imagination and freedom of expression (Improv theater)

As you put together a playshop, or just leading one or two games keep these categories in mind and choose according to your intentions for the group. Do they need to be energized, or are you looking for a variety of ways to teach principles of connection, compassion and mindfulness? Perhaps your goal is to help them build relationships and experience genuine connection. Often you will want to do all of this and more. There is usually enough time to address multiple goals with a good list of games.

If some participants are hesitant to play at first, it's important to emphasize the non-competitive nature of the games, and that together we will all create a sense of safety.

With adult groups, when I mention that we are going to play for a while, many people react as if it is a scary proposition. That person probably has a play deficit. For many adults, by the time they are adolescents, play is primarily a competitive situation and the win/lose scenarios of competition becomes very unenjoyable.

There are some games here that are mildly competitive and these activities can be used in such a way as to bring to everyone's awareness the difference between competitive and cooperative play. You can use a slightly competitive but very silly game like Gotcha to get everyone laughing. Or you can use an obviously competitive game like Stand-off in juxtaposition with a game that requires cooperation to succeed, like Human Spring, to let players feel the difference and reflect on how they react to each.

Introduction

For some people the risk in play is not in losing, but in appearing foolish. This can be especially challenging with teens, who are hyper-conscious of how they come across to their peers. Most people will gladly risk being playful and silly when they feel safe, but it is vital to be patient and understanding that this is an opportunity they may not have had in quite some time. Your job is to establish a safe, non judgmental space and facilitate the growth of community with those same qualities. Given the high-pressure environments in which most of us live and work, it is a relief for many adults, and children alike, to experience a place where play and games are meant to be a fun experience for everyone. The activities in this book are designed to help facilitate maximal inclusiveness.

Creating a safe environment for this exploration is your responsibility as a play leader. It is also a privilege. I think of these cooperative games as, "Exercises for the Interpersonal Heart!"

Establish a safe and fun tone by being inviting, enthusiastic, and playful even in introducing what you are about to do. You might want to remind them that there is much more going on than meets the eye with these Integrative Social Play exercises. There is a great quote from Plato, "You can lean more about a person in an hour of play than a year of conversation."

In the realm of playfulness, everyone has permission to explore the possibilities within themselves. Emphasize that mistakes are okay. And fun equals success.

Since play brings people quickly into a present-moment experience, and can bring up many feelings, it is valuable to take a few moments for reflection and awareness during, and especially at the end of a play session. Ask the players to take a moment and notice how they are feeling. Be aware of any anxiety and resistance that may come up for anyone and you can address it compassionately. Many people have been hurt during play or have become very judgmental of themselves when they make mistakes, so games can sometimes bring up these thoughts and feelings. Consider how you want to address the need for grounding and reflection and you can build these into your game flow.

Whenever possible, start in a circle to create a sense of the group as a whole. Do be aware of group size, as some circle games work best with only ten to twenty people (the game description includes a recommended size for each activity). In a large group (about 30 or more) it is good to begin with an energizer such as Gotcha, and then move into some big circle games that let players learn about each other with games like Have You Ever, or The Cool Breeze Blows. Name Games are always important, but in large groups they can take a long time, so it is

The Heart of Play

good to do a few energizers first to make sure everyone is engaged.

If you are working with a lot of people, you may wish to break them into pairs and small groups after a few circle games, to promote more intimate interactions and allow for a more diverse selection of games.

This manual also includes some tag and active games that you might use with groups who want to move a lot. As children grow into later childhood (8-11) and adolescence they enjoy a good challenge. If you lead some of the more competitively based games, a nice conceptual framework that you may want to relate is from Jenna Marcovicci, a well-known teacher at the Omega Institute who for many years taught "The Dance of Tennis." He talked passionately about the idea that all players are your partners in any game. For example, your opponent across the net in tennis is essentially your partner; she has agreed to come and play the game with you according to the rules. Yes, you may keep score, and there may be a winner and loser at the end, but this person is still your partner in creating the drama of the game.

Choosing the level of competition and silliness is based on your evaluation of the group's openness and energy. Games such as Elephant/Rabbit/Palm Tree or Groove-a-Liscious are fantastic when groups are ready for it, but they can garner resistance if players are still worried about making mistakes. Much of that will depend on your ability to pull them into the experience; they will love it if you make it safe, funny, and engaging.

You may need to specifically address this and ask inviting questions like:
"Are you ready to get a little crazy?"
"Are you willing to laugh at your own mistakes?"
This will set the tone for non judgmental fun and alert them that they need to let their guard down in order to fully enjoy it.

Simple theater games and exercises are excellent to intersperse in most play sessions. Games such as Memory Loss, Gibberish Translator, and What Are You Doing... are played in dyads or triads and are relatively easy to teach. In addition to those listed in this manual, there are lots of improv game books and an array of games available online. One book I especially want to recommend is, *Playing Along,* by Izzy Gessell.

Introduction

Key Concepts

The following are a few concepts and pointers to keep in mind when leading play.

— Fun —

First and foremost is fun. This Heart of Play manual is about bringing people together, enjoying each other, feeling connected and having fun. One way to do that is by sharing play with joy in your heart, being playful, engaging and even silly at times.

— Creativity —

Bring as much to each game as you can, with variations and adding your own elements and characters. Being a little zany can be a form of creativity.

Introduce the games with stories when possible. Make up a fantasy story that supports the game. I love the books written by Karl Rohnke because he always tells great stories to introduce the games, but that is not my style.

I have tried to make the description of the games simple to follow and concise for maximum utility.

— Clarity —

In fact, that is how I tend to teach. I have always tried to be really clear with directions, and I want to be as concise as possible. I err on the side of keeping the directions brief and starting to play the game as soon as possible. Then stopping along the way to clarify anything, rather than going on too long with game descriptions and have people get bored.

Using a list of games that you have created ahead of time can help with delivering a crisp session that adds to its clarity.

— Collaboration —

It is always fun to plan a play session with a another teacher. Compare notes beforehand if you can, so you are both on the same page.

Inviting the players to make suggestions, as in many Improv games, is another way in which this collaborative magic can happen.

The Heart of Play

Before getting everyone's attention and launching into verbal instructions, remember the acronym **DDADA**:

Describe (the Activity) – Share the intentions of the game, and teach the rules playfully and with enthusiasm. Remember though that brevity is the soul of playfulness.

Demonstrate (the Activity) – A quick demonstration helps all those visual and kinesthetic learners.

Ask (Questions) – Ask everyone if they understand and re-clarify if anyone is at all confused.

Do (It) – Start playing the game as quickly as possible. After all, that's what everyone is there for.

Adapt (Whatever you need to) – If something isn't working, stop, reclarify the rules if necessary and suggest some changes, or ask the group for some suggestions on how to change the game to fit the needs of everyone.

Another very important concepts for keeping everyone active and engaged is **MAP**. This stands for *Maximum Activity Plan*. Ideally everyone should be as fully involved in games and exercises as possible. For example, the game of kickball is not a game with a good MAP. One person kicks and runs and usually one or two fielders get involved—and everyone else is standing around watching.

A game like Elephant/Rabbit/Palm Tree is a great circle game, but if there are thirty people in the circle and only one It in the center there are a lot of people just watching. Once the game gets going and everyone understands how it works, you can improve the MAP of this activity by adding an extra It or two (or three or four!).

A game like Asteroids has a great MAP, where everyone is playing. And Tag games where everyone is moving, like Elves and Wizards Tag or Everybody's It, naturally have great MAPs. There are a few guidelines with these games to maximize engagement. The first is to balance the number of Its with the number of players. A good ratio is to have one It per ten players. The other main thing to keep in mind is the size of your playing field. For a running tag game like Elves and Wizards tag, setting the boundaries too close can make the game crowded

Introduction

and not safe, and too far apart and there is too much running involved and not enough action. And older kids need a bigger space than younger kids. Usually an area the half the size of a basketball court is suitable for 20 to 30 players of any age. And you can always adjust the boundaries according to the situation.

There are situations where it is fun for a group to be observing other people play. That is the beauty of many circle games. But it's still important to remember the concept of a MAP.

Attention Getters

Facilitating play is an art requiring a set of skills. One of the most important is being able to get the group's attention, getting them to focus without resorting to yelling, or blowing a gym teacher's whistle, or—worst of all—telling them to, "Shut up!"

One good way, an old standard, is to raise your hand and then everyone who notices follows by raising their hands as it spreads to everyone.

Another favorite is to say, "If you can hear the sound of my voice clap once… If you can hear the sound of my voice clap twice," etc. Usually by three claps everyone is paying attention.

Amplified microphones are great when there are large numbers of people, but don't worry if you don't have one. Using these techniques and really projecting your voice when you need to will get you through most everything.

Some friends of mine who work with large numbers of teens set up a call and response system. They often use lyrics from popular music. A recent one was the leader would shout out. "I wear my grandpa's clothes." And the response would be, "You look incredible." Pretty cool when you hear 70 teenagers shout that back to the leader.

One attention getter that I learned from my dear friend Julia Martin, the director of ReTribe, is the Call & Response. She teaches her students, "When I say: A hush came over the crowd, you responds with: Hush... Okay? Let's try it. A hush came over the crowd—"

"Hush…" Which they dramatize with tone of voice and hand gestures.

Simple but effective.

As you practice leading playshops, you will develop your favorite tools for smoothly gathering up everyone's attention. Use a variety of attention getters, and most importantly, remember to be patient, yet insistent, allowing the group a moment to come into being focused, quiet, and ready.

The Heart of Play

Working with Large Groups

If you have a group larger than 30 people it isn't always ideal to play in a circle. You might break people into smaller groups of eight or ten.

You could first play an energizer like Tiger/Pistol/Person in triads and then have each group find two other groups of three to make groups of nine. Then play a series of circle games in those groups simultaneously. The room will be buzzing and brimming with energy and laughter.

Games such as Group Juggle, Slap Pass, Scream Circle, Knots, Count Ten and Energy Ball work well with 8 – 10 people in a group. Choose perhaps three or four to play depending on how much time you have. Before these groups disperse you could have them do a Core Group Formation, and then later when you call out, "Core Group Formation," the smaller circles could reunite. There are many ways to move in and out of various-sized groups. Experimentation is the way to go.

Transitioning

Having a smooth transition between games can make the difference between a great play session and one where maybe not everyone was fully engaged the whole time. There are many ways to make these transitions, a few of which are listed in the games section of this manual. However you choose to transition, the important thing is to keep everyone engaged and not have lag time where players are uncertain of what to do. Think of the MAP for your entire games session, not just for each game individually.

Transitions are also a good time to introduce mindfulness components to the playshop. Between games you can invite players to walk mindfully around the room, noticing any sounds, smells, or sensations in their body. Ask the players to focus on their breath, feel their bodies in the room. Then have them look around, and tell them that the first person they make eye contact with is their next partner.

Another kind of transition, and a challenging one, is when you instruct the players to choose partners or form into small groups. Children will grab their best friends and this can lead to feelings of exclusion among many of the others. Fortunately, there are lots of creative ways to choose groupings and partnerships.

A standard way is to count off around a circle. Other ways include having

Introduction

everyone put one, two, or three fingers in the air, and then finding someone else with the same number of fingers in the air as you do. Or, say, "Choose a partner who has the same color clothing as you do."

"Choose a partner whom you haven't played with today."

"Choose a partner who has similar colored eyes."

"Choose someone who has hair close to as long as yours."

Or hand out cards with animals on them, and they have to find the person or persons with the same animal as they do. Let your creativity inspire you, remembering to create inclusion and lots of opportunities for players to play with different people. Choose your transitions based on the size groups you want to use, and your goals for the session (emphasizing mindfulness, interpersonal connection, cooperation, and so on).

Game Sequencing

It is important to understand the flow of energy, to go from a simple ice breaker to a name game, to working in smaller circles, to partner games. Experiment and find your own sequencing and change it according to the group size, the people playing and the objective for that play session.

Here is s typical game flow I have used many times for groups of around 30 people for an hour-long playshop. (Transitions are shown in italics):

Start seated in a circle of Chairs. Introduce the play session.
- ✓ Gotcha
- ✓ Have You Ever

"Everyone push the chairs back and stand in a circle."
- ✓ Name and Movement Replay

"Everybody put up one, two, or three fingers and find two other people with the same number of fingers you have to form a group of three." Adjust as necessary (a stray number can switch if needed)."
- ✓ Tiger/Pistol/Person

"Join two other groups of three to form a group of nine."

The Heart of Play

- ✓ Slap Pass
- ✓ Count Ten
- ✓ Knots
- ✓ Core Group Formation

"Walk around the room in no particular direction. Just keep moving into open space. Keep walking, and now imagine there is a string from the ceiling gently pulling upward on the center of your head. Notice how that feels. Now walk as though your hurrying to catch an airplane... Now freeze. The person closest to you is your partner. Spread out in pairs around the room.

"Find a chair to sit in."
- ✓ Memory Loss
- ✓ Gibberish Translator

"Come back to the large circle for some final group fun."
- ✓ Elephant/Rabbit/Palm Tree or Human Machine

Then shout out, "Core Group Formation!"
- ✓ Take time in core groups for reflection – go around and share anything that surprised you, or anything you learned that you enjoyed. What did you notice in your own response to the activities?

Then gather the group into one circle to share gratitude or closing thoughts.

Feel free to change group size throughout the session; paired activities can be interspersed as transitions between other games, as can moments for shared reflection.

Teen Sequence

Here is another list of games that can fill a one-hour session for teens or middle-schoolers, starting off with energizers, followed by active games:
- ✓ Stand-off

Introduction

- Human Spring
- Four corners
- Gotcha
- Ho
- Name and Movement replay
- Team Ro Sham Bo or Evolution
- Elephant palm tree
- Human Machine

Outdoor Play Sequence

Here are some fun games for an outside play session:
- Moonball
- Hog Call
- Group juggle
- Everybody's it Tag
- Asteroids
- Elves and Wizards tag
- Lemonade

Safety

    Your first priority should always be making a game physically and emotionally safe. It really sucks when someone gets hurt playing. That's why players should always feel free to choose their own level of participation. As play leaders, as we try to nurture self-awareness in others, we must trust the self-knowledge they come to. Part of creating a safe environment is setting a nonjudgmental tone, not only toward so-called mistakes, but also toward non-participation.

    Physical safety is pretty straightforward, but emotional and psychological can be trickier. Some of the activities could be a bit uncomfortable for some of the players at any given time, but especially at the beginning. You need to be sensi-

The Heart of Play

tive to that. Maybe they are worried about looking foolish in front of their peers; maybe because they have been hurt by competitive play in the past. Encourage them to stay aware of these feelings but stretch themselves into that discomfort, and to trust that they will not break.

For physical safety, be sure to tell players the boundaries of every game, and before you start make sure the playing area is safe of any rocks, etc. If playing a Trust game, instruct everyone on how to safely lead a person who has their eyes closed or is blindfolded. Even in a simple game such as Have You Ever, just moving across a circle and changing chairs can be unsafe if people are playing too aggressively, or are not aware of their own bodies and of others moving in the space around them. When playing tag games that involve running, remind all the players to stay in control of their bodies. If need be you can stop the game, re-clarify the need for safety, ask for suggestions from the group, and if necessary, end the game. Safety should be everyone's first concern.

Broadly speaking, some games are physically risk-free, such as playing chess. Some games are a little more "extreme" and helmets are required. Some people are driven by a risk-to-fun ratio, and it's why I have included a section of games that I call vigorous or wild play. Certain children will need more full-on challenge and physicality than others. Providing a range for all children to engage in is good. Care and attention are always the watchwords.

Keeping play safe emotionally and psychologically can be more challenging sometimes. Some of the activities could be a bit uncomfortable for some of the players at any given time, but especially when first getting started. You need to be sensitive to that. Creating emotionally and physical safety is so crucial to making sure play stays playful.

And yet, kids do get hurt feelings. Children have not yet learned the emotional regulation or skills to handle their impulses. Physical mistakes happen. Children get upset when playing. Hopefully, with some of the time-tested games in these pages, and the teaching points described in each game, you will feel more confident in leading play activities, helping you to course-correct disruptive behaviors and guide the children into playing well together.

There is always a mixture of play-personality types in any group setting. It gets to be an art to bring everyone in sometimes. It helps to have options and different kinds of play to reach different people helps, so as you build up a repertoire of games try to make diverse. Having a wide range of interpersonal skills also helps—this is where the Nurtured Heart Approach comes in quite nicely.

Beyond play-types, everybody brings their own special set of emotional

Introduction

states that contribute to the group energy. Every group feels different. Some of them falling into the fun, easy, enthusiastic or amazing; some of them clearly falling into the category at the other end of that spectrum.

Sometimes there can be a mismatch of energy where one player is too intense, and another player feels beat up on. Then it's not even about the game anymore; it feels personal. As play facilitators we are responsible for the kind of play that happens. When using games that are more physical, it simply becomes more and more important to emphasize safety first. The magic of active play is that when it is accomplished well, it creates an exceptional state of emotional safety, to know you can trust the other people to play well, safely, carefully enough to not hurt anyone. This forms deep emotional bonds between the players, in sports and in noncompetitive play.

In the Adventure Game Theater, before beginning the very physically active drama, complete with monster attacks and sword fighting, we would all come together as a group, stand in a circle while holding hands, and ceremonially initiate the beginning of the live-action story by saying the guiding phrase, "All safety, all health, and (all empowerment as well)—Let us play!"

Debriefing

The processes of debriefing and post-game reflections are explained at length in the book *Nurtured Heart Play*, as the Nurtured Heart Approach itself is an effective modality for Social Emotional Learning. But I will offer some guidelines here that will help make any game a good vehicle for SEL experiences.

Be clear with your intentions and SEL objectives for the game

For example, if during the game you want the participants to be aware of cooperation, then throughout the game, be sure to point out when that is happening. This can be clearly stated at the beginning of the game so that the players are aware of these intentions. Or you can ask for reflection upon the completion of an activity about whether the goals and intentions of the game were met.

Highlight the qualities of greatness expressed during the game

During play, children are often in their joy, so this is an ideal time to reflect to them the greatness they are exhibiting, and to point out when qualities like

The Heart of Play

enthusiasm, creativity, cooperation, and kindness, are being expressed. Often children are left to just play during recess, or at home during their free time, which is fine, however, it can also be a beautiful time to enter into their experience and reflect their greatness back to them, effectively reinforcing those qualities.

The power of appreciation, gratitude, and recognition

A fundamental need for everyone is a visceral and real-time experience of being seen and heard. This is especially true for children. Taking a few moments during and after play to offer specific, direct, and truthful validation of what is occurring that is positive will be helpful in building the skills of social emotional intelligence.

For example, "Tom, I saw that you were really kind to Emily during the playing of this game."

"Joseph, you showed great problem-solving skills during this team-building game."

The possibilities here are endless. These can be fluidly added throughout your leading of play activities.

The brilliance of resetting ourselves and forgiving mistakes

If there are disagreements around rules or mistakes happening, we can always declare a "do over" and try again. I am a great believer in playing by the rules. In that way everyone understands the boundaries necessary to make a game or activity work well. However, within play there are times where feelings get hurt, accusations happen about the breaking of rules, and demands for fair play are sometimes expressed out of anger. This is a golden opportunity to validate feelings, discuss what happened, make reparations where needed, and to clarify or change rules when necessary. Then, even if there was quarrelling, there is always the option to reset ourselves back to playfulness and get ready to play again in the next moment.

The power of reflection – Debriefing the experience

Dan Siegel, author of many books on the neuroscience of learning, emphasizes the importance of reflection in the learning process. Daydreaming, for instance, is actually a very healthy and normal part of learning for children. So along these lines, opportunities for different kinds of reflection need to be built

Introduction

into all areas of learning. Much can be processed after a game is over by asking the participants to reflect upon their experience.

In Experiential Education this is typically called a debrief. After you have played a game you can create the opportunity for people to share about their experience during the activity. The group gathers and takes the time for reflection. The depth and complexity of the debrief will vary on the age of the players and needs of the group.

When I work with adults doing team-building, I ask the questions like: What did the group do well? What could we have done better? And how did it feel to be a part of the experience?

Here are some other specific frameworks for a teacher/game leader when working with students who will need more guidance in looking at what actually took place during a game.

1. What did you see happen during that game? What did we do? (Here you are looking for particulars of what actually occurred. Simple specifics.)

2. Repeat back what you heard from the group. For example, after the game Have You Ever, I may say something like: "Okay, so you walked across the circle without bumping into anyone. What else? What happened for those of you who started to go to a seat and someone else beat you there? Did you fight for it? No, you didn't. You went to the next one that was empty. What else happened?"

3. Then I go into any character qualities being expressed. I start by saying something like: "So now that we know what we did during the game let's talk about what qualities it took to do these things. What did it take to not run into someone as you were skipping across the circle? Yes, it took self-control and awareness of others crossing the circle and of your own body..."

4. I then tie it into other aspects of life. For example, "So, when are some other times at school or at home that you have self-control or self-awareness? Or, when are times at home or school that you need to have better control or awareness? What are some examples?"

I may also ask, "Did you know that you had such amazing control of your body?" And asking them, "What are some other times that you have shown self-control and self-awareness."

My goal here is to create first-hand experiences of success, both in the game and in other aspects of their life. Maybe this game is their first success at that quality. This really becomes a discussion about successes and moving them forward through their mistakes.

5. Sometimes I ask, "What was it like for them to be acknowledged, or to acknowledge someone else?" This helps students to reflect on how it feels to hear themselves being acknowledged. Then following it with a question about how they can acknowledge others in other aspects of life. Depending on the group, I also give them the opportunities to acknowledge themselves and others right then and there.

6. At the end of the debriefing, I acknowledge everyone for their willingness to participate and allowing themselves to be open, caring, and vulnerable in the group.

Many educators are torn in today's world, between the need of meeting core curriculum standards and meeting the social-emotional needs of their students. How can they possibly take the time to play a game and have fun when there is so much to accomplish? What many educators are finding is that by taking the time to do team-building experiences, by building in SEL lessons, by building community in their classroom, or adding in mindfulness experiences, that their classes function more smoothly and effectively.

More learning happens when children feel connected, safe, and are having fun. Students can learn the skills of self regulation, focus, feeling and expressing empathy. Using energizers, cooperative games, trust activities, theater games, etc., Integrative Social Play lends itself as a natural complement to a whole support system to any SEL program, character education curriculum, or mindfulness based training, boosting the overall energy.

As simple as it seems, taking some time during the day to play, and then reflect on it, will have great benefits. When the games are targeted and well facilitated, only a few minutes a day is needed to have a positive impact on the learning potential of the students. Each teacher, therapist, parent, counselor, or youth group leader will find their own leadership style, which really should include offering recognition's and appreciation throughout play, and taking the time to reflect on the experience will serve to remind everyone how valuable it is to connect to each other in this way.

Debriefing is more powerful than it might seem when just reading about

Introduction

the technique. Giving kids a chance to process their experiences on this level and share their feelings is all too rare in the overly competitive and grade-based world.

Working with Different Ages

My expertise has been mostly using New Game and Cooperative Games with school-aged children, teens, and adults, emphasizing fun and connection. Games with these kinds of rules can be a great way for children to learn concepts of listening, boundaries, fairness, physical awareness, and many more concepts. However, the challenge is knowing what game and activities will work with different ages. Here is a short overview of some general qualities of different age groups that may support you choosing games that will work best. In this manual I did not list an age range for each game as I have found that it varies depending on the play-maturity of each grouping, and with some simple variations most any game in this manual can be played with most any age. There is, however, a section of games for younger children that will work with most children 6 to 8.

Pre-school and Kindergartners

At this age children are just beginning to learn how to behave in, and function as a group. They do really well in small numbers, which is why teachers have them play quite a bit in stations of three to five. Children this age are deeply into imagination and fantasy play. They love having stories read to them. They love to move their bodies and play with objects. They love to sing, to draw, to play with toys, and to dance. They also derive great joy in playing games where everyone joins in together.

When playing with preschool and kindergartners, I primarily use Original Play, which is something I have trained extensively in. For more information go to www.originalplay.eu

So the simplest movement-based, singing and imaginative-based activities are the best for preschoolers and kindergartners. There are lots of great resources available for this age group that focus on movement education. One music organization, Education through Music uses traditional singing games such as Farmer in The Dell to teach group awareness and language skills. However this age group also starts enjoying playing simple group games together, so enjoy the chapter entitled games for younger children. Please note that many games throughout this book can be used and adapted to work with these younger children.

The Heart of Play

I originally learned parachute games from the New Games Foundation and, for sure, parachutes are always a hit with the youngins. There are lot's of great books available on using parachutes, so I haven't included any games here.

1st and 2nd grade

Children at this age start really enjoying group game experiences. The emphasis, however, needs to be on cooperation and an everybody-wins philosophy. Often the play leader really needs to be extra aware of safety, so simplified versions of games like Have you Ever, and Who Changed the Motion, are lot's of fun for them. Hopefully, in their gym classes they have done enough movement awareness to be able to move safely thru space with others. This is a learned skill. So some active tag games like Everybody's It tag, Lemonade, or Elbow Tag will be okay as they mature in their abilities to follow rules, self regulate their energy in a group, and play safely together.

The emphasis needs to remain on movement, imagination, and fun.

3rd and 4th Grades

Around this age children really start enjoying challenge and full-on group experiences. Many kids at this point join sports leagues. When taught by very good coaches who emphasize movement, fun, skill building and participation these sports experiences can be rewarding and full of great learning opportunities. However, this is not always the case and often children can get quite caught up in feeling they have to win at all costs, which can lessen their enjoyment of playing for the fun of it, for its own sake, playing spontaneously and compassionately with others.

Playing games that have built-in challenges while still having an everyone-wins philosophy can be very beneficial for both the child who loves to win and the ones who don't like being competitive. Games Like Everybody's It, Elbow tag, and Lemonade are great examples of games that kids this age will enjoy.

5th grade and up

Once kids hit later childhood and into adolescence they can handle the complex rules of most any game. The challenge here is when they start being overly self-conscious. Sometimes their own internal judgment about making mistakes and having to win prevents them from enjoying some of these games. Games such

Introduction

as Group Juggle and Gotcha can be used to emphasize that it is okay to make mistakes. And that can loosen the participants up before doing something silly such as Elephant Palm Tree or Evolution.

This is the age where organized sports become developmentally more appropriate as long as the coaching and teaching stays age appropriate. Even in coaching and teaching sports, the play leadership principles still apply. Keeping a good MAP, maintaining emotional and physical safety, making sure there is inclusion, cooperation and empathy built in to all that is taught. Teaching mindfulness and doing quality reflection that is game-specific will have great value. Some of this is learning and developing the very character traits that will truly create long term success in life.

As much as possible, I have tried to make each game a one page description so you can copy it and have it right with you, "out in the field," to refer to when facilitating. Most every game has a entry called Variations. These give you ideas on how to change a game to better meet the needs of your group, or simply as another way to enjoy the game. Just with these variations you have double the amount of the games written here, and then you can always make up your own and give them fun names. Maybe I will learn of it someday.

Also, there is a section entitled Teaching Points. These are key elements to help make the game successful and reminders on what to be aware of as the game is being played. Remember, you can take any game and use it to highlight different elements of character. I give you a few ideas and then I leave it up to you to come up with your own as you play.

This book is a cry from the heart to save childhood development from the throes of over-institutionalization and the good intentions of a misguided society. If you embrace these games, you are helping to right the ship. So make up new games. Change the rules. Connect the games to deeper teachings when possible. Most importantly, have fun and play from your heart.

Play on!

The Heart of Play

After I took my first trainings in New Games I was so excited that I launched my first play business teaching cooperative play to teachers, and in particular PE teachers. Many teachers shared how much they loved the focus on cooperative play. I continued on in my own personal studies. I read the cooperative sports game books by Terry Orlick. I took trainings with Project Adventure. And then I discovered the work of Fred Donaldson, the founder of Original Play.

Finally, after many years of freelance work, I took a job teaching P.E. at a small private school in upstate NY. I introduced the school to Fred's work and we implemented it with the preschoolers and kindergarten classes. Sessions consisted primarily of basic movement activities and the simplest games. It was play at its best.

The Heart of Play, Games Manual

— Over 200 Activities for Connection & Joy —

The Heart of Play

Name Games

Name Games can be a great way to begin a group activity, especially when most of the players are newly acquainted. You might start with a couple of energizers just to get everyone playing freely, without needing to know names right away, but don't wait too long. Knowing names is important for a group to feel fully connected, and since it takes time and repetition for people to learn a bunch of new names, the sooner you start the better.

These games fit seamlessly within the overall play structure, so you can pepper them throughout the session as needed. Or do two different name games in a row. Since Integrative Social games are helpful in the formation of a community-feeling within the group, whether it is that people are coming together for just an hour, for a whole school year, or longer, this category of games is not only important but rich with possibilities of playfulness.

Names can be hard to learn quickly, but the good news is that we have lots of games we can use to make it fun from the start. Some of the games use mnemonics, kinesthetics and musical memory aides that teach skills that can be applied to academic learning.

> "Play is vital to all humanity. It is the finest system of education known to man."
>
> Scarfe, Neville V.

Name Games

BUMPITY, BUMP, BUMP

(10 - 30+ Players)

A fun and silly way to play with learning names, this is a good game when most players know some names, but maybe not everyone's really well. Can also be played even when everyone knows everyone's name.

Set Up
1. Have everyone get in a circle.
2. Ask everyone to turn to their partners on their left and right.
3. "Okay everyone, we have to learn this silly phrase. Repeat after me. Bumpity, Bump, Bump! Again—Bumpity, Bump, Bump."
4. One person starts as the It in the middle. Demonstrate how that person walks up to someone, points at that person and says either, "Right, bumpity, bump, bump," or, "Left, bumpity, bump, bump." The person pointed at must say the name of the person to the right or left, whichever the It says before completing the saying, "Bumpity, bump, bump!"

Game Play
"Okay It, go up and point at someone."

When a person makes a mistake, which is either not saying the correct name in time, or by saying an incorrect name then that person replaces the It in the middle. If correct the "It' continues on and chooses a new person to point at.

Variations
Come up with other silly phrases to use in place of Bumpity, Bump, Bump.

Also, if playing in a small circle, the It can just spin around, stop, point, and then go into the phrase.

Teaching points
If there are lots of people playing add more "it's". This is a fast paced game where everyone will be learning everyone's name, even when players don't remember in time.

The Heart of Play

INTRODUCE A NEW FRIEND
(10 - 30+ Players)

This is a great game for a relatively new group as a way to have partners focus on what is special about each person.

Set Up
1. Have the players find partners, preferably someone whom they have not met before, or do not know well.
2. Give the pairs a few minutes to have each person tell their partner a couple of things that they would like other people to know about them: accomplishments, hobbies, favorite sports teams, favorite music, or favorite book, etc.
3. Then have them gather in a circle to introduce their new friend.

Game play
Have the players stand and introduce their partners, telling the group a few of the interesting things they learned about them. For example, "This is my new friend Sue, and she loves to play soccer, and she also loves chocolate ice cream." The person introduced stands and bows as the group applauds and cheers. Then it is the other persons turn to introduce their new friend.

Variations
You can vary this game by how many things the partners can share. It can just be one thing or several. Another variation with a large group is to have everyone walking around with their partner, linking arms if they want, and introducing themselves to other pairs. Take the next five minutes and introduce yourself to five other pairs.

Teaching Points
Encourage a little theatrical flair in the delivery of the information, as if the person is a celebrity of some kind. We all deserve to have that kind of attention once in a while.

Name Games

NAME & MOVEMENT REPLAY

(5 - 40 Players)

The simplest, easiest, and one of the most fun name games you can play.

Set Up
1. Have everyone in a circle.
2. Explain that each person will do a movement and say their name.
3. Tell the players, "The only thing you need to do is remember your own name and movement."
4. The leader demonstrates doing a name and movement. And then the whole group repeats that name and movement.
5. For example, John steps forward, says his name, and bows at the waist. The group then says John's name and does his bowing movement.

Game Play
So now that everyone sees how the game is played the next person to the leader's left (you could go to the right) shares their name and movement, and then everyone repeats it. This goes all the way around the circle, giving everyone a chance to create their own movement associated to their name. Once it is complete tell the group now we are going to do it three times as fast. Ready go. Maybe a third time around even faster.

Variations
A slightly more complex version of this game, and still delightfully fun, is to say your name, and then say what you like, while doing a movement that represents what you like, i.e., "My name is Joe and I like to surf," and as you pretend to surf, everyone repeats it and says, "Your name is Joe and you like to surf... I am Sue and I like to knit..."

Teaching Points
Remind everyone to keep it simple. Tell them, "Just trust your body and make a movement." Sometimes people are shy and don't trust their creativity. Encourage them to not think about it. "Just move your body as you say your name and see what happens."

The Heart of Play

NAME AND MOVEMENT AND ALLITERATION
(5 – 40 Players)

A fun and creative way to learn names, and kids learn what alliteration means.

Set -up
1. Have everyone standing in a circle.
2. Very similar to name and movement replay, in this version the first person says their name and adds a quality, or an adjective that begins with the first letter of their first name. Also ask for a movement that goes with this.
3. For example, the leader starts and demonstrates, "I am Silly Susan" and she makes a silly gesture. Everyone then replays that back to her. "She is Silly Susan!"
4. The next person says, (for example) "Hi I am hopping Harry", hopping as he says it. Everyone responds, "He is Hopping Harry… or, Courageous Carol", as Carol hold her arms up showing courage.

Game Play

The leader demonstrates doing their name and alliteration, and then passes it to the left, whereby that next person has the attention while doing their name and alliteration, etc.

Variations

If it is a small group, each person can repeat the person to their left, the name and alliteration, before doing their own. Or, for even more difficulty, they have to say each person that has gone before them. Change the game to what the person likes. My name is Joe and I like to surf and Joe pretends to ride a surfboard.

Another fun variation is after going around the circle, have the players mingle around the room, going up to other players and do that persons name and alliteration. "Hi Hopping Harry, I am Silly Susan, etc."

Teaching points:

If the group is larger than 30 people this will take some time, so be sure they are ready for this level of focus.

Name Games

NAME WHIP

(10 - 30 Players)

A fun fast paced name game.

Set Up
1. Have everyone get in a circle. Explain that the group is going to go around and say their name, and then the next person will say their name—and we want to do it fast as we can, really whip it around.
2. Ask everyone to enunciate their names as clearly as possibe.
3. You as the leader can start the whip...

Game play:
Ready go! "Sue, Bob, Christopher, Tammy, Enrique, etc..."

Okay now that we have done it in the clockwise direction, let's go the other way. Ready. Go! "Howard, Shayna, Melanie..."

Now that we have whipped names around, what name do we think we can whip around the fastest, Bob, Sue? Okay I am going to start with Bob in this direction and Sue in this direction. One person will get hit with both, so they have to be sure to pass both of them in the right direction.

Okay, Sue got around first, so let's time how fast we can pass it one direction. (This is very similar to the game Ooh–Ahh, so please refer to that game for more variations.) Wow, 15 seconds. Can we beat that time? Let's see.

Finally, let's see which name would be the most challenging to whip around. Hmm, Elizabeth, Chamiqua, Barry... Let's try it.

Variations:
Try doing it in slow motion, or do it by really exaggerating the pronunciation of the name, or do it softly, or do it loudly.

Teaching Points:
To see how fast they could do it injects some challenge, and boosts enthusiasm. When you do the two names in opposite directions the person that gets them both can easily get flustered, in a fun way.

The Heart of Play

SING YOUR NAME
(5 – 40 players)

A fun way to add in some playful singing to form a fun and effective name game.

Set up
1. Form a circle and designate a starting "performer".
2. Demonstrate the singing of your own name, or nickname.
3. Have the group sing the name back to you in the same manner.
4. Instruct the players to avoid using the same melody.
5. Tell the group that this game will require a willingness to use your voice playfully and creatively.

Game play
The first person steps forward and sings out the syllables of their name, perhaps with an introductory, "My name is Bri -an."

The group then responds with, "You name is Bri-an".

The next person then sings their name, etc.

Variations
If the group is more advanced you could have them sing their name in a particular style, such as opera, country, or hip hop. Styles could be suggested by others in the group like in an improv game.

Sing and Spell. Make a tune out of the letters of the name, and repeat.

Teaching Points
This game can be a challenge for some people who feel shy about singing and using their voice in this way, as they are the center of attention for a moment. Therefore, this activity can help with confronting those anxieties. Because of the potential for artistic expression in this simple exercise, it can be a fun part of a session even with people who already know each other's names.

Name Games

TOSS A NAME GAME
(10 - 30 Players)

A simple, fun and semi-active name game.

Set-up
1. You need a few soft throwable objects. Fleece balls or some nice, plush animal toys are great.
2. Tell the group that this is a memory game, so do your best to remember at least one or two other names as the ball gets passed around the circle
3. Take one of the throwable objects and pass it around the circle.
4. Each person says their name when the ball is in their hand.
5. Did everyone remember at least one persons name?
6. You may want to pass it around a second time.

Game Play
When it comes back to you, the leader, you take the throwable object and pick out one person whose name you remembered. Then say that person's name and toss it to them. That person now says a new person's name, and tosses the ball to them. Continue with this for a number of tosses. Now, add second ball into the game, reminding people to say that person's name loudly enough to get their attention to the toss that is coming to them. After a while, add a third ball into the game. At the end, can anyone name all the names?

Variations
After a while, add the rule that when a person tosses the ball to you, you thank them by name. For example, Bob says "Madison!" and tosses the ball to Madison. Madison says, "Thank you Bob." Also, it can be fun to suddenly toss in a funny throwing object like a rubber chicken.

Teaching Points
Remind the players to make nice underhand throws that are easy to catch, and emphasize drops are okay. Also, if you want to toss it to someone whose name you have forgotten you can always ask, "What's your name?"

Also, make sure everyone is included. After a while you can stop and ask, who has not received it yet, have them say their name and toss the ball to them.

Discuss the value of learning and practicing memory techniques that can be applied to other schoolwork.

The Heart of Play

YOU ARE SUSAN!

(5 – 40 Players)

A bit different than a simple name game, this activity is an experience that can be wonderfully empowering.

Set up:
1. Tell the group that this is about truly stepping into your own power and allowing yourself to stand and hear your own name.
2. Due to the repetitive nature of the experience it truly helps people to remember the names—and we need to know everyone's name, so focus is important.
3. You can do this in a circle or with each person walking up to the front of the group.

Game play:

The first person steps forward and says their name with pride and confidence, "My name is Susan."

The group then responds with, "You are Susan, Susan, Susan! Susan steps back and the next person in the circle steps forward and says their name. My name is Roberto. You are Roberto, Roberto, Roberto, Roberto! Go around the circle and have each person declare their name and have it repeated.

Variations:

Have each person step forward and declare something they believe is true about themselves. I am Susan and I am strong! The group then responds, "You are Susan and your are strong!" Or, "You are Susan and you are creative!"

Teaching Points:

There is something very powerful about people repeating your name in this manner and yet some people will be very reluctant to step forward and be present to this experience. It is important to coach each person to let this experience wash over them, and to let in the power of a group of people chanting their name. If doing it in a classroom or on a stage, encourage players to walk with confidence to the front of the room and stand still with pride. Debrief this experience asking the players how it felt to be the center of attention. This is also excellent for the whole group to maintain their focus during the experience.

Howard Moody

Ice Breakers & Energizers

With a lot of overlap between these two groups, depending on how the games are used, Icebreakers generally come before Energizers. Especially for a new group that needs to come together, where there may be hesitation, shyness, and even fear of not being accepted by others. People may be entering into a new social environment with general anxiety. That's why these well-structured games, cooperatively based, and enthusiastically led, can be so powerful and so important to the overall creation of great play session.

Creating a sense of community through laughter, joy, and fun sometimes requires a jump-start. All the games in this chapter are great for that purpose. Sometimes the group just needs to lighten the mood, to get the energy up and flowing, to move around and laugh. These games can also be great stand-alone activities you can bring into your classroom—or into the beginning of a meeting—or later, whenever things are stagnating. Most of these are also very simple, yet not too silly or risky for people to just jump into. Games can be toned up or down by the style of facilitation, and by tweaking the elements with variations.

There are other games within this book that fit the essence of Energizers. Most Circle Games could be in this category, as could a number of the basic Improv Games. For example, What are you doing?, Memory Loss, and Mirroring are simple and fun and make good energizers. Mindfulness games such as Four Changes, and Freeze Dance can also get the momentum flowing. Even a simple tag game can really energize a group. Heck, you could put some music on and toss yogurt container lids around the room like little Frisbees and totally jazz things up. After all, you are the Play Facilitator.

Even though all these games are quite simple, there is so much that happens on the level of social bonding and creating feelings of belonging. Since the social-emotional health of children is vital to their success in life, with these games you have a opportunity to impart a life-enhancing energy that will have far-reaching benefits for kids—perhaps psychologically ice-breaking.

The Heart of Play

ALPHABET RACE

15 - 50

A team-building challenge that reminds the players that spelling is fun.

Set Up
1. Make two sets (or more) of alphabet cards.
2. 4X6 inch cards work well. 26 cards, one letter per each card.
3. Mix them up and spread them out on two tables, or you could put them on the floor.
4. Divide the group up into teams of 8 – 12 players each.

Game Play
The leader shouts out a word. For example, "DOG." The first three people run up to the table search thru the cards and grab one letter per person and then stand in order spelling the word correctly. The team to do it first gets a point. Play a number of rounds varying the length of the words thus the group has to first figure out how many people to send up. The facilitator can scramble the letters quickly between each round.

Variations
Turn the cards upside down and the team has to run up and turn the cards over to find the right letters. This makes it quite a bit harder and more chaotic, however it eliminates teams trying to put the letters in order when they put them back after a round. Or ask questions that the group must first answer. No double letters in the word of course. There could be more than one correct answer. A five letter flower. Tulip or Daisy! A four letter sport. Golf? A seven letter spice that is orange-ish in color. Tumeric!

Teaching Points
As with any relay, the emphasis is on the fun and developing good communication amongst the team. Be sure to note that you have to use words with only one of each letter. You could also choose words in themes. Fun, Humor, Laughter, Jovial, Heart... or add in words such as Zero or Quickly, to use those unusual letters. It can be best to write out your list of words so as not to choose words that have two of the same letter in the word.

Ice Breakers & Energizers

BALLOON VOLLEYBALL
(10 - 30 Players)

A full-on-energy game, guaranteed to bring laughter and delight.

Set Up
1. Have each person get a partner.
2. Everyone sits down on the ground across from their partner, who is actually now their opponent thus making two lines, each team being its own line.
3. The partners place the soles (sole to sole contact) of their feet together and must keep connected in this way throughout the game.
4. Ask for a couple of volunteers to be retrievers.

Game Play
Give each opponent pair a balloon with which to start. The game is very simple. The objective it is to strike any of the balloons with your hands, and try to get it over the heads of the other team, far enough so it is beyond their reach. Players can lie down and stretch back to grab any balloons they can reach while still maintaining sole-to-sole contact. They can now toss the ball up like in a tennis serve and launch the ball back into play. Retrievers can toss the balloons that are out of reach back into play, thus making the game continuous--until for the last minute when the retrievers stop retrieving. See which team can knock more balloons over the other team's head and out of their reach.

Variations
You could have players seated on pillows on the ground, or on designated spots if lying down is not an option.

Teaching Points
Before the game starts, be sure it is okay for people to be supine. If anyone has a back problem or any other physical issues, have them be a retriever. Another key safety concern is reminding players not to swing their hands so hard as to hit another person's hand with too much force. Sometimes players across from each other will try to strike a balloon at the same time.

It is not necessary to have retrievers, however, the game can end pretty quickly otherwise, which is fine. Just start another round. The retrieving role can also be fun, especially for people who don't want to play such a vigorous game.

This game can be a great abs and core workout.

The Heart of Play

BIRTHDAY LINE-UP (& OTHER LINE-UPS)
(15 + Players)

Line-ups are a great way to learn a few interesting facts about people.

Set Up
1. For a birthday line-up, tell the group that they are to form a line (it can be curved or could even be in a circle), organized by their birth date, from Jan 1st to the end of the year.
2. This challenge has to be done without talking.

Game Play
"Ready everyone? You have one minute to complete this challenge, Go!" After letting them know when the time has ended, go around and see how the group did. People can reorder themselves in the process of sharing.

Variations
Other Line-ups could include: Alphabetized by their first name, Where they live closet to or farthest from the workshop location. How many siblings they have. How many years they have worked at this organization.

Another fun variation on this theme of silent line-ups is to give them shapes to make. You could have the shapes drawn on a flip chart. For example make two circles with a dot in the middle of each circle. Make two triangles. The fun is in silently figuring out who is the dot or how many people on each side of the triangle,

Teaching Points
It may be helpful when you start a line-ups for a group to know where to start the line. Debrief what strategies developed for communication without talking. What strategies were most successful? Who took leadership, and who was willing to just pick up and follow other people's ideas?

Ice Breakers & Energizers

BIRTHDAYS
(25+ Players)

A great large group energizer.

Set Up
1. Gather everyone together close in a bunch.
2. Tell everyone they are going to find everyone born in the same month as them.

Game Play
"You have 1 minute and 27 seconds to find everyone born in the same month as you are. Go!"

People will start yelling their month or holding fingers up indicating the month. Give them a count down. "You have 20 seconds left to find your birthday mates... and 5,4,3,2,1, Stop. Let's check to see if everyone has found their group." Call out each month and have people wave to you, and let anyone not in their month go join them. Ask them to now share their dates in their month group to see if anyone has the same birthday. "Who has the same birthday?"

"Now that everyone has shared their dates, we are going to do the Birthday Wave. Can everyone squat down a little bit? When I say go, January is going to leap to their feet and scream January. As soon as their feet hit the ground February jumps up shouting their month and on it goes. Ready, set, go!"

Variations
For some good team building have each group do a short skit about their month. Give them 3 - 5 minutes to work on it then have them perform their creation.

Teaching Points
One of the fun aspects of this game is in the quick set-up. This game is great with large numbers of people. If there are only 25 people in the group there will probably be a couple of months not represented. However in a group of 50 or more usually all the months will be populated and almost always someone has the same birthday as someone else in the group.

The Heart of Play

BOOP
                                              (as many groups of 4 as you have balloons)

A beautifully cooperative game.

Set Up
1. Make groups of four and have them hold hands in a circle.
2. Give each group of four a fully blown up balloon.
3. The objective in this game is to not let the balloon hit the ground.

Game Play
Have the groups start by keeping the balloon aloft without breaking the connection of their held hands. After a minute or so of some fun and cooperation the leader starts calling out different challenges: "Keep the balloon up using your shoulders only." After 20 or 30 seconds of this try another body part. "Try it with your elbows only. Okay, now your knees, your feet, your head" etc.

"For the final challenge, get the balloon really high in the air and try to keep it up with your breath only." This cannot be done for very long, although it can be done and usually ends up with everyone laughing and falling on the ground.

Variations
This can be done without holding hands with partners or a threesome. A simple game of "hacky sack" with a balloon. For younger children just giving two or three players a balloon and playing a little cooperative play time with a balloon is always fun.

Teaching Points
Number 12 size balloons are large and easier to work with than smaller varieties.

Be careful with calling out using your head only as you don't want two people jumping in with their heads. It is okay to do it; just remind the players to be fully aware of each other at all times.

Ice Breakers & Energizers

BRAAK WHIFF

(2 - 20 +)

The name of the game, is the closest possible vowel and consonant spelling of the sound that a deflating balloon makes when you release it.

Set Up
1. You need a large indoor play space.
2. Each player gets a balloon and then everyone gets a a partner.
3. Each pair goes to the end of one side of the room,
4. The objective is to blow up your balloon but don't tie it off. You will be using it to work your way across the room to contacts the far wall.

Game Play

So the first player of the pair releases their balloon and watches to see how far it travels. You can do a dramatic countdown, 3,2,1, Release. The other person of the pair then goes to where that balloon lands, stands there and then releases their balloon. This is not a timed race. It is simply to see how many released balloon tries it takes to get across the room.

Variations

You could make this a timed race which will add a little breath control to the game as players will have to blow their balloon up quickly. There will obviously be a decision process as to how much to blow up the balloon before releasing.

Teaching Points

This game is particularly fun to play as it is obvious that it is not skill that usually creates the success. It is pure random release of air. Sometimes strategies of pushing the balloon forward can be helpful or another strategy may be not blowing the balloon up very far. A great time to discuss with players that random chance can be a fun variable in playing games.

A good game to play before Boop or Balloon Volleyball.

The Heart of Play

COMMONALITIES

(Groups of 4)

A fun way for people to learn new things about each other in a fast-paced way.

Set Up
1. Get in groups of 4, and have everyone kneel.
2. Explain that the players will take turns offering a fact about themselves.
3. If the other three players have that all in common, they jump up and yell 1. Then another fact is offered and if they all share that in common, they jump up and yell 2. Make sure that players are not saying things that are obviously true for everyone i.e. I have fingers. I was born. I have a mother. Although something like "my parents are still married," or "I play a musical instrument," or "I have a brother would be allowable."

Game Play
"Okay, everyone begins and you must jump up and yell out your number to declare which number you are on, and whichever group gets to 10 things they have in common first will get our applause."

Or give the groups a certain time limit to come up with as many commonalities as they can within the two minute framework.

Teaching Points
It's great to have each person take a turn, however, if the group just does it randomly with players shouting out an idea, that is fine too. If necessary, you can emphasize that each person should take a turn, but in that case, make it okay for a person to pass if they can't think of something quickly on the spot.

Variations
This could be done in group of 3 or 5, but probably more than 5 people would get too unwieldy to match. This could also be done in a slower-paced way, with people just sitting down and not having to jump up to cheer. Just have them write down the things they have in common. Perhaps set a certain time limit and see which group comes up with the most.

Maybe even have each group then share their one commonality that is the most unusual.

Ice Breakers & Energizers

CONSENSUS

(15 – 40)

A fun mix of theater, team building and just plain old fun.

Set Up
1. Divide the group up into four separate groups in each corner of the space.
2. Tell them that they have to come up with a symbol or tableaux that when others look at it they will be able to guess with it is. Nothing too difficult or unsafe such as a human pyramids. Perhaps a merry go round, or a banana peeling, or the Statue of Liberty.
3. It can have moving parts. Remember to keep it simple.
4. Give them about two minutes to brainstorm and come up with their symbolic representation. Go around and have each group show their symbol and have people guess what it is.

Game Play
So now you have four symbols, i.e., a Tree, a Bank being robbed, a Washing Machine, and a Rock Band. Now the groups must huddle up and pick one of the four symbols that they will now do at the count of three at the same time. The idea is in as few rounds as possible, without talking too loudly so the other groups would hear, nor giving away what symbol they have chosen by setting their bodies in the pose before the leader says to go, to have all four groups be doing the same symbol at the same. Thus they have come to Consensus.

"For round one you have twenty seconds to come to consensus as to which one you will do. Maybe it is your own, maybe you were impressed with the Rock Band, and your group will do that. So take twenty seconds to come to Consensus. Ready, 1,2,3, do it. Ooh, look, two Rock Bands, a Washing Machine and a Tree.

"Get ready for round two. You have fifteen seconds to come to consensus, ready 1,2,3—Oh look we have three Trees and a Rock Band.

"Ready round three. You have ten seconds to come to consensus. 1,2,3, Amazing. We have four trees!"

Variations
Try doing it with more than four groups.

Teaching Points
This a great game to talk about afterwards, reflecting on what it took to come to consensus. The structure of the game is to give the groups very little

The Heart of Play

time to come to consensus. How did that feel for the players? Who decided for the group? Who took leadership in making the decisions? Sometimes groups will purposely not try to come to consensus. Possible just to have more fun, but also perhaps it is fun to just be a contrarian. Again, interesting to discuss. When does that feel fun and when doesn't it feel good in life when someone plays that role?

> Kids must learn to move their bodies through space safely before they can play more complex games or sports. Dance, gymnastics, and swim programs are all great ways for children to learn how to move freely and safely. Perhaps the best of all is just doing free play outside in nature. Since there is an increasing tendency to be inside sitting in front of a video screen, it is more important than ever to create situations where kids have access to climbing on play-scapes, being in nature, running around outside, jumping rope, and riding bikes, and a myriad of other forms of play that come along with the territory.
>
> Kids don't choose their surroundings. Parents and teachers shepherd them around, and if there is not adequate playtime for optimal brain development, its the fault of the adults. And that's what is happening in the world today, a collapse of playtime, below a minimum critical mass for full physical and psychological development.

Ice Breakers & Energizers

CREATE A TABLEAUX

(8 – 30)

My 3rd grade PE class would request this game over and over. Great game for adults too.

Set Up
1. Divide the group into two equal sized groups.
2. Each group brainstorms secretly on a scene that they will sculpt using the other teams bodies.
3. One group will be the sculpted team first and the other the sculptors.
4. When ready, instruct the sculpted team to close their eyes and the sculptors come over and more them into position.

Game Play

Team A is the first sculpting team. So group B closes their eyes and team A comes over and moves the people into the statue, the "tableaux" they want this team to be. For example, they move the players into various positions as if they were playing baseball. When everyone is placed have the sculpting team move away. Count down 3,2,1, and have the sculpted team open their eyes. Now they look around, while staying frozen, and try to guess who and what they are. Hopefully they guess correctly. If they can't guess after 30 seconds reveal to them what they are. Now switch roles. Team B is the sculpting team and team A is the team to be sculpted.

Variations

Have the sculptors make an abstract piece of statue art. The group opens their eyes and names the statue.

Teaching Points

Be sure to demonstrate what safe touching and guiding looks and feels like. The touch needs to be gentle and guiding the person safely in the direction toward the pose team B wants that person to be in. So if they want a player to kneel on the ground, they can gently ask them to kneel and help them get down while keeping their eyes closed. It is best to choose situations where people will recognize what they are. Rock band, circus, yoga class, recess, ballet, etc.

The Heart of Play

CREATION GAME
(15 or more)

A fun way to run and yell and let out lot's of energy and to teach a little bit of science at the same time.

Set up
1. You need a really large area to play in. A full field!
2. Gather everyone in a huddle and tell them we are going to simulate the beginning of all creation.
3. Gather everyone in real close, like an extended huddle. "At the beginning of time, once upon a time, there was the Big Bang. As far as scientists know, somewhere around 14 billion years ago there was this great explosive event that created the entire known universe...

Game Play
Everyone gets close together and make a tight ball. We all start humming with that dynamic potential energy. You could either give a countdown or let the humming get louder and then everyone peels off in an explosive energy and runs outward.

The big bang happens and everyone yells and runs off screaming to the edges of the universe (the play area). When they reach the end of the play area they pause, take a breath or two, and then return to the original huddle. Everyone huddles together and hums, ready to do it again.

Variation
Create your own fantasy: A wizard sending out all its apprentices to cast spells. Or in a smaller area how about bees flying out to gather pollen and returning to the hive.

Teaching Points
The key to this game is creating the scenario of the big bang. Before the game begins encourage everyone that this is a great opportunity to yell. So be sure to be in a space where it is okay for everyone to yell freely. There was the original belief that universe was slowing down and would collapse back on itself. Now it is believed that is still speeding up and expanding.

Ice Breakers & Energizers

EVIL MAGICIAN
(12 - 40)

This game was originally called Killer, but a better context for this game that is more appropriate with younger players is that of a fantasy scenario. Though there is something delightful about suddenly acting like you are dying an excruciating death compared to being put to sleep. Teach what is appropriate for your group.

Set up
1. An evil magician is lurking about who puts people to sleep.
2. The magician does this by winking at their victims, which acts as a sleep spell that takes ten seconds or more to go into effect.
3. Everyone is trying to find out who the magician is. If two players can correctly identify who the magician is then the magician is put to sleep. This is done by a player putting his or her hand in the air and saying, "I accuse." Another player must say, "I second it."
4. These two players (on the count of three, without talking to each other) point at whomever they believe is the magician. If they are correct: the magician falls asleep immediately. If either one is incorrect: then they both fall asleep, the wizard remains at large, and the game continues.

Game Play

The game begins by secretly choosing one player to be the evil magician. Have all the players close their eyes and tap one player on the head. This player is the magician. Everyone begins milling around saying hello and shaking hands. This is an excellent opportunity for players to introduce themselves. The magician also shakes hands and tries to secretly wink at the unsuspecting mortals.

As players fall asleep perhaps one bold person will make an accusation and another person will second it and the magician will be caught or perhaps the accusers are wrong so they fall asleep and on the game goes.

Variations

When playing with larger groups (over 20 players) you can actually play the game with two magicians. The challenge is with the accusation process. When the accusations are made and the accusers point at the same person and that person is the evil magician then they have caught them and that magician dies. If they point at two different people, if one of them truthfully says they are not the magician, then the accusers fall asleep. If perchance they have both pointed at a magician (therefore neither one of them can say they are not the magician) then

The Heart of Play

obviously the accusers are both correct and both magicians are defeated!

Another way that the magician can signal is when shaking hands. The magician wiggles their middle finger on the palm of the persons hand they are shaking. Or play a daylong version of the "kiss of death," which I learned from Karl Rohnke of Project Adventure. One person is chosen as the killer and they kill other players by sending them a kiss from a few feet away when no one is looking. In this version players who are killed wait a few minutes or perhaps even an hour or so later to die. Or play that the magician is casting a love spell and the players must swoon and fall down love-struck.

Teaching Points

This game is delightfully fun and probably most appropriate for slightly older children. At first, players might forget to wait to fall asleep, and it will be easy to tell who the magician is. Also if two accusers point and are wrong, one of the players will invariably say I know it was him. It may take a couple of reminders for the players to understand the importance of the secrecy of the game.

I originally learned the game as "killer." So depending on your comfort level with using certain terminologies do what is appropriate for you and your group

> For students to thrive in school and classroom settings they need that deep connection to their teachers, mentors, aides counselors and fellow students. Creating an environment of safety, engagement and trust is vital for students to feel ready, willing and able to learn. It's all about building relational trust. The games, exercises and concepts in this Heart Of Play Manual are ideal for doing just that.

Ice Breakers & Energizers

EVOLUTION
(10 – 50 Players)

Is evolution a result of random chance, or is there intelligent design? Only God really knows.

Set Up
1. Anyway, in this game there are four steps to evolution.
2. The first is the egg who squats down and says, "wobble, wobble, wobble."
3. Then there is the chicken who "waddles and quacks."
4. Then there is the dinosaur who makes "big roars" and moves their arms imitating a T-rex or a raptor.
5. Then the final symbol is any designation of supreme beings. Super heroes, the signing group the Supremes, or Greek Gods.

Game Play

Everyone starts out as an egg. Pair off with someone else who is an egg and do a game of rocks/paper/scissors. Make sure everyone does the same rhythm: 1, 2, 3, shoot, or rock's-paper-scissors-shoot. The winner evolves to a chicken. If it's a tie, do rock/paper/scissors again till someone wins. Then any chickens get together play R/P/S and the winner evolves into a dinosaur. If you are a chicken and you lose, you devolve back into an egg. So each time you win a round you evolve into a higher level, or if you lose you devolve to the lower level and find someoneelse of your own kind.

When you reach the level of Supreme Beings, gather with the other Supreme Beings and root on the others trying to evolve. One fun way to do this is being the singing group the Supremes and singing the song, "Stop in the Name of love, before you break my heart, think it o'o'ver." Or with younger kids they can be Super heroes.

Variations

Create different levels of evolution or different periods of growth. Maybe egg/embryo, cat/dog, monkey, human.

Teaching Points

You will want to end the game before everyone makes it to be a Supreme being because not everyone will, and it can get frustrating to devolve and stay stuck at the lower levels. Karma?

The Heart of Play

FFEACH
(10 – 40 Players)

A fun team relay and theater game all rolled into one. I learned this from Steve Butler and Karl Rohnke. FFEACH stands for Fast Food, Electric Appliances and Comic Book Heroes.

Set Up
1. Divide your group into teams. Two, three, or four teams will work well.
2. Make a set of cards for each team with a name from one of the three categories on the card. Maybe about ten cards in each set. The sets can be similar but not exactly the same, and they can be set about 20 feet away from the group, depending on the size of the space you have to play in.
3. This is a miming game. Demonstrate how a player runs up and looks at a card to and then they go back to their group to mime that name.
4. Tell the group they can come up with symbols for each category.

Game Play
The game begins with the first person from each group running up and looking at the first card. They run back to their group, probably signaling one of their three symbols that represents one of the categories and then begins miming out what was on their card. When the group guesses correctly, the next person runs up and gets a card. Play until they have completed all the cards in their stack.

Variations
Another way you can play this is where one player from each team comes up and huddles with you as the facilitator. You whisper to the group which thing they are going to be acting out. They run back, act it out, and when the group guesses correctly the player runs back and tags the facilitator. Whoever gets back first gets one point for the group. Keep a running score. Good for when you have multiple groups in a large area.

This kind of relay has all kinds of cool variations. I first learned it as Animal categories. Birds, Beasts and Fish. Other ideas: Modes of Transportation, Cartoon Characters, Historical Figures. In an English class or history class you could change it from a miming game and have them use words to describe characters.

Teaching Points
The fun is in the acting, not necessarily the competition. Names I've used in each category, Fast Foods: Big Mac, Milk Shake, French Fries, Pizza, Hot Dog

Ice Breakers & Energizers

etc. Electrical Appliances: Blender, Toaster, Microwave, Refrigerator, Washing Machine, etc. Comic Book Heroes: Hulk, Batman, Wonder Woman, Rogue, Spiderman, etc.

> Creating your own games – When I first learned New Games, what really stuck out to me was the concept of changing the rules to meet the needs of the group. Over the years my favorite play experiences have been ones where I created my own games. I co-created a whole live-action role-playing theater game process. I believe the success of it all was largely due to the fact that Brian Allison and I were always willing to try new rules, constantly experimenting. We would grade the changes based on our own play rating scale, the Fun For All Factor.
>
> One game I immensely enjoyed creating was when I was as PE teacher I had recently purchased a set of four 5' x 10' sections of wrestling mats so I could teach some gymnastics and wrestling in gym class. I noticed that when they were rolled up they made these really cool tubes. I then remembered a game I had see on one of those Battle of the Stars TV shows. I decided to stood up the four tubes in quadrants of the gym. I put two soft foam balls in play, added some Team Handball rules, plus a few other details and I created the game called Tubular SlamBall. Still one of the favorite games I have ever played.
>
> So make up your own games, experiment with rules, ask your group for new ideas to try. In other words, play with it all!

The Heart of Play

FOUR CHANGES

(2 +)

A simple yet fun and connecting partner activity. Great for focusing, observing and paying attention to details.

Set Up
1. You can play sitting in chairs or standing up.
2. Each person gets a partner. One person will be the guesser and the other person will be the changer.
3. Ask the partners to choose who will be the guesser and who will be the changer.
4. This game is all about observation and noticing what gets changed

Game Play
The guesser looks very carefully at their partner for ten to fifteen seconds. The guesser now turns around. The changer now changes four things about their appearance. They take the pen out of their shirt pocket, They untie one shoelace. They roll up one shirt sleeve a little and take off one ring. When that is complete they tell their partners to turn around and try to guess what the four changes are. When they have finished guessing they reverse roles.

Variations
With younger children give them a longer time to observe. Also you can make more than four changes to make it harder. You can also do this with people in places. Invite ten or so people up to the front of the room and form a line. Have someone go out of the room and have a few people change places and the see if they can guess who moved and put them back into order. Or move a few things around in the room and have the person guess what got moved.

Teaching Points
A great opportunity to discuss what we observe and how things can change and how we can sense it but maybe not quite know what is changed.

Ice Breakers & Energizers

FOUR CORNERS

(10 - 100)

This is a fun exercise for people to get in touch with diversity and how we all have different preferences.

Set Up
1. Somehow delineate the four corners of the space with cones or shoes or anything.
2. One corner represents "I love it." Another one, "I like it." Another, "I don't like it." And the last one, "I hate it."
3. Explain how the game will consist of the group dividing themselves up and moving to the corner that best represents how they feel about the question being asked.

Game Play
Begin asking questions and then the players move to the corner that best represents how they feel about the question. People who are ambivalent can stand in the middle or between two corners. This can be used to highlight any particular subject. Questions like, "How do you feel about science fiction movies?"... Video games?"... Pizza... School...etc. Ask lots of questions and afterward make the observation that we all have many different opinions and perspectives about everything.

Variations
There is a similar activity I have experienced in various forms. It goes by the name of Crossing the Line. Usually used with teen groups to explore various deeper themes. The four corners game is simpler version of this.

Teaching points
You can use this game in a very lighthearted way, or you can ask more emotionally charged questions. Of course that can frame the reflections after the game.

The Heart of Play

GOTCHA
(10 -40)

An excellent game to use the term reset to help the students realize how a reset is a simple and effective way to become centered and experience that state of readiness.

Set up
1. Have everyone in a circle, standing or seated.
2. Have the players place their left palm facing upward, about waist height, next to the person on their left. Then everyone places their right index finger onto that left palm of the person to their right.
3. "This game is called Gotcha, so when I say the word Gotcha again everyone tries to grab the finger of the person to their left that is in their palm. while at the same time lifting their right index finger trying to escape being captured by the person to their right.

Game Play
The play leader pauses for a moment of suspense then shouts out the word "Gotcha," and everyone reacts. The leader then asks the players to RESET back to the starting position, and play continues.

It is fun to also do a head fake before saying the word "Gotcha" trying to get people to do a false start. Always leads to some laughter. The leader can then choose other players to be the gotcha-callers. Also switch hands for balance.

Variations
You can do this game in partners very effectively—just have the players face each other (and repeat the above directions). Also try different words as the go word. "When I say "surprise... Ready... Super, ahh, superman, ahh—surprise!"

Teaching Points
This is a great opportunity to emphasize the fun of playing rather than just winning. The game is so silly that it lends itself to laughter and surprise. Also you can emphasize how excited we can get when anticipating the action and how it is good to breathe and stay relaxed, and then to reset ourselves ready to play again.

Works with groups of any size and most any age.

Ice Breakers & Energizers

HOG CALL

(10 - 40)

Hog Call is a grand excuse to make a lot of noise (and is a nifty means of breaking the ice, especially with a group that has just met).

Set Up
1. Have the group pair up, and instruct them that you want them to share a matching set of words; i.e. peanut-butter, Marco Polo, yin-yang, etc.
2. One person will be the first word, and the other person, the second word.
3. Ask each pair to announce their choice, in order to enjoy the humor of the more inventive selections, and to make sure there are no duplications.
4. Explain that once the game begins, just as in calling a hog with SOOEEE, the most functional means will be to shout your part of the phrase and listen for your partners response.
5. Of course you will be doing this with your eyes closed and walking slowly!
6. For example, if I shout PEANUT, my partner will be saying BUTTER. Be sure to instruct the players to have their "bumpers up"; i.e. arms out toward the front, hands up and palms forward so when they bump, their hands can be GENTLE shock absorbers – in order to provide personal protection while moving around sightlessly.

Game Play

Have the players who are the first part of the phrase go to one end of the play area, and the second part of the phrases go to the other end. Instruct the players to close their eyes (or put on blindfolds). Then ask them to shuffle right or shuffle left in their lines and to turn around twice, and then do their best to find their partners. As the facilitator, be sure no one is moving toward anyplace unsafe.

When partners find each other amidst the cacophony of sound, they may open their eyes and observe the other "hog callers" trying to find their partner.

Variations

If you are in an area or location where shouting would be disruptive ask the players to find each other by whispering. Or you can do this in large circle with partners on opposite sides.

Teaching Points

Remind the players to move slowly to maintain safety while walking with eyes closed and you as the leader makes sure no one wanders away.

The Heart of Play

HOW'S YOURS?

(4 – 10)

A simple guessing game that elicits lots of laughter.

Set Up
1. Choose someone to be the guesser and they go out of the room.
2. Then the group discusses what part of their body that they all have in common that will be the secret choice. For example, their elbow. The guesser will be asking the player's the question, "How's Yours" and responses should best be answered in one word. Occasionally a multi word answer will be appropriate.

Game Play

The guesser comes in. They then ask various people the question, "How's Yours." "Tom, how's yours," "Mine is hard." "Arika how's yours?" "Mine is wrinkly." "Jose how's yours?" "Mine is pointy." The guesser then guesses, "Elbow!" "Yes!"

Fun choices of body parts, Toenails, Tongue, Skin, Lips, Ears, etc. Also, obvious interior parts of the body are cool: heart, brain, lungs, etc. There are also lots of funny and generic answers that can be used. Fine, Special, Paired, Warm, Smooth, or Covered or Exposed if clothes are, or are not, covering that body part.

Teaching Points

This game can be a bit "suggestive," so only use in a group that has a familiarity and comfort level that this will be okay and not make people feel uncomfortable or inclined to act inappropriately. Many body parts can be described as smooth, warm, moist, hard, etc., so take this into consideration and it can still be funny and fun in the right group.

Also remind the players to perhaps not give the most definitive clue first. So, let's say the secret body part was toenails. "Painted" or "blue" could be quite good clues to help the guesser guess, however, if it was the first response it might give away the answer too soon.

Variation

Perhaps if you are studying biology you could focus exclusively on interior parts of the body.

Ice Breakers & Energizers

HUMAN SPRING

(2 - 40+ Players)

A great follow up to the exercise Stand Off.

Set Up
1. Have everyone choose a partner who is close to the same height and size.
2. Two players face each other, standing about two feet apart with their feet shoulder width apart.
3. They put their hands up, palms facing each other.
4. Demonstrate how when they gently fall towards each other they contact palms and then push off of their palms to come back up to standing. After a few gentle falls and push back ups, the players then each take a small step back, thus increasing the angle and the challenge.

Game Play
Make sure everyone spreads out in the space and has enough room. Encourage going at their own pace and enjoying the dance of falling forward and pushing pushing away. Remind the players to only go as far as it feels safe. The person who weighs less needs to fall forward a little further. Important safety point. At no time are they to lock or interlace fingers when their hands come together. Demonstrate for the players how to have flat palms with fingers together to push off from safely.

Variations
Two people place their palms together and then move their feet backward while supporting each other by their palms connecting and pushing into each other. Like making a bridge. You could even add for the players to say to each other while they are holding this bridge pose, "I trust you." Adds a nice sense that it takes each player trusting each other to hold each other up.

Teaching Points
This coupled with the game Stand Off is a a great opportunity to talk about how it feels to be in cooperation as opposed to competition. Ask which they preferred and why?

The Heart of Play

IN PLAIN VIEW

(Any Number of Players)

A very simple observation game ideal for a space like a classroom that is filled with lots of stuff.

Set up
1. One person is chosen as the hider of the object. Everyone else stands around the room.
2. Choose really any object that can be seen by everyone from wherever they are, so perhaps not as small an object as a pencil. Rather a ball, a book, a hat, etc.
3. All the players close their eyes, and the hider walks around the room and places the object "In Plain View."

Game Play

Ready everyone 3,2,1 open your eyes. As soon as you see it without saying anything or pointing at it, sit down. See who are the last few people to spy the item. Randomly choose a new hider of the object.

Teaching Points

Remind the hider to walk all the way around the room so it seems like they have gone most everywhere in the room to hide the object.

Variations

The players could all be sitting down and they just raise their hand when they see the object. Perhaps pick three objects to hide and choose three people to hide the objects. So, the players have to spy all three objects before they sit down.

Or have the hider hide something in a much more challenging way, such that players must move around the room. The object must be able to be seen from at least one angle, but in a way that the players will have to look more closely. Remind the searchers that once they have seen the object to not give the spot away, but just sneakily go back and sit down in their seats.

Another kids favorite great for small groups of kids is, "I spy with my little green eye (or blue of brown) something in this room that is yellow." Each player takes turn describing and/or pointing at something. "Is it that banana?" "No." "Is it that picture of a sunflower?" "No." Is it the sun on that poster of the solar system. "Yes." That person who guessed correctly gets to pick the next thing in the room.

Ice Breakers & Energizers

JUMP IN, JUMP OUT

(10 - 30 Players)

A fun game that demonstrates that when learning something new it's okay to make mistakes, and actually a great way to be silly and laugh at ourselves.

Set -up:
1. Everyone stands in a circle and holds hands.
2. Explain that the fun in this game is doing our best to follow directions, but inevitably you will mess up and that is OKAY!
3. Next explain that there are four commands. Jump in, Jump out, Jump right, and Jump Left.
4. Demonstrate how this looks and then have everyone do this with you. When a command is said repeat the command and then do the action trying to do it in unison with everyone.

Game Play:

During the first round, just give out about 5 or 6 commands. Do what I say and repeat the commands after I say it. Jump In, (everyone repeats the phrase "Jump In" and jumps in). Jump out, Jump right, Jump in, Jump left, Jump right, Jump Out. Great everyone did well. Now in this next round I want you to say the command I say but physically do the opposite. Demonstrate once how this would look. I say, "Jump In" and you say "Jump in" but in actuality you all Jump out. Do a few commands and you will see many mistakes being made. Great now for this third round when I say a command, I want you to do that physical action but say the opposite of what I say. Again demonstrate once. I say "Jump Right" you do Jump Right but as you are doing that you say "Jump left."

Variations:

If people have any physical limitations, do it by just stepping in or out, or stepping right or left.

Teaching Points:

Holding hands adds fun to the game, however, if a group doesn't feel comfortable doing that, you can still play the game without holding hands. As the leader, it helps if you have practiced this a couple of times so you yourself won't make too many mistakes, but invariably you will mess up too. Ask the group afterward which was harder to do, the same action while saying the opposite or saying the same and doing the opposite.

The Heart of Play

KNOTS
(8-12)

This is a fun and interesting problem that gets people close to each other.

Set Up
1. Separate the players into groups of approximately nine players each.
2. If there is less than seven players in a group, the problem is too easy, and more than 12 can be too difficult, although a large game of Knots can be wonderful if the group is up for it.
3. To form a knot, have everyone in the group stand shoulder to shoulder in a circle and place their hands into the center.
4. Now everybody grabs a couple of hands, making sure it is not two hands of the same person, nor the hands of a person standing right next to them.

Game Play

Now that there is a sufficient entanglement, ask the group to carefully untangle this knot without breaking the connections between the hands. Tell the players it is perfectly okay to readjust their grips to keep their hands from getting all twisted up (but not to release and regrip to solve a knot problem).

Now comes the true test to see who the analysts and activists in the group; those who will try to figure out the problem and those who will dive right into it and start climbing over and under. Usually a combination of both approaches will be helpful. The group should end up as one big circle or perhaps into two intertwining circles.

If the knot seems impossible, bring in the famous Knot Doctor (the teacher). Determine where the best place is to make an incision (pull apart a pair of hands and reconnect however needed) and see if this will provide the "knot-aid" to solve the problem.

Variations

Have everyone join hands in a circle. One or two players are chosen to be out of the circle as they are the "untanglers." Have the group go over, under and around each other until the group is sufficiently tangled up and then have the untanglers come in and direct the group how to move and become one circle again.

Ice Breakers & Energizers

Teaching Points

This game takes a great deal of cooperation, listening and comfort level with touch. With a group of nine, the "knot" problem can usually be solved, meaning untangling into one circle, or two intertwined circles. The rewards can be great for a group of children who are ready for this challenge, however be sure to emphasize being gentle, listening and taking care of each other. It is also helpful to tell a group when they join hands to not just thrust them into the center of the circle. Reach up or reach under to grab a hand. Also remind the players to be sure they have just one hand they are not grabbing someone's wrist that is holding another person's hand.

> I read an article on the relationship between kids participating in sports and their parents. On the point of speaking with the gifted athletes and asking them about the support they had from their parents, and what difference it made in their enjoyment of the sport, and in their overall success. The author came to the conclusion that more than being praised for their performance, most importantly, the simplest and most supportive expression of all was, "I love watching you play."

The Heart of Play

MAGIC 7 / 11
(Groups of Three)

A simple math and matching game.

Set up
1. Get into groups of three.
2. Explain that this is a simple game of trying to achieve a set goal that will be determined at the start by adding up fingers that each player shoots out.
3. Choose players to demonstrate this to the whole group.
4. You face your partners and on the count of three, by pounding your fists together, saying, "1,2,3 shoot," then you shoot out 0 – 5 fingers with one hand. The idea is, without conferring or planning in anyway, to magically get to the pre-set goal of 7. Once accomplished, try for 11.

Game Play
Everyone in their groups of three does the first one all together. Ready, "1,2,3 shoot!"

Anyone that gets to exactly 7 receives a big cheer from the group. Okay, ready, "1, 2, 3, shoot."

After a few rounds, see who hasn't yet accomplished their two goals. For those that have, try one more challenge. Take two hands and try to get to 21. "Ready, "1, 2, 3, shoot."

Teaching Points
Ask afterward if anyone trying to get to twenty-one realized each person could put out 7 fingers, since 21 is divisible by three. However, once you give out this secret you will have to choose a different number next time. Also, were there any other strategies people tried to be more effective?

Variations
Try it with different numbers. Try it in groups of four.

Ice Breakers & Energizers

NIGHT AT THE MUSEUM
(12 - 40)

A fun way to have everyone play with being still and being observant.

Set up
1. Everyone takes a position as if they were a statue, tableaux, or mannequin in a museum.
2. One player is chosen as the security guard who walks around the museum.
3. The statues' objectives are to move into new poses when the museum guard isn't looking.

Game Play
"Ready everyone? Take a pose and wait for the guard come in." The still players will choose to come alive and move when the museum guard isn't looking at them and move hopefully in a way that the guard will not notice. If the guard notices them he or she points to them and says something appropriate like, "I saw you moving." That means they have been caught and are sent off into the "storage room." Or you can have these caught players join the guard and continuing walking around the museum trying to catch the moving statues.

Variations
At our recent New Year's retreat for ECRS (Eastern Cooperation Recreation School) my friend Dylan came up with this variation and it's great. Everyone gets a partner and makes a statue with this partner. The guards are partners too, and they move about the museum looking at the paired statues and, of course, the paired statue will move to a new pose when the guards aren't looking. The guards need to really ham it up and not try to catch people right away.

Teaching Points
Games that require a person to be the guesser can lend themselves to kids accusing each other of not playing fair. In games such as these, you can use the concept of "Total It Power." If the It says you moved, you did. Or you can have the teacher/facilitator work along with the chosen It, thus helping them to be fair.

The Heart of Play

NO, NO, NO, YOU MEAN
(4- 10+)

A fun word game.

Set Up
1. Explain that this is a simple word game and that the object of this game is to give an incorrect definition of a word, but the word that is defined must rhyme with the word, closely rhyme, or share close alliteration with the word that has been incorrectly defined.
2. You can have the players in a circle or just seated at desks.
3. You can break a bigger group up into smaller circles.

Game Play
The first player picks a word and defines it incorrectly. The next player in line must correctly guess what word the player was actually defining and then give an incorrect definition of that word. Sounds complicated, but it's not.

For example, one player starts and says, "A cat is what I hit a ball with." The next player would say, "No, no, no you mean a bat, which is what I wear on my head."

Then the next player would correctly identify the word saying, "No, no, no you mean hat. A hat is what a cat eats for breakfast."

"No, no, no you mean a rat, which is a club at a college."

"No, no, no you mean a frat, a frat is a milk shake."

"No, no, no, you mean a frap is what you take in the woods..."

Variations
Do a gibberish version. "A purrsoup is a special soup made for cats that makes them purr." "No, no, no you mean, purrsloop. A purrsloop is Italian butler who works on a boat.

Teaching Points
Although it is easiest to stick with rhyming words, using words that are similar in any way allows the word game to make interesting shifts. If a player can't guess what the word is or come up with a new definition, then let the next person try it. This can be a very funny game. Remember to point out that some people are better with words than others.

Ice Breakers & Energizers

ORDER UP

(10 – 40)

From Jacquie Adain, this is a very simple, seated version of Simon Says.

Set Up
1. This game is played with everyone sitting in a circle.
2. There is one leader who calls out the commands.
3. Show the group that there are only three movements. The first command is called, "Order Up." When Order Up is called everyone brings their hands up by their shoulders in position as if it were a robbery.
4. The next command is, "Order Down," and then the players following the command of the leader puts their hands down on their legs.
5. And then the final command is, "Nibbledy Bibble," which is patting your hands on your legs alternately quickly as if in a drum roll. The Nibbledy Bibble command does not need the word "Order" before it.

Game Play
So the leader starts the game, "Order Up... Order down... Nibbledy Bibble."

"Up..." At this point, the leader has said "Up" and moved their hands up but did not give the correct command of, "Order Up," which is a mistake to follow. Invariably, the players will follow the movement and not the verbal commands. When someone makes a mistake, choose a new leader. Choose someone who made a mistake to be the next caller.

Variations
Can you play the game with a couple of new commands. Maybe "Order Wave," and you wave both hands. And "Order Dance," and you move your hands and shake your torso as if dancing. Or make up your own. If sitting is not ideal you could play the game standing.

Teaching Points
Players may make mistakes purposely to be the next leader so use a different method for choosing the next leader.

The Heart of Play

QUICK LINE-UP

(15 - 40)

This is one of the few New Games that's played in a square rather than a circle. It is also a great way for teams to test wits and group spirit.

Set Up
1. We start by lining up shoulder to shoulder in four teams, each team forming one side of the square, with everyone facing the center.
2. One person goes into the center of the square as the spinner. The spinner stands still for a minute, facing one of the teams.
3. Each team must now remember the order in which it is lined up–that is who is next to who in the line, and second, where they are lined up in relation to the spinner.
4. A team can be facing the spinner; it can be to his or her left, or right side; or it can be behind them. If we're not clear on this, we're going to be lost very soon.

Game Play

Once we all know where we are, the spinner spins around a few times and then comes to a stop, (facing a different team presumably) and calls "Quick Line-Up!"

That's the signal for everyone to regroup around the spinner in their original positions. To do this everyone will have to scramble across or around the square (without collisions please) and get into the right spot in relation to the spinner and his or her teammates. As soon as each team is in its original order and its original orientation to the spinner, all its members join raised hands and shout, "Quick Line-Up!"—indicating that their team is without question the most together of the four.

With an older group, give the fastest team a point and play a number of rounds and the first team to a certain number (say, 4) wins. The spinner can be clever by moving out of the square to another location or can also move again before the players are all lined up making them change directions in mid-movement.

Teaching Points

If the spinner makes a 180 degree turn then the lines are now opposite of their intended position so the tendency is to just rush across the square so the potential for collisions is present. People have to be playing safely in their bodies and with playfulness as their primary focus. If they are too competitive people will not feel safe and have fun in this game.

Ice Breakers & Energizers

ROBOTS

(10 - 100)

A very fun game for all ages. Great with large numbers of players.

Set Up
1. You now can have your very own robot. In fact, you can have two.
2. Have everybody get into groups of three.
3. Call up two people to demonstrate their own unique robot locomotion and danger signal, and explain a robot only moves in one straight line and has a proximity detector. So when it gets within two feet of something or someone the robot emits a danger signal. Have each robot demonstrate their own unique locomotion and danger signal.
4. Then demonstrate how each robot is controlled by three different commands. A tap on the right shoulder turns the robot in a 90 degree angle turn to the right. A tap on the left shoulder turns the robot 90 degrees to the left. And a tap on both shoulders at the same time turns the robot 180 degrees around.
5. Do a practice run with these two demonstrating robots. Turn you robots on, tap them on the shoulders and when a robot emits a danger signal " beep-beep-beep...." the robot stays stationary until the robot master redirects the troubled android.

Game Play
Have the groups of three decide who is the first robot master and who are the two robots. One person is the robot master who starts up and guides their robots. Before starting, the robots can demonstrate to their masters their own unique locomotion and warning signals to help distinguish them from other robots.

"Okay robot masters, there is a switch on the back of your robot, turn your robots on and go!" After a minute command everyone to stop, have the robot masters collect their robots and have the players switch roles, with the new robot demonstrating their unique locomotion and danger signal before they start. Play at least two more times so each player gets to be a robot master.

Teaching Points
It is very important to remind the players that the robots must move in straight lines and that they have proximity detectors so that they stop before contacting another robot. This keeps the game very safe.

The Heart of Play

STAND OFF
(Partners)

This is one of the few games in this manual that distinctly has one winner and one loser.

Set up
1. It is important to demonstrate Stand Off correctly.
2. The players need to find a partner that is approximately the same height as they are.
3. Call a volunteer up to help demonstrate the game.
4. Then have them stand about two feet apart, which they can measure by being a bent arms length apart. They are to stand with their feet together.
5. This is a balance game and vitally important for safety that their feet are together.
6. They then place their palms out towards each other.
7. The object of the game is to strike the other players palms with your palms and to knock them off their balance point. You cannot move your feet. Either player can fake. And you also lose if you contact anything but the opponents palms. Play best two out of three.

Game Play
After demonstrating the game, have the pairs spread around the room. Make sure no one is going to be pushed backward toward another person. Remind everyone to put their fee together. Ready 1,2,3, go. Have the players play a best two out of three or three out of five. Switch partners and play again.

Variations
Players sqaut down and play in this squatted posture.

Teaching Points
This is a great game to play in partnership with Human Spring. Stand Off is an obviously quite competitive game. Human Spring totally cooperative. Have the players play each and ask them which one they liked better. Good for a discussion about the importance of cooperation even within competition.

Ice Breakers & Energizers

TEAM RO-SHAM-BO

(10- 40)

A great way to build the energy of enthusiasm and team spirit.

Set up
1. Explain that this game will start with pairs and then end up as one team at the end.
2. Demonstrate how to Play Ro-Sham-Bo (otherwise known as Rock, Paper, Scissors).
3. Review that each symbol defeats another, Rock breaks scissors, scissors cut paper, paper covers rock.
4. Agree on the rhythm of the chant with each person pounding their fist into their open palm, "Rocks, Paper, Scissors, shoot," or "Ro-Sham-Bo shoot." On the command of shoot each person throws out one of the three symbols.

Game Play
Everyone pairs up. Each pair plays a game of Ro-Sham-Bo. Whoever loses now gets behind the person that won and becomes their cheerleader. For example Sue defeats Joe. Joe gets behind Sue and cheers her on as she looks around and finds another team to play. So Sue pairs off against Kelly's team. "Go Sue go." Kelly defeats Sue, so now Joe and Sue get behind Kelly's team and cheers for Kelly. Play until you have two large teams and then the final contest with one team wining. "Yeah, it is Madison's team that wins."

Variation
Each pair plays a best two out of three challenge.

Teaching Points
This game lends itself to a fun way of cheering on teammates and then having your allegiance quickly shift and the players support their new leader. The cheering may get loud, so be ready to have the teams cheer in whispers if neccesary.

The Heart of Play

TIGER/FIREWORKS/PERSON
(3 - 39+)

A fun game of intuition and connection.

Set Up
1. Ask the players to put one two or three fingers in the air.
2. Tell them to find two other people with the same number of fingers in the air and to make a group of three, and then to put their hands down to indicate they have found their group, or to sit down in their group of three.
3. This game is about our intuitive or psychic abilities.. To test ourselves we need to learn the three magic symbols.
4. The first is a ferocious tiger, bearing its claws and growling. You demonstrate by spinning around, with hands up by your face, Raaar! "Okay, let's practice it, Ready, 1,2,3, Tiger!
5. The second symbol is Pistols, and they are very special pistols that only shoot fireworks. Demonstrate by pointing index fingers in the air and going "Pcooo—Ooo, Aah! Ready 1, 2, 3, Fireworks!"
6. The last symbol is a Person, and it is a very passionate person. Demonstrate blowing a kiss with both hands. Ready, 1,2,3 Blow a kiss.

Game Play
"Now with your two partners stand back to back to back. The object of the game is that when I count to three, you are going to whirl around and do one of the three symbols. The object of the game is to psychically and magically match your partners (without talking).

"Tune into each other, visualize one of those three symbols. Ready, 1,2,3, go! Alright who matched? To truly prove you are psychic you have to do it two times in a row, so let's try it again. Ready, 1,2,3, go... Who matched?

"Lets do it a third time."

Variations
Have each person in the group make up their own unique symbols and play it again.

Teaching points
Ask the players to reflect on how it feels to match and be connected. Ask them to talk about what did they sense about how their partners would choose.

Ice Breakers & Energizers

TOUCH BLUE AND FREEZE

(10 - 50)

A great game for gentle and safe touching.

Set Up
1. Everyone get really close.
2. "We are going to get in "touch" with each other in a playful way. This game is called Touch Blue.

Game Play
"Ready! Everyone, touch something blue on someone else and then freeze."

Give everyone a few seconds to find something blue to touch. "Now say goodbye to blue and touch something green on someone else and freeze."

Other fun calls to make are, "Find something shiny... letters... numbers... logos... colored shoelaces, etc."

Then you can end with, "Touch someone who you do not know well and share your name and share a really good movie you have seen in the last six months."

Variations
With young children in a classroom you can have them touch objects. "Everyone touch something round... Touch something smooth,.. Touch something green... Touch a picture of an animal... Touch a triangle... Touch a square..."

Teaching Points
This game can be a great opportunity to talk about what safe touch looks like and feels like.

You can also add the rule of electricity. If, for example, you say touch something pink and only a few people have pink on and a lot of people are touching that person, and it is crowded, you can touch the person who is touching that person, and thus by the game playing principle of electricity you are connected.

The Heart of Play

Circle Games

There is a natural connecting quality to being in a circle together, one that creates a true sense of being part of a group. Everyone can look into each other's eyes and read each other's body language. Many schools are beginning to embrace the importance of just sitting in a circle and sharing. There is also an awareness that playing games in a circle also helps young people learn the value of the group process. Teachers of the Responsive Classroom model use "circle time" as a core component of their modality. Whenever possible, I start play-shops in a circle. It is a great way to create that sense of, "We are all a part of this team whose objective is to create as much fun for everyone as possible."

Sometimes when I have large groups of 40 or more, I might not start in a circle, however, at some point I break the group into subsets of nine or so people, and have them play games in small circles.

Often in circle games there is the concept of shared leadership and sharing the focus. Many circle games involve the passing of energy in some way such that each person gets the focus of attention for just a few seconds or moments. Or there is a time when someone is in the middle and the whole group focuses on that person. Since there is a need in all of us to be seen and heard, circle games provide a robust structure for this to happen. This is a great way to learn and practice the skill of give-and-take of attention in group settings.

Even in well established groups, if you regularly meet in a circle you could dive into this section and pick out a few games to play and plug them right into your day. As I said in the intro to the previous section, many of these circle activities are also great energizers. At the same time, Circle games and sharing are also a great way to end a day, a chance for some fun and reflection..

Circle Games

BEHAVIOR MODIFICATION

(15 - 40 Players)

Otherwise know as B.F. Skinner, named after the psychologist who developed the concept of operant conditioning.

Set up
1. Have everyone seated in a circle
2. Ask for two volunteers, who will go out of the room. They are to be the guessers.
3. Then choose two people who are to be the models for the group and they get up and stand in the middle of the circle.
4. Now ask for suggestions from the group about what pose or statue they can be. It could be a simple pose like standing and leaning on each other back to back or a simple statue perhaps of a simple scene with the two players in relationship. For example a baseball pitcher and catcher.
5. Have the two models rejoin the circle and call in the guessers.

Game Play

Tell the guessers that there is a pose, a position that they need to discover. The group will help them by only giving non-verbal positive reinforcement. Gentle clapping to louder clapping to very loud clapping and cheering when they have accomplished the task. This is just like the kids game warmer and colder, however no feedback is given when they move away from the desired positions. Only positive non verbal reinforcement is given.

The key is for the whole group to be skillful in their positive reinforcement. When either of the volunteers moves toward the desired position give them positive feedback by clapping.

Teaching Points

Let the guessers know that if either of them move in a way that gets closer to the desired goal they will get rewarded. So remind them to move separately and they can talk to each other and make suggestions. I have seen some really unique scenes created. A lion tamer and lion, tango dancers, William Tell shooting the apple off of his child's head with an arrow, etc.

If the players are not making progress you may have to stop and give a hint to the two players. For instance, that their arm is close to the correct position, perhaps they could try adjusting their fingers. Occasionally the guessers will get stuck so the leader may have to give them a hint: one of you is an animal..."

The Heart of Play

COME ALONG
(10 – 40 Players)

Essentially a cooperative version of musical chairs.

Set up
1. Have everyone sit in a circle of chairs.
2. Choose someone to oversee playing the music.
3. Choose one person to be the first leader, who has no chair to sit in.

Game Play
The music starts playing. The leader walks around on the inside of the circle, reaches out a hand, and picks someone to join hands with them. That person stands up and joins the leader as they walk/dance inside the circle. That chosen person then reaches out with their free hand and chooses another person to join the moving line. After several people have been added, the music is stopped and everyone that is up on their feet in the line must let go of hands and scramble back to an empty chair. The person left becomes the next leader. Start the music!

Variations
You could also have a few players playing drums or instruments, or signing a song, thus having live music. Just be sure to choose someone as the conductor, who is in charge of when the music stops. If the group is large, choose 2 or 3 leaders to start.

Teaching Points
Depending on the ability and agility of the group, you may need to make the rule of no running. If it is a large group, you may have two people be leaders, thus having two lines. Be sure that everyone gets chosen within the first few rounds. As the play leader, you can be the music director, making sure lots of people get chosen. Sometimes children may purposely not try to get a chair, so they get to be the next leader, so remind players that the purpose is to try to get to a chair safely, and to just let it happen randomly to see whoever gets to be the last person without a chair.

Circle Games

CORE GROUP FORMATION

(8 – 12 Players)

From Playfair, this is a simple, fun exercise with small groups. If you are playing with larger numbers, it is often helpful to break into smaller groups.

Set Up
1. After playing some games in this smaller group, tell them, "This has been your core group for a while, so come up with a chant and a symbol that represents your group." This could be, "We are family," and then they all hug, or it could be, "We're number one," and they put their finger in the air. Let them brainstorm and then create. Remind them to keep it simple.
2. Have each group show the other groups what they have created.
3. "Now that you have your core group chant and symbol let's make the Core Group Formation. Make a tight circle, put your arms around each other's waists, and then lean back, supporting each other, like a big lotus flower opening up and then count quickly to ten."
4. Tell them to say good bye to their group, and that sometime later you will say the three magic words, "Core Group Formation!" At which time, everyone must chant their chant, do their symbol, and find all the players in their group, and then do the formation. The group that does it first will be designated as super-cool…The fun of this is not really to see who is first it is for the fun of getting back into their core group in an exaggerated, spirited way!

Game Play

Sometime later in your play session (or in the day), shout out the three words, "Core Group Formation". The players do their symbol, do their chant, and find their group. A big cheer for the group that made it first.

Variation

Could be used with triads or smaller groups to find each other during the play session.

Teaching points

The fun of this activity is in the creation of the unique symbols and chants and then the surprise of when you call out for them to find each other. If you have a really large group with a number of core groups you may wish to give them the suggestion of where in the space they want to meet. Maybe right where they are.

The Heart of Play

COUNT TEN

(8 -15 Players)

This is simple and fun problem-solving game that focuses on listening and being present.

Set Up
1. Gather a group of 8 – 10 (or more) players into a circle, or they could just be sitting at their desks.
2. The challenge will be for the group to count to ten, where no one can say two consecutive numbers. by random participation, one number at a time, without pre-planning who is going to say which number.
3. No one can direct it, nor can there be any pattern, meaning if three people right in a row next to each other said 1,2,3, that would be a pattern.

Game play

The object of the game is to do this without having two or more people say the same number simultaneously. For example: someone, anyone, starts by saying "One," then someone says, "Two," then someone quickly sneaks in, "Three," and then perhaps two people say "four" at the same time... Aah, back to the beginning again because two people said a number at the same time.

Variations

For a greater challenge try counting to 15 or 20, or try it with a group of 15 or more people counting to 15 or 20. This does make the challenge quite a bit harder. After a group has succeeded, have them try it with everyone's eyes closed. Another rule can be added to make the challenge a bit harder. When someone says a number neither person to their right or left can say the next number.

Teaching Points

This is a great game in a circle of approximately ten people. It get's harder as you add more people. You can stop the group and have them brainstorm what will create greater success. Being patient, slowing down and listening are usually successful strategies. Making eye contact also usually helps. Remember no pre-planning strategies.

Circle Games

ELEPHANT / RABBIT / PALM TREE

(10 - 40 Players)

A great game to emphasize that mistakes are okay, and that it is just fun to play.

Set up
1. Arrange the players in a circle, and start by giving everyone some practice in forming the characters of this jungle world game (which always involves three players reacting together to create the shape with a center person and two others).
2. An elephant is composed of one center person who turns into a long trunk, while the two other players (one on each side) become large floppy ears. The trunk is made by sticking your right arm out and wrapping your left arm under and around the right arm and grasping your nose. The ears are made by the players on the side making a big half-circle with their arms.
3. A palm tree has a tall trunk that reaches for the sky (the center person), flanked by two arching palm fronds (or coconuts).
4. The third animal is the rabbit. The middle person makes the big ears and big teeth. The two side people thump their outside foot.

Game Play

The game begins with the leader standing in the center of the circle. Their job is to point to a person and say either (1) Elephant, (2) Palm Tree or, (3) Rabbit. The signified person and the person to the left and the person to the right must perform the specific pantomime before the It player counts to ten.

If the sequence is not done correctly or not done in time, the offending person must take the place of the person in the circle. If the sequence is performed correctly, then the It goes over to another player, points, calls out a symbol and counts to ten, until someone eventually makes a mistake.

After a while the players get more proficient making the symbols, so add the rule of Bippity, Bippity, Bop. If the It points to someone and starts saying, "Bippity, Bippity, Bop," the person the It points to must say the "Bop" before the person saying the phrase, "Bippity, Bippity, Bop" does. If not said in time, that person becomes the It. Used strategically this rule makes it easier for the It player to catch someone making a mistake.

Add more than one person in the middle to increase the action—and add more symbols as the group gets better at forming the first three.

The Heart of Play

Variations

Add many more symbols.

Other symbols: Super Model: Middle person walks the runway, two side people take pictures.

Viking ship: Middle person makes Viking helmet with horns, the two outside people row while vigorously saying "hooo, hooo, hooo."

Jello: Middle person jiggles, while saying "Watch it wiggle," and the outside people join hands around the Jello to make the bowl.

Have the group make up their own symbols.

Teaching Points

Also introduce the concept of "Total It Power," meaning the person pointing is the one who decides if anyone made a mistake. This is a wonderful tool that generally eliminates arguing. If the It person says you made a mistake, you go with it because whether you did or not doesn't really matter—and being in the middle is lot's of fun too. Arguing, not so much.

> The creation of something new is not accomplished by the intellect but by the play instinct acting from inner necessity. The creative mind plays with the objects it loves.
>
> Carl Jung

Circle Games

FIRE ON THE MOUNTAIN

(15+ Players)

A fun mixing game that I learned From Frank Aycox.

Set Up
1. Everyone gets a partner.
2. The partners then stand one in front of the other making two circles: An inner circle and on outer circle each facing into the center of the circle. Have a bit of space between each pair.
3. One odd person is in the center as the caller.

Game Play
The center person starts making a repeated clapping rhythm with their hands and everyone joins in with the rhythm. This is the signal for the outer circle to start walking clockwise (it could be counter clockwise, just choose one direction to start with). After some good rhythmic clapping for 15 or 20 seconds, the center person throws their hands up in the air and shouts, "Fire on the Mountain."

This is the signal for all the inner circle people to do the same thing.

All the players who have been walking around the outside of the circles must now scramble to move in front of anyone who has their arms up, which will be all the inner circle people, and take their place in front of them.

Meanwhile the caller since they are in the middle should be able to quickly find a spot in front of someone. If everyone is comfortable with a bit of touch, when an outer circle person lands in front of a player with their arms up who just shouted "Fire On the Mountain," that person places their hands on that persons shoulders—thus anyone who still has their hands up is an open spot. One person will be left without a spot in and thus they can be the next caller.

Teaching Points
This is one of those scrambling to get to a spot game. Remind the players to play safely in their bodies and not push each other. Also, after a couple of rounds the circles will have gotten substantially closer together, thus less space, so have the players take a couple of steps back and play again.

Variations
All you musical people out there, create a song or a call and response to go with the clapping.

The Heart of Play

GROOVE-A-LISCIOUS
(8 - 15)

This is truly a fun and zany game.

Set -Up
(This game takes more explanation than most, so introduce each rule one at a time and play it for a bit.)
1. Get everyone in a fairly tight circle and explain that this is a game of passing energy, and just for a moment everyone will have the energy and focus.
2. First, show the group how to pass a wave around the circle by moving their hands as if passing a little wave in one direction, saying—"whoosh."
3. Pass this around a couple of times.

Game Play
Obviously this would get very boring, so now demonstrate how anyone can put their hands up, facing the person's direction who just passed them the "whoosh," and say, "Whoa!" This stops the Whoosh and sends it back in the direction it came from.

Play this for a bit and then you will see that sometimes it can get stuck with people on each side of someone saying, "Whoa."

Next, introduce the rule that when it comes to you anyone can zap the energy to anyone else in the circle by slapping their hands together in a pointing-slapping fashion, and getting eye contact with the person they are zapping, and saying, "Zap," nice and loudly. The person who has received the zap now has two choices, to either continue the Zap to someone else, or to start a new whoosh in either direction. "You cannot Whoa a Zap." These are the first three rules, so play this for a bit.

Later introduce an energy changer, called Groove-a-liscious. When it comes to you, you can wave your arms in front of you like a dancer getting groovy, and say Groove-a-liscious, and everyone mirrors you and says "Groove-a-liscious."

Later, you can also add a Non-sequitor, which means you can do anything you want for a few seconds, and everyone mirrors you. After either a Groove-a-liscious or a Non-sequitor, that person then must get the game going with either a "Whoosh," or a "Zap." Play a little more.

Finally there is the rule called, " Freak Out." When the energy comes to you, you can say, "Freak Out." and everyone now has to run around and change places in the circle. The person who said, "Freak Out," starts with one of the other choices.

Circle Games

Variations

For younger children perhaps start slowly and just do whoosh and whoa You can also designate two or three players who "have the power" to do Whoa. Then after a couple of minutes change the players who have the Whoa power.

Teaching Points

This game is great from the standpoint that, basically, each person has the focus for just a second or two, as they pass the energy, or if they are doing Groove-a-liscious or a Non-sequitor for no more than just a few seconds. This is great for some children who have a hard time sharing the energy, and just want the focus on them. The structure of the game is such that they can do something silly and get attention, but just for few seconds. Be sure to remind anyone to do their silly thing and then pass it on.

Games such as Consensus, Elephant Palm Tree, Memory Loss, etc., rely on the players having a good imagination and on their being creative. One winter I was teaching a mindfulness program for a school where I designed a lesson on imagination and creativity. I did a presentation about our brains and how we have a left hemisphere and a right hemisphere and they have different functions. I explained that our left brain is our "L" brain. It is literal, linguistic, labels everything, and makes lists. While our right brains are where imagination, creativity, and seeing the big picture live.

Since so much of school operates on a left-brain basis, and where learning is focused on getting the right answer, we tend to need more creativity and imaginative play. And kids love it. We have to champion these programs that give students permission to develop more of the skills associated with right-brained learning where there are often very many right answers.

Remember, Albert Einstein said: "Imagination is more important than knowledge."

The Heart of Play

GROUP JUGGLE
(10 - 20 Players)

A great cooperative game.

Set -up
1. Have the group form a circle.
2. One person will be designated as the starter. The starter has a number of soft tossing balls available.
3. The starter starts by tossing a ball to anyone across the circle. This first person will throw to that same person every time.
4. This second person raises their hand, or crosses their arms or puts a foot froward to indicate they have already received it, and then tosses the ball across the circle to a new person. This continues until everyone has their hands up, indicating each person has caught the ball once and the pattern is complete by the ball coming back to the person who started it.
5. Remind the players to remember who they tossed it to.

Game play
Repeat the pattern to make sure everyone knows it, and then commence adding more balls gradually. If people drop the balls just get the balls going again. Remind the players to watch the person who is throwing to you, and to throw underhanded (usually), making the tosses easy to catch.

Try adding a command, such as, "Now in slow motion," or, "Now in hyper speed," or try reversing the throwing pattern.

Variations
With younger children you can have them in smaller groups and roll a couple of balls in that same person-to-person pattern.

Teaching points
Ideally played with about 10 - 15 players this can be done with more players, however, it takes a bit of time to set the pattern. A great opportunity to reflect on how we all tend to be more successful when just focusing on one basic task at a time, such as, watching the person you receive it from, then turning and tossing it to another person. Ask players how they can apply this to their everyday life. Focusing on one task at a time, even amidst the chaos of everything around them.

Circle Games

HAVE YOU EVER

(8 - 40)

Here's another variation on the switching chairs theme. A great getting-to-know-you game.

Set Up
1. Each player, except one, sits on a chair (or something like a pillow or jacket to designate their space), and these chairs are in a circle.
2. The extra person goes to the center of the circle.
3. Demonstrate to the group how this person will now ask a question in the "Have You Ever" form, then anyone who answers yes to that question gets up immediately and SAFELY moves to another chair.
4. The person in the middle must also be able to answer yes to the question they ask.
5. The person in the middle also attempts to find an open seat (and usually has an easy time of it). The player who does not get a seat is the next person in the middle and asks the next question.

Game Play
The middle person asks a "Have You Ever question". "Have you ever ridden a bike?" Anyone who answers yes to that question immediately gets up and finds another chair. The person who does not get a seat asked the next question.

Sometimes players will get stuck when they have to think of a question on the spot, so recommend travel questions, i.e. "Have you ever been to New Hampshire?" With younger children the teacher may actually ask the questions or be in the middle and help the middle player think of a question.

Variations
Anyone who answers yes to the question comes to the center and gives each other a high five. Variations for younger children are described in The Cool Breeze Blows for Anyone Who...

Teaching Points
This game is ideal for 10 – 40 people. If chairs or not available it can be done with people standing in a tight circle and the last person to find a space in the circle is the next questioner.

It is important to remind players that the object is to not contact anybody,

The Heart of Play

to be safe with their bodies and to not dive into chairs. Remind them continually. With kids who have not played cooperatively before they might start pushing. Stop and reclarify the no contact rule as necessary.

> When I first arrived at the private school in upstate NY where I worked as the PE teacher, I was on recess duty everyday for the student in grades 5 through 8. They loved playing kickball. However kickball is a game where the best athletes tend to dominate the play. The other kids tend to admire these athletic kids and they want to play with them, and the less athletic kids feel left out, and with the athletes running into their area to catch the ball, or the kickball being thrown too hard to get them out. It was getting to be a problem.
>
> So after a couple of weeks observing this, I banned the game of kickball at recess. I could have changed the rules to make it better for everyone but I decided yanking it was the better choice at that time. The game just didn't have a good MAP (maximum activity plan) for that group at that time.
>
> Of course some kids weren't happy, but I explained this was temporary, and we could look at bringing it back at some point, but for now they just had to play other games. Not too hard a plight, and life went on just fine...

Circle Games

HO

(15 - 50)

A great game to start building energy with a group.

Set Up
1. Have the group make a large circle.
2. Demonstrate how you, the leader jogs across the circle making eye contact with one person and then stop in front of this person.
3. That is the signal for that chosen person and the leader to jump up at the same time, slapping the persons palms in a "Double High Five," therefore a High Ten, and they both say, "HO" loudly together.
4. The leader then takes that persons place in the circle and that person then runs across the circle and picks a new person.

Game Play
After the group gets the idea the leader selects another person, then another person so you may have four or five people moving across the circle to run and go "Ho."

Remember to mention safety, as it is important to time the jumps and meet your partners energy, slapping in synchronicity and not knock someone over or miss their hands. This is a very high energy game, so remember to tell players to be aware when there are more than a couple of people jogging across the circle.

Variations
Have the players just give a simple high five and not jump. Or choose a different exclamation. Maybe "Yihaa!" or a loud "Yes!" or perhaps shout that persons name.

Teaching points
Great for circles of thirty or more players although fine for a group of fifteen to twenty. If it is a smaller group just make sure they spread out and make the circle big enough.

The Heart of Play

HUMAN MACHINE

(8 - 30+)

A game of creativity, imagination, movement and sound.

Set up
1. Everyone can be in a large circle or seated in an audience style set-up leaving lot's of space for the activity
2. Demonstrate how everyone is going to build a collective machine by adding in one person at a time.
3. Demonstrate with two or three people to start so that everyone sees how it is done.

Game play
One player starts the game as the first part of the machine. This player steps into the center and does a certain repetitive movement, and does a corresponding repeating sound as if a part of a machine. Another player then joins this player and adds another movement and sound that blends with or complements the first player's sound and movement.

One-by-one the players join this ever growing machine becoming the cogs and gears in this machine. After all the players have joined (or those that want to—it's also fun to just watch the machine being built) the movements of the machine the speed up and the sounds grow louder.

To end the game have the players speed the machine up and then slow the machine down until it comes to a complete stop.

Variations
Eventually the machine is just working too hard, and "boom" it collapses from over exertion. Also have the students brainstorm for what the next machine makes. Oh, it makes balloons. Ready, let's build a machine that makes bubble gum...

Teaching Points
Take a moment to recognize the incredible creativity and cooperation that the group just exhibited. Point out how they clearly followed the rules. Children love the creativity of this game however it can lend itself to some chaos. Set very clear boundaries as to what is okay. Initially it may be best to state that the there is no touching. Later it can be you can contact another person (after all machine

Circle Games

parts are connected) but not lean on them. Also this game can be great way to reflect on the day. Ask the students what has been the key value for that day. Maybe it was listening. Let's build a machine that represents listening.

> You want games that have lots of activity for everyone playing. So I gave the kids foam swords and taught them how to do cooperative sword play. I made big hula hoops. I bought lots of frisbees so they could play frisbee golf or ultimate frisbee. I encouraged them to play on the jungle gym. I bought net goals that could be used for soccer or team handball. These are all games that have a better MAP than kickball. It helped them to be better sports when playing Four Square, and to not argue. Better to do a "do over" than to argue over a line call. I engaged the more athletic kids into playing basketball which also has a much better MAP than kickball.
>
> Eventually I allowed the students to play kickball again. An interesting thing happened—they hardly ever chose to play it.

The Heart of Play

HUMAN STATUES

(8 - 30+)

A great opportunity to witness creativity in action and to recognize all the amazing values expressed both by the group and individuals.

Set up
1. Everyone can be in a large circle or seated in an audience style set-up, leaving lots of space for the activity.
2. Demonstrate how everyone is going to build a collective statue by adding one person at a time.
3. Demonstrate with two or three people to start so that everyone sees how it is done. Tell them if they do touch another person that they are not to put their weight on that person.

Game play
One player starts the game going into the center and creating a pose that they can hold for at least a minute. Then another person goes into the center and joins this other person and makes a new pose that joins with, complements or adds to this making of a growing statue. More players join until the leader or the group feels it is done. Perhaps ask for suggestions for the name of this statue.

The players then leave one at a time in the same order they went in with and this last person that went in stays and holds that pose and then a new statue is built starting with this last persons pose.

Variations
Just do one full statue without having anyone leave at the end. Or divide into smaller groups of players and make statues in a museum. Have some people walk around and view all the statues in the unusual museum.

Teaching points
Take a moment to recognize the incredible creativity, cooperation, stillness and balance that the group just exhibited. Point out how they clearly followed the rules. It is not necessary for the players to touch, however, the game works well when some of the statue pieces can be in contact. Set very clear boundaries as to what is okay. Demonstrate what it looks like to be in contact without having to support the persons weight in any way.

Circle Games

OOH-AAH

(20 – 50+)

When I first saw Bill Michealis teach this activity I learned so distinctly how the leading of a game, the energy with which you facilitate the game can make all the difference. This is a bit of an energizer, a bit of team building game, and also a great closing activity. You definitely need a good size group for this. At least more then 20, and the more the merrier. I have done it in circles of 80 to 90 people with great success.

Set Up
1. Gather everyone in a circle.
2. Ask the group to hold hands and explain that we are going to pass two sounds around the circle in opposite directions.
3. So starting clockwise send an "Ooh." Then going the other way start an "Aah."
4. After those have gone thru a few people start another "Ooh" then another "Aah," and then another.
5. Then watch it as it is passed around and then the fun of course is where they cross and watching someone deal with this conundrum.
6. Rarely do groups ever get all the sounds all the way around, although occasionally it does. Also, sometimes an extra one gets created.
7. After this has been accomplished and everyone has laughed, ask them now let's see how fast we can pass an "ooh." around the circle. Ask if there is someone who can be a timekeeper in the group who has a stopwatch on their watch or cell phone.

Game Play

Start an "Ooh" in one direction and time how long it takes to pass the it around, beginning and ending with you as the leader. With a group of thirty it will usually take about 15 - 20 seconds.

Ask the group how much faster they think they can do it. People will say twelve or ten seconds. Invariably someone says a decently low number and the group will all make sounds and declarations of doubt. No they can't do it in 6 seconds. I usually pick a time as the goal that seems too difficult, but close to a low one someone suggested, but not too low. So in a group of thirty I might say let's shoot for under 7 seconds appeasing the person who said 6 who almost everyone thinks is crazy.

The Heart of Play

Almost always the group cuts their time in half. And you say, "Look, we just cut nine seconds off our previous time, so now we have done it in eleven seconds. We only have to cut four more seconds off the time."

I ask the group for suggestions as to how they can do it faster. Getting closer is a good suggestion. Let's try it. Or maybe the suggestion is to go in the other direction try that. Other suggestions are everyone turns their head in one directions. Doesn't usually help but you can try it. I suggest they loosen up their arms and heads little bit like a good jazz musicians, Ooh, aah!" This doesn't help much either but it feels good.

So now I bet the group is close to the goal maybe improving a couple of more seconds. You can make a bit of a joke about where in the circle it moved quickly and where maybe it didn't. Sometimes if I want it to end I share the "secret", which is anticipation. You know it is coming to you so just keep it going, Just like in the wave at a sporting event. Once everyone gets this it will go faster. If they don't reach their goal tell them no one is going to care if they are a little bit ahead of the wave. Just get it flying around the circle. Sometimes someone will be really smart and say, "Can we say Ooh" all at once. In essence, this fits into the challenge. I have seen large groups off forty or fifty people send it around in a wave of about 8 seconds. Groups of twenty I have seen them do it in under 4 seconds. It is just how fast can the wave go. Ready, OOOO!

Variations
Try using different sounds.

Teaching Points
Enthusiastic and dramatic facilitations is the key to this game.

Circle Games

PASS THE CLAP

(6 - 20)

A fun circle game that is all about rhythm and energy.

Set Up
1. Demonstrate how the leader turns to the the person on their left (or could be right) gets eye contact and together they clap at the same time.
2. That person then turns to their left gets eye contact and passes the clap.
3. The goal is for the claps to happen at exactly the same time and for the claps to be passed in rhythm.

Game Play
Start the claps and after a round or two pick up the pace just a bit. Then introduce that a person can change the direction of the clap. This happens when the receiving person who has just received the clap doesn't turn and face the next person. Instead they stay facing that person and clap a second time. Thus it gets sent back in the direction it came. The challenge is to do it in the same rhythm and the person who just turned and passed the clap really has to pay attention when this happens because everyone has gotten used to turning and passing. Now the clap heads in the opposite direction.

Variations
There are many of these passing games in circles. Use your imagination as to what imaginary energy you might want to send. Imagine different kinds of balls you could throw, or imagine they are ninja throwing blades, and imagine yourself being a great ninja who can catch a throwing star.

Teaching points
The object isn't to go faster and faster, however it is fun that once the group gets the rhythm to build up the energy with a bit more speed. This game is about feeling the energy of the group. Playing circle games such as this creates a sense of the group as one entity working together to create a fun shared experience. It also helps with attention and focus.

The Heart of Play

PASS THE SOUND AND MOVEMENT

(8-20)

There are lots of passing games using sound and movements. Here is a basic one that is simple and fun.

Set Up
1. Have everyone get in a circle.
2. Demonstrate how each person will mirror the sound and movement that is created by the leader as best they can.
3. Once it goes all the way around the circle, the next person in that direction creates a new sound and movement, which is then sent around...

Game Play
The leader turns to the next person in the circle and does a sound and movement. This person immediately replays that same sound and movement. This person then turns to the next person and recreates this same sound and movement which is then mirrored/replayed and on it goes around the circle, like a wave. Remind the players to do this quickly. Best to try to not think, just move your body and do the sound and movement. After everyone gets a feel of this have each person keep the wave going but they now change the sound and movement slightly. As in the game telephone the sound and movement will naturally want to change. Go around a few times and see how the sound and movement has transformed.

Variations
Pass the sound and movement across the circle. The person receiving it mirrors that sound and movement and then creates a new one that they pass to another person. Have each person make the sound and movement bigger and louder until the last person makes it really exaggerated.

Teaching Points
When the players are asked to change the sound and movement slightly, the idea is to not think about what you are going to do. Just react and allow the change to happen naturally.

Circle Games

SCREAM CIRCLE

(8 - 20)

Surprisingly simple yet so very fun.

Set Up
1. The players stand in a tight circle. Everyone looks down at all the cool feet making up the base of this circle.
2. Each player picks one pair of feet to look at.
3. This is the person they have secretly chosen.
4. Upon the leaders command of, "1,2,3, Heads Up," everyone snaps their head up and stares at the person whose feet they have chosen.
5. If that person they are staring at is looking at someone else nothing happens.
6. If the person they have chosen has also chosen them, and they are staring at each other then both players scream in surprise.

Game Play
So ready now that the group knows that they are picking just one person the leader says, "Heads down, ready? 1,2,3, Heads up." Are there any screams? It's really fun when no one has chosen each other and there are no screams. Wait a few seconds and then, "Heads down, ready? 1,2,3, Heads up..."

Repeat a number of times.

Variations
Have two circles and the players change circles after they scream. Or you can do this as an elimination game so when players have chosen each other and scream, they are eliminated from the circle. The circle closes in and then do it again until one or two players have survived. It actually goes quite quickly, then you can play again.

Teaching Points
Ask the players not to scream so loudly that it will hurt the ears of the other players in the group. It is more a scream of surprise.

The Heart of Play

SLAP PASS

(8 - 15)

This is a simple theater warm up game. It helps the players to focus and stay totally present. Only needs to be played for about 30 – 60 seconds.

Set up
1. Gather everyone in a circle.
2. Demonstrate how the slap is made by rolling one palm over the other as if rolling a small piece of dough between their palms in a rolling, slapping motion. You can also add a sound, such as Zap!
3. Show how it can be fun to send it back to the same person who sent it to you, keeping everyone on their toes.

Game Play
One person initiates the zapping of the energy by slapping their palms together as if shooting an energy bolt out their hands and directs the energy bolt to someone else. This person then passes the slap onto another person. Try to pick up the speed. Only necessary to play this for 30 seconds or so. Don't let the group get bored.

Variations
Players can play with the energy before sending it, and the other player can receive the energy based on what is being sent. And then send a new energy bolt of their own. The energy could be a ninja throwing star or a football pass or blowing a kiss. Or it can be just passing a sound with the energy, and the player mirrors the sound and then makes up their own new sound.

Teaching Points
A great game to build a sense of connection and to enliven the energy of the group. A great opportunity to emphasize being ready and paying attention.

Circle Games

VEGETARIANISM

(15 – 40)

Great lead in to the games Have You Ever?, and The Cool Breeze Blows.

Set Up
1. Have all the players sit in a circle seated in chairs, except one who stands in the middle.
2. This middle player is going to play detective and try to find out who hates what vegetable.
3. All the seated players think of the one vegetable that they hate.
4. They keep their choices secret.

Game Play

The person in the middle names off a number of vegetables that come to mind and then says, "Switch!" The people who had their vegetables called must switch to another chair or spot, of course the middle person also tries to get to a now vacated chair. Whoever is left without a spot becomes the next detective in the middle. If the person in the middle calls out "Vegetarianism," everyone has to go. At the conclusion of the game go around the circle and ask everyone to name their most hated vegetable to see if anyone did not get named.

Variations

Have everyone choose their favorite fruit and play the game calling out fruits. "Kiwi, strawberries, bananas, switch." Or the person can call, "Fruit Basket," and everyone has to move and change places. Another way to play is to scatter pairs of chairs around the play space and the players are in partners and sit in the chairs. They secretly each have their favorite fruits. One partnership does not have chairs so they are the callers, and if either of the partners fruits get called the partnership gets up traveling together by holding hands to find a new par of chairs to sit in.

Teaching Points

Remind the players to be safe in their bodies and that the object of the game is to not touch anyone while changing places. Try a round or two moving in slow motion or like zombies to reinforce this.

The Heart of Play

Games for Younger Kids

This games manual is intended to cover a wide spectrum of ages. There is a difference in the way a three year old plays, and a five year old, and a seven year old, etc., but they all benefit greatly from the social-emotional aspects of these activities, which integrate and overlap many developmental stages. While each year of early childhood has its own specific needs in terms of what is most appropriate and children vary in their development, in a larger, more general categorization, for kids from toddler thru age seven, dramatic play, free play, object play, and movement-based play are the primary modes.

As children reach elementary school age they start wanting more group play. They want to play with their peers. This section is a selection of games that work well with children ages five through eight year old. This includes a number of circle games, such as Many Ways to Get There, The Cool Breeze Blows, and Pass the Funny Face.

Many of the games throughout the rest of this book, maybe with a few adaptations, can be made to work with younger kids. Games in the mindfulness and improv theater games section can also work nicely with this age group. Conversely, some of the games in this chapter are also great for adults and older kids. For example, the game Lemonade is one of my all time favorites with all ages.

Of course, I have also always loved parachute games. Lots of other books on play include them, so for the sake of brevity I am not going to describe them here, but they can also be great for these younger players. Also, I highly recommend for everyone who works with children from age three to eight, to take a training with Life is Good Playmakers. Also, go the web site for the Great Activities Publishing company, as there is wealth of resources there for this age group.

So bring the magic of social play to these young minds, and share the love!

Games for Younger Kids

ALL HANDS ON DECK (GRADES 2 +)
(10 – 30 Players)

A fun game of making decisions and joining with others to do what is called.

Set Up
1. The captain of the ship calls out the various commands and the players must follow correctly and/or join with the proper number of players.
2. If someone makes a mistake (goes in the wrong direction) or they can't fit into a group, because there aren't the correct numbers, they are eliminated or sent to "Walk the Plank."
3. With younger children I just have them jump off a mat into the pretend ocean, and then they immediately rejoin the group.
4. For older kids I may have them do ten sit-ups or five push ups to get back into the game.
5. Determine the boundaries of the space, what represents the front, back, and two sides of the space.

Game Play

Do a complete run through of all the commands before actively playing the game. The game starts with groups of four or five player all sitting in a line and saluting the captain. This is, "All hands on Deck."

The captain then begins calling out other commands:

Starboard: Everyone runs to the right side of the boat.

Port: Everyone runs to the left side of the space

Bow: Everyone runs to the front.

Stern: Everyone runs to the back of the space.

Sea sick: Two people holding hands and one person leaning over their grasped hands and pretending to get sick.

Man overboard: One person becomes the floating object and the other person lays across their body.

Lifeboat: Three people. Two sitting and holding their hands out as if they are a lifeboat, and one sitting in the middle of the boat.

Crows nest: Three people kneeling making a circle, and one person has their hand on their forehead looking out to Sea.

"Okay, everyone now that we have learned all the commands, let's play. All Hands on Deck."

The Heart of Play

Variations

Make up your own imaginative commands and their corresponding formations. Mermaids bathing on the rocks, a whale swimming by, working in the galley etc.

Teaching Points

Elimination games can be fun, but they can also get too competitive. The fun is in the dance of this game. As you can tell the different calls represent a different number of people and thus the combinations are constantly changing. Occasionally you can have the game go all the way down to the last few people however games of elimination are only fun if the group is ready for and wants that challenge. After the players have learned the commands, other players can take turns being the captain and calling out the commands.

> In 2002 I designed a PE program for students with autism at an alternative school that was created specifically for students with Aspergers Syndrome. I had noticed over the years that a few kids on the autism spectrum who attended our theater program, The Adventure Game theater, seemed to do quite well in our camps. They enjoyed the focus on play, role-playing and fun.
>
> So the creator of the ASPIE school, Valarie Paradis heard of our work and asked me to help her create an alternative PE program. I could only attend once a week, but the time I spent there was truly suggestive of the power of playfulness as a core competency that creates connection and belonging for this group. This eventually led us to creating, in collaboration with The Wayfinder Experience, an alternative summer camp based on role-playing. We eventually presented at a national autism conference on the success of our work, which was unanimously regarded as transformational.
>
> At the conference I was introduced to the work of Pam Wolfberg from San Francisco State College. Pam's program truly embodies the value that play has to offer to everyone, and in particular young people "on the spectrum."

Games for Younger Kids

ANIMAL CATCHER

(10 – 30)

(From Artie Kamiya – Great Activities Publishing company.) My kindergartners and 1st graders would play this game all day long.

Set Up
1. Put a mat or some designated coned area at one end of the play space.
2. This will be the "cage" or "compound" where the animals are kept.
3. Before the game begins ask all the children what animals they want to be.
4. Then narrate a little story as to how you are the caretaker and how you accidentally walked away from the cage forgetting to lock it, and that will be the signal for them to run away.

Game Play

All the players run away. Run after them, tag them and capture them and bring them back to their cage. Then add the rule that if another player can run back to the cage and tag another animal they are freed before the animal catcher gets back to the cage.

Variations

Add the scenario that you have little tranquilizer darts (use soft fleece balls or foam balls) and you toss them at the animals and they are hit by the ball they are put to sleep and you can grasp their hands and lead the sleepy animals back to their cage. Also enlist other players to be helpers to lead the tranquilized players back to their cages. Now any free players can run back, tag them (wake them up) and the game goes on.

Teaching Points

Children love to be chased by grown ups. Chasing and fleeing are an essential part of play that children naturally love to do. Maintaining just the right mix of playfulness, excitement and running can be great exercise and so much fun.

The Heart of Play

CAR WASH
(10 - 40 Players)

One of those fun simple New Games I first learned. A fun intergenerational experience.

Set up
1. Find a very soft grassy area, soft carpet or on mats.
2. Have players form two lines facing each other with about four feet between them. They get on their knees.
3. Explain to everyone that this is a car wash.
4. Have a few spare people start on one end. These will be the first people entering the car wash.

Game Play
The first person on the starting end gets on their hands and knees and will go through the line. First that person declares what kind of car they are, "I am a Honda Civic—"

"Okay here comes the Honda…" This person now crawls through the car wash and the players on the sides gently brush, buff, and wash the car as it passes. When that player reaches the end, they join the end of one of the lines and now become one of the washers. If you have two longish lines, start another car as the first car is half way down. "I am a Lamborghini—"

"Here comes the Lamborghini…" After a few cars have gone and everyone gets the hang of it, the first players at the beginning of the car washer lines become the first in line to be the cars that are washed, thus everyone get a chance.

Teaching Points
It is good idea for the facilitator to be at the start of the Car Wash, and to announce the cars, thus supervising the flow. This is a game that involves touch, so only use it where everyone feels safe. However, imagine doing it with preschoolers during an intergenerational party. It helps to teach young people that they can touch playfully and safely when the adults are modeling this for them.

Variation
Maybe it is carnival ride and the children could be on scooters, or walking down a line, and the people on the sides are different characters, or scenes, or statues like in the It's a Small World ride at Disney, and then the person going through the line has to guess what they are.

Games for Younger Kids

FUNNY FACE HOT POTATO CATCH

(6 - 12+)

A fun little creation of my own that works well in small circle. Great for a family at home.

Set Up
1. Start by playing a simple game of catch.
2. Tell the players that the ball is hot so they can only hold it for a second or two.
3. Remind them that smooth tosses which are easy too catch are best.
4. You can even precede this game with playing name and catch where you learn people's names by saying their name and tossing them the ball.

Game Play
After everyone has the idea, add a second ball into the game. The rule now is a player who ends up having two balls at the same time must make a funny face and a funny sound. Then quickly they toss the balls back into the game. Later, a third ball into the game. The game works well when the players are not purposely trying to get a person to have two balls. It is more fun when it just happens. Remind the players that tosses which are on target and easy to catch make the game more fun for everyone. Then add a fourth ball or even more if the group is large enough.

Variations
When two balls are possessed, the player has to explode and collapse onto the ground. Or you can play this with younger children with balls you can roll. The collisions of the balls is always fun.

Teaching points
This game will not work well with players that want to throw the ball too hard at the other players. Talk about how easy passes are more catchable and will make the game flow better.

The Heart of Play

HURRICANE

(15 +)

A fun game that emphasizes some qualities of nature.

Set Up
1. Gather in groups of three.
2. The three of you will be making a hut with one villager inside.
3. To do this, one person squats down and the other two people stand and place their palms together, making the walls and the roof of a building over the squatting person. This is the villagers hut.
4. There are three commands in this game. Famine, Earthquake, and Hurricane.
5. When Famine is called, the villager must leave their hut and go find an empty hut to re-inhabit.
6. When Earthquake is called the walls collapse and must then run and reform over another villager.
7. When Hurricane is called everyone swirls around and then must reconstruct with different players making a new hut and villager.

Game Play
The leader (you as the teacher can start in this position) shares a short story. "Oh it is beautiful day, everyone is happy in their homes, but wait, the earth starts shaking... Oh, it is an earthquake!" The walls collapse and run around and start reforming. Of course you as the leader, the story teller, is sure to become a wall and then the last person who does not have a home – (so you will have to balance the number of players so there is one extra) becomes the next story teller."

"It seems the sun has been very hot this summer and we have had so little rain. Yes it is a Famine. All the squatted people have to leave their house looking for food and so they crawl into a new hut in a new village. A new story teller may say, "Oh look at those gigantic clouds, and so much wind. It is a Hurricane!"

Variations
If you have two extra players they can tell the story together.

Teaching points
This is a fun mixing game and the most fun is for the extra person to tell an imaginative, yet concise, story before each round.

Games for Younger Kids

LEMONADE

(8 – 20)

A great game for intergenerational play, this is an acting game and a tag game all rolled into one. Ideal for mixed ages. Good to have an adult with each team.

Set Up
1. Each team has a safety zone at opposite ends of the playing area. Mark that with cones or some kind of markers and also demarcate a center line.
2. The teams gather in there safety zone in a huddle and pick a profession or trade they will pantomime, such as surfing, and a place that they will be from, such as California (that may be a clue to the trade they have chosen).
3. Choose one team to go first. This team joins hands and takes a big step toward the other team and says, "Here we come."
4. The other team replies while taking a big step, "Where you from?"
5. To which they get the response "California," as this team takes another step forward.
6. The inquiring team asks while stepping forward, "What's your trade?"
7. "We sell lemonade," is the standard answer as the team steps again.
8. The guessing team comes back with a final, "Well then show us some if you're not afraid," (which means begin acting out, miming their job, their occupation).

Game Play
By then the teams are about five feet apart at the center line. The first team pantomimes the trade they have chosen, while the second team tries to guess what it is. As soon as someone on the guessing team guesses correctly, the first team starts to run back to their safety area. The other team chases them, and anyone tagged before they reach their safety zone becomes a member of the tagging team. Then it is the other team's turn to choose a profession and a location, and the game continues back and forth.

Teaching Points
When playing with younger children it is important to have an adult help lead the discussion and the choosing of the occupations. Make sure when players turn around and run that there is no one behind them. Remind everyone to tag gently. You can always use flags to pull rather than tagging directly.

The Heart of Play

MANY WAYS TO GET THERE

(10 – 40)

(From Artie Kamiya) Great game for young children. How many ways are there to travel? Bike, walk, car, train, plane... In this game we get to travel across the circle any way we want.

Set Up
1. Have everyone in a circle, seated on the floor is fine, or it could be in a circle of chairs, or even standing.
2. Have a few spaces empty in the circle.
3. Tell the players there are many ways to travel across this circle, safely and creatively. Someone could walk slowly, or you could hop, or walk like a robot, or a zombie, or a snake, or really any movement pattern or expression with their bodies.

Game Play
Start with just one person traveling across the circle, and everyone can applaud or just be in wonder at this person's creativity. Then ask for another volunteer, and everyone watches as this person explores their own unique movement creation. After a bit of time have two or three people travel at once. If the group is ready to move safely all together, give them the full on experience and have everyone travel across the circle all at once.

Variations
Ask the group for other ways they could move across the circle. Maybe as a flock of birds, or how about bunch of frogs. In my laughter yoga classes when I teach this to adults, I call this the Ministry of Silly Walks in honor of the Monty Python Skit, and we all laugh along with the silly creations.

Teaching Points
A great game for children to offer support to each other for their own uniqueness.

Games for Younger Kids

MESSY BACKYARD

(10 – 40)

So very simple and yet so very fun.

Set up
1. Gather all the soft throwable objects that you have.
2. Then divide your play area into two sides. It could be two sides of basketball court, or two sides of a volleyball court.
3. Put out all your soft play objects evenly onto each side.
4. Divide up into two teams.

Game Play
The object is very simple. On the start signal just throw the objects on your side of the playing area onto to the other side. After 30 or 45 seconds of play stop the action. Take a look and see which team accomplished getting more objects onto the other side at that moment.

Variations
If you only have objects like tennis balls, play that the players can only roll them. Or play in a small indoor space with rolled up balls of paper.

Teaching Points
The fun is in the throwing, not really in the comparing. You can tell a fun story that your mom has asked you to clean up your back yard, so you decide to try and throw it into your neighbors yard, but of course they decide to throw it back so then it just becomes fun to keep on throwing things.

> A little side note: the other evening I watched an episode of Mythbusters. They sought out to discover if there was some anatomical reason why boys seemed to throw better than girls. I had often said in my gym classes that the statement, "someone throws like a girl," was truly an ignorant and sexist statement. Then I would have everyone in my class throw with their non-dominant arm.

The Heart of Play

> Mythbusters brought numerous girls and boys of different ages and had them throw, then they did slow motion studies, and then did exactly the same thing that I had done in my gym class and have everyone throw with everyone looks pretty uncoordinated throwing with their nondominant hand.
>
> At first they thought they thought there were some genetic and anatomical differences and the girls of the same ages did not throw as fluidly and the boys. Then they brought in female collegiate softball players and found no differences. The college softball players had the same efficient form as the major league baseball player. The velocity may be a bit less due to the stronger muscular structure males have, however the accuracy and the form was the same. It really is a matter of young boys have more are exposed to and choose to participate in more throwing activities then girls tend to. But when given the same amount of practice girls can throw with the same efficiency and accuracy of motion as boys.

Games for Younger Kids

MOVE AND SHAKE IT UP

From *Life is Good Playmakers*, this is a fun way to release energy.

Set up
1. "Hey everyone, do you sometimes have all that energy in your body where you just got to move it? Well, let's give ourselves that opportunity."
2. "So let's all stand up."
3. "I'll demonstrate first."
4. "Let's shake our right arm. Ready arm shakes, arm shakes, arm shakes, arm shakes....and stop."

Game Play
Start adding other body parts. Do this by asking the group, "Okay who has another part of the body that they want to move and shake." Carol raises her hand. "Carol what do you want to shake? Your leg. Show us how to do that. (this a great way for children to choose to be seen as they are chosen to demonstrate this). "Okay everyone, leg shake, leg shake, leg shake and stop..." And on it goes for a few more parts of the body. Choose different players to demonstrate which body part. Be sure to emphasize if someone suggests to shake the head that you should shake your head carefully and gently. (See also the game Countdown.)

Variations
If the group has enough self control and you have the space and time you could have them move around the space and call out different fun movement commands. "Everyone, let's move and sound like a monkey, ooo, ooo, aahh, ahh and stop. Okay everyone, let's move like a dinosaur, arrr, arr, arrr... and stop."

Teaching points
Games like this are a great way to teach self regulation. Taking the moment to let them know that is time to stop by saying it in a calm clear way and using your hands in a calming and stopping gesture helps the players know it is time to stop. You could also take a moment at the end and ask everyone to take three deep breaths and ask them to feel the energy in their bodies.

The Heart of Play

OCTOPUS
(10 - 30 Players)

A simple yet classic game that young children love to play.

Set Up
1. Make a playing area about the size of a basketball court.
2. Have all the players line-up behind the line at one end of the area.
3. Choose one player to be in the middle, who is the Octopus, and they have a soft throwing ball.

Game Play

The Octopus calls out, "Fishies, fishies cross my sea." That is the command for everyone to run to the other side of the playing area. The octopus throws the ball at the players and anyone hit by the ball is now frozen and squats down on one knee and is now an extension of the Octopus. Now that everyone is on the other side, the Octopus calls out again, "Fishies, fishies, cross my sea." But watch out, anyone that is frozen can reach out with their tentacles while staying on one knee, and if they touch anyone running by, those players also take a knee and are now a part of the ever-growing Octopus.

Variations

The players can stand rather than squat on one knee, but must not move their feet when trying to tag. Also create new scenarios, i.e., Alligator, or Gorilla in the middle. Also, the Octopus could just tag with their hands. Another option is rather than squatting on one knee the players, when frozen, can just be frozen standing, like they are stuck in the mud, waving their arms like they are seaweed. In this stuck in the mud version, the runners can crawl through the legs of the frozen players—and this frees them to keep on running. The frozen players are no longer using their arms to tag, so perhaps add a couple of more taggers in the center to start the game and see if the runners can unfreeze enough players each time to keep the game flowing.

Teaching points

One reason to squat on one knee is that it's a good resting place and it's easier for a player to not cheat by moving their feet from that spot when trying to tag someone. The challenge here is that whoever gets caught first is there for a while, so make sure the game goes quickly because the fun of the game is running through the octopus-obstacle-course. Ideally, play a few rounds so everyone gets that opportunity.

Games for Younger Kids

PASS A FUNNY FACE

(6 – 20)

A great game to elicit laughter and honor silliness.

Set Up
1. Have everyone sit in a circle.
2. The object of the game is to make really funny faces.
3. Have all the players warm up by scrunching their noses, puffing out their cheeks and wrinkling their forehead in preparation for making funny faces.
4. Add a little fantasy to the game by telling the players that, a magic spell has been cast over the group changing everyone's face.
5. To be saved from the spell, funny faces have to be passed from person to person around the circle until it gets back to the first person again. Then the spell will magically disappear.

Game Play
To start the game, the leader or a designated first person makes a funny face and displays it to the group. They then turn to their neighbor who mirrors this expression. These players both turn to the group to get verification that the mimicking player has done an adequate job of mirroring the face. This second player now changes the face into another funny face, and turns to their neighbor and the process continues. It is important to remind the players to show the group their funny face in the mirroring process, as this keeps the whole group involved in the fun.

Variations
A person makes a funny face and points to anyone in the circle who now must mirror that face. That person then make a new face and point someone new.

Teaching Points
Since this game is focused on just two players at a time, make sure the group is ready for this level of patience. Really, the fun of this game is being entertained by each pairs mirroring of the funny faces.

The Heart of Play

SET EM UP / KNOCK EM DOWN
(10 - 30)

About as simple a game as it can get, but the young ones love it.

Set Up
1. Set up cones—or other objects that stand up—all around the play space.
2. Divide the players into two groups.
3. Tell the first group that their job is very simple, it is to knock down the cones.
4. They must use their hands only.
5. The other groups job is to set them back up.

Game Play
Give the first group a 5 - 10 second head start. "First group, ready, go!" Then give the second group their go signal. After 30 seconds have them stop. See how many cones are knocked down and then switch roles.

Variations
Each of the knock-down crew has one or two throwing objects like soft foam balls or fleece balls. The goal is to run up to a cone and then throw their ball at the cone to knock it over. They can get as close to the cone as they want or further away to challenge themselves.

Teaching points
Kids will want to kick the cones to knock them over, but it is better to have them use their hands only. Kicked cones can get launched into the air and can become unsafe.

Games for Younger Kids

SNAKES

(10 - 30)

A great simple movement games for early elementary children.

Set Up
1. Can be played on a gym floor or outdoors on a paved space or it could be on grass too.
2. Cut lengths of rope approximately the length of a standard jump rope and give them to about half the children.

Game Play
The children then move around the space dragging the ropes as if they are snakes. The other players try to step on any of the ropes being pulled behind them. If a player steps on the rope and it stays stuck beneath their foot then they become a snake puller and the other player becomes a snake chaser. Make the rule you cannot immediately step on the snake that was just exchanged. Give this new snake puller the time to start moving.

Variations
Put balloons on the end of string and the chasing players now try to stomp the balloons to try and break them. Not as easy as it sounds. If successful, that player runs over to the extra supply of balloons on strings and grabs one and become the new puller.

Teaching points
Remind the players who are pulling the ropes, the snakes, to shake them steadily but not wildly as they pull them behind them. Also, once they feel that the rope has been stepped on and stopped to then let it go and not try to pull it loose. Not recommended to play this game with standard jump ropes that have plastic handles on the end as that extra weight of the handle can have a whip-like effect. Standard close line rope, or climbing ropes will work better and be safer.

The Heart of Play

THE COOL BREEZE BLOWS FOR ANYONE WHO
(10 - 40)

A great getting-to-know-you activity.

Set Up
1. Everyone is seated in chairs.
2. Demonstrate to the group how when a statement is said in the form of the "Cool Breeze Blows for Anyone who..." and the answer to the question is yes then they get up and move to another chair.
3. For example, "The cool breeze blows for anyone who... likes vanilla ice cream."

Game Play
The teacher/leader calls out the first few statements. After a few rounds the leader can ask for suggestions as to how players could move in different manners, i.e., slow motion, bunny hop, like a robot, etc. Remember to keep it safe.

Then the leader can ask for volunteers to give the statements. "The cool breeze blows for anyone who ate pizza last night."

Variations
Pick categories. You can do this by everyone going around and naming their chosen category, with repeats allowed or you can do it secretly with everyone just choosing in their mind. For example, everyone chooses to be a kind of fruit. Then the leader names a number of fruits and then says, "Switch" and those fruits have to switch places. Or if the leader says, "Fruit Basket," and everyone has to switch. Other categories could be presidents, or insects, or mammals.

Teaching Points
Remind the players to move safely.

Games for Younger Kids

WHAT TIME IS IT MR. FOX OR MRS. FOX
(10 - 30 Players)

One of my favorite games that I picked up from Artie Kamiyas wonderful Book, *The Elementary Teachers Book of Games*.

Set Up
1. All the players line up at the far end of the play space.
2. Mr Fox (the teacher or other designated caller) is at the other end.

Game Play
The players at the far end all call out, "What time is it Mr. Fox". Mr fox calls out a time. "It is 4 o'clock." The players then take 4 steps toward Mr. Fox. The players ask again and this is repeated with the players taking the same number of steps of the hour that is called out. When the players are close enough to Mr. Fox such that Mr. Fox feels he can catch someone, when the question is asked, "What time is it Mr Fox", Mr fox yells "It's Midnight'" and chases after the players as they try to return to the starting line. If they are tagged before they do they join Mr Fox as the taggers for the next round. The last person left or tagged can be the next Mr Fox or choose someone randomly. This game lends itself well for players to take the risks that they feel safe doing so, which allows some players to take smaller steps than others.

Teaching points
For safety, be sure that the children have space behind them so when they turn around and run no one is behind them. Best for the teacher to be Mr. fox the first number of times the game is played.

> From O. Fred Donaldson's book, Playing by Heart, four year old boy David, "Play is when we don't know we are different from each other."

The Heart of Play

WHO CHANGED THE MOTION?

(10 – 30)

A great game for concentration and learning to follow a leader.

Set Up
1. One person is chosen as the guesser and this person leaves the play space so they can't see who is going to be chosen as the leader.
2. Everyone is seated in a circle and a leader is then chosen.
3. This chosen leader starts a simple motion i.e. slapping their palms on their thighs, scratching their nose, or waving their hand above their head.

Game Play
The guesser is called back and steps into the center of the circle. As the guesser turns around looking at the players the leader changes the motion and everyone follows and does that movement. The leader should change motions as often as possible, trying to not get caught. The guesser can have three guesses to correctly guess who is the leader.

Variations
A game that is very similar is, Whose the Leader. Everyone close their eyes and picks someone in the circle who will be their own personal leader. Now everyone takes a simple pose, i.e. arms crossed, hands on their belly, etc. At the count of three everyone opens their eyes, looks at their leader, and takes the pose of that person, and only moves when their leader moves. Because your leader has chosen someone else they are following, there is this weird moment right when everyone open their eyes. Usually in about 15 to 30 seconds it comes to an end, meaning everyone has a set pose they are now in. Point to who your leader was. See what poses are, the ones at the end, and ask who started with that pose. Remind the players no one should initiate any action. Do it again with weirder poses.

Teaching points
Remind the players who are seated near the leader to look across the circle to the players who are directly across from the leader and in that way they won't give away too quickly who the leader is. Also encourage the leader to change the movements as often as they can.

Howard Moody

Active Games

Since my early background was in sports, and then New Games and Physical Education, I have a great love for full-on active games. These often involve a lot of running around, and require a certain level of body awareness, agility, and athleticism. Therefore, some of these activities might not be right for everyone. Going back to the chapter on Play Leadership, remember to choose games that have a good MAP, games that spark teamwork, physicality, and the right level of challenge for your group.

In this section you will find fun variations of dodgeball, balloon games, relays, adapted versions of capture the flag, and more. Many of these active games do involve an element of competition and physical challenge, and yet these are some of the most fun (when taught well, and played well), and can create an exceptional experience of connection.

I am a great believer in cooperative play, and I refer you to Terry Orlick's books in the Resources section. There is a reality though, that the world has many influences that reflect an overly competitive mind-set, with deleterious effects on society. From a developmental standpoint, we are introducing too much competition at too early an age to children. I wish we were are all doing more Original Play, cooperative games, creative movement, dance, free play, and playing in nature, than we do. However, since children are seeing the sports world, playing competitive video games, and playing these with their peers, they will be given an imbalance of competitive tendencies.

As a play leader you can help to balance the scales by creating teaching moments, helping students learn the value of cooperation, collaboration, and respecting their fellow players, even within a competitive game. At about age eight, moving into second or third grade, children love playing active group games that involve exuberant movement and some competition. Many children crave this kind of challenge. The trick is to emphasize the skills and qualities of cooperation, fairness, teamwork, and compassion, thus helping young people to remember to have fun, include each other and be connected.

Many of these active games also involve lots of opportunities for the players to work together. By the time children enter about 5th grade, many of them want more and more challenge, and they may be playing lots of competitive sports and buying into the winning-is-the-most-important-thing mentality. The

The Heart of Play

question is, can we have a variety of people with differing physical abilities playing together, having fun, and challenging themselves, playing a game where everyone is in the flow?

Since the real skill of play leadership is in being aware of the needs of all the players and honor them. There may be certain individuals who are uncomfortable with full-on vigorous play, who are not okay with having balls thrown at them, for example. Help these students make conscious choices, whether to sit out a game, or have the whole group discuss how to include everyone and still meet the needs of the group. Traditional dodgeball, for example, has been banned in many school districts. That is probably a good thing with those red, rubber playground balls, which are a recipe for injury. But for many players dodgeball is a lot of fun, maybe even a favorite game. I have included some variations of that classic game that use foam balls or fleece balls, which are very safe and make it more fun for most everyone.

And that's what it's all about.

> Play is the only activity in which the whole educational process is fully consummated.
>
> Scarfe, Neville V.

Active Games

ASTEROIDS

(10 - 50+ Players)

If there is any one game that I can declare as my favorite active game this may be the one. Asteroids is a full field version of dodgeball. A collection of soft, fluffy, or foam balls is needed, preferably one per player. I like fleece balls, otherwise known as yarn balls.

Set up

1. Gather everyone together and give each person a fleece ball.
2. Describe that once the game begins everyone start throwing the balls at each other.
3. If you are hit by a ball. You must go to one knee and toss away any ball that you have in your hands, at least ten feet away from you.
4. If any ball now come rolling by you such that you can retrieve while keeping your knee on the ground, you are now free and can stand up and continue playing.
5. Another great trick is that if someone throws an "asteroid" at you and you catch it—they are now frozen.
6. No throwing at anyone's head. Head shots don't count.

Game Play

Everyone gathers together and does a countdown from five to zero, and then everyone throws the balls high in the air. As they come down they are like asteroids falling to the earth and you can't touch them till they hit the ground and cool off, which is instantanously. Play as long as you want, as the game may never end with people becoming unfrozen as much as frozen.

Teaching Points

Remind the players that if they run too far afield the chances of a loose ball landing near them is much less. Let the players discover that a very fun role is to be the helper, someone who picks up loose balls and rolls them, or gives them to frozen players and unfreezing them.

Sometimes certain people do not like having things thrown at them. Very understandable. Have them play the role of a healer who just collects loose balls and gives them to players that are frozen to unfreeze them, and who is immune to being frozen.

The Heart of Play

DRAGON DODGEBALL
(12 - 30)

A fun challenge that requires the players to cooperate together to be successful.

Set Up
1. Make a large circle of the players.
2. It is optimal to have something marking off the perimeter of the circle, such as cones or gym spots.
3. The players on the outside are given a soft ball to throw.
4. Two people are chosen to go into the middle.
5. One person is in front of the other and the person behind puts their hands on the shoulders of the person in front of them, thus making a dragon. The person in the front is the head of the dragon and the person behind is the tail of the dragon.

Game Play

The object of the players on the outside of the circle is to throw the ball to try and hit the tail of the dragon, i.e., the person in the back. The head of the dragon gets to block the ball anyway they can to prevent the tail from being hit. If the tail is hit the player who threw the ball now becomes the tail, the tail moves up to become the head, and the head become a regular player in the circle, and the game continues. It takes cooperation from the outside players to pass the ball to get the dragon to move to keep up with the passes and keep the head in position to block. For more dynamic play, add another ball and another pair in the middle.

Variations

Put one chair in the middle and one person becomes the chair guard. What's great about this variation is that the players are throwing a ball at the chair and not at a person.

Teaching Points

This is great game to teach the importance of passing the ball. You can also make the rule for greater safety that the ball has to contact the dragon from the waist down.

Active Games

ESTI RUN

(Any number of Players)

A fun activity that will help players learn about estimating time.

Set Up
1. Pick a set distance (say one lap around the field) for the kids to run.
2. Ask them before they begin how fast they think they will run that distance. Have them make a guesstimate of how long it will take them to run that distance.

Game Play
"Esti Run. Ready everyone? Go!"

Be at the finish line calling out the times. The goal for each player is to try and hit their mark right on the time. So it is not a race as much as it is playing with skills of estimation.

Now that they have run it once see if they would like to refine their time and do it again.

Variations
You as the teacher or coach pick set times each runner must try to run the distance. Say for example one lap around a traditional track which is 440 yards long. Divide the group up into timed sections. Okay, who thinks they can run this lap in 90 seconds? Your one group. How about 2 minutes. Your another group.

Teaching Points
Great opportunity to teach the kids about pacing in running. In organized running sports the concept of pacing is vitally important, which is the reason many runners wear watches and track their times.

The Heart of Play

FOOOP

(circles of 8 -12)

A great follow up after having played Moonball. Just be aware that you will quite easily burst a beach ball or two in the playing of this game, but it is worth it.

Set Up
1. Take a 16 or 20 inch beach ball that ahs been fully inflated and remove about a fourth of the air out of the ball.
3. Form a group of about 8 to 10 players and have them make a tight circle almost shoulder to shoulder. With younger kids I will often put gym spots on the ground and tell them they must stay on that spot and they cannot step forward.
4. They may step backward but not forward.
5. Explain the object of the game is to keep the ball going using their hands without stepping forward. Players may step backward to hit the ball back into the tight circle. Kind of like the game Hacky Sack, but with hands.

Game Play
Take your slightly deflated beach ball and start smacking it around the circle. Because the ball is slightly deflated it makes that funny sound, FOOOP! It's like a rally in volleyball going back and forth quickly. If you have 9 or more players, and the players clearly follow the rules of not stepping forward, then the ball will have a tendency to fall on the ground into the middle. In that case you can actually place a person on their back in the middle with their hands and feet up like a turtle upside down on their shell, and they can keep these balls that fall in the middle up in the air. Kids love being the "turtle" and it is imperative that you only do this if the players know not to step forward.

Variations
Add two balls into play! Or just play a game of moonball with a slightly deflated beach ball.

Teaching Points
This game will only work well if the players do their best to not move off of their spots, thus staying in their own space, and trying to keep the ball in play. If you smack it too hard it will go flying out of the circle. The big fun is in having a really good rally.

Active Games

FOUR CORNER RELAY
(12 - 24)

Relays can be fun and yet they can also be pretty competitive. The beauty of this relay is it takes some strategy, a little bit of skill, and a whole lot of luck to be the winning team.

Set Up
1. Place 4 hula hoops in each corner of your defined play area about twenty to thirty feet equidistant from each other.
2. Divide your group into 4 equal teams of 3 to 6 players. Each team stands by their hula hoop.
3. The simple rule is each team can only have one runner at a time and only one ball can be picked up at a time.
4. Place 11 balls in the center of the playing area.
5. Explain to each team that they are to send out one player at a time to retrieve a ball from the center pile and run back and place it into their hoop.

Game Play

At the start, a player from each team runs out, grabs one ball, comes back and places it in their teams hoop. Then another player comes out until all the balls have been retrieved. Now each team probably has three balls in their hoop and one team will have two. The play stops at this point. Explain to the teams that to win the game they must have 6 balls in their hoop. The same rule applies with only one player from your team running at a time.

Now they are free to run to any other hoop to take one ball from that hoop and return with it to their hoop. Since the other teams cannot stop any players from taking one ball at a time, the key is to watch other teams hoops to make sure they are not getting six. Meanwhile, the referee will toss one ball into the middle about every fifteen seconds with up to 5 or 6 more balls added into play.

If the players are incredibly aware, this game can stall out with no winner emerging, so perhaps another ball or two could be added into the middle at some point.

Variations

Once players know how to play the game you can start the game and play can go on continuously from the start with no stopping.

The Heart of Play

Teaching points

For safety, remind the players that they could be running right toward each other if they choose a similar path.

This relay has loads of energy. It takes a bit of luck because if two or three other teams decide to run to your hoop to grab a ball then there goes some of the hard work the team spent in getting the balls.

Make sure the players standing by their hoops are not interfering with other players coming to grab a ball.

> The right to play is the child's first claim on the community. Play is nature's training for life.
>
> Froebel, Frederick (1782-1852)

Active Games

GA - GA

(8 - 30 Players)

This is an all-time favorite active game for many kids. It seems that this game came over from Israeli summer camps and has been incorporated into lots of camps and PE programs with many places building permanent Ga-Ga courts.

Set Up
1. Set up a ga-ga court. Ideal is 8 (6 or 8 foot) long tables laid on their side. This makes the perfect octagon. (It could be a septagon too.)
2. You can also use a multi purpose room that might be twenty or so feet wide and long.
3. Find a good bouncy play ball. A volleyball is good or a four square ball can be used. I have had the best luck with a softee trainer volleyball.
4. The players strike the ball with their fist only, and if it strikes another player on the legs, below the waist they are eliminated. They step out of the octagon. Sometimes the rule is only knees or below which makes it more challenging.
5. The best strategy is to squat down and put your fists in front of your legs to block the ball.
6. You cannot kneel on the ground.
7. If a players strikes the ball and it sails out of the octagon without touching anyone then they are eliminated.
8. If it bounces off of someone above the waist and goes out that can be a do over.

Game Play
One person tosses the ball up in the air so that it comes down in the court, and when it bounces the players say, "Ga, ga, ga," and on the third "ga" anyone can move forward to strike the ball to start.

Anyone who gets hit on the legs steps out while the game still keeps on going, it doesn't stop when someone gets hit unless there is dispute. Another important rule is that you can't hit the ball twice in a row, with the exception of bouncing off a wall.

Play till there is just one person left.

Variations
Play no elimination. Just count the number of times you get hit.

The Heart of Play

Teaching points

Games such as this take really good body awareness to play well and to self referee. Be sure the players are negotiating any potential conflicts well. Either you as the leader can be the referee, or if there is a disagreement the players can declare a "Do over." A great opportunity for players to develop honesty, fairness and body awareness. This game moves fairly fast and given that the ball bounces off the walls it isn't only the best athletes that succeed. It's fast moving and fun. If it is taking too long for the last few players to get out, just end the game—call it a tie—and everyone comes in for the next round. It's good sometimes to play games that don't play all the way out to the end.

> When I first learned New Games I was substitute teaching for a gym class one day and the 7th grade students were doing a volleyball unit. Someone would serve and almost every time the team could not get the ball back over the net. These students hadn't yet learned the skills necessary to play volleyball in a proficient and therefore fun way.
>
> So I lowered the nets, got everyone close together, and had them see how many times they could hit the ball cooperatively. All of a sudden they started to have fun. So here is great game that was, in essence, cooperative volleyball. And soon they developed the skills to play well enough to enjoy the "real game."

Active Games

GOLD RUSH

(12- 24)

A great version of capture the flag that works in a smaller area and with smaller numbers.

Set Up
1. Set up a playing area about the size of a basketball court with a midline.
2. On each side are five hula hoops, placed in approximately each corner of the territory and one in the center.
3. One hoop in a far corner is the jail.
4. The other three hoops in the corners are safe spaces. Safe spaces are hoops that an invading player can stand in and be safe.
5. The one in the middle is the goal or flag area. Place three "gold nuggets" (these could be three soft foam balls or fleece balls) into that middle hoop.
6. If you are on your side you cannot step into this goal area.
7. You are free to stay in this center hoop for only ten seconds.

Game Play

The players objective is to run into the other teams territory, get into the hula hoop with the gold nuggets, grab one gold nugget, run out and get back to your side safely without being tagged.

If you are tagged while on the other teams side you have to go to jail, escorted by another player. You can be freed from jail by being tagged by one of your own free players

If you have a gold nugget you can toss it to a teammate (not in a safe area) however you cannot toss it across the mid dividing line. When you cross onto your side with a gold nugget you have successfully retrieved, toss this ball out of play. The team who gets the three nuggets first wins.

Variations

When in jail and you are tagged free, you get a free walk back. Go out of bounds and walk back all the way to your back line, and reenter the game. If players are in jail for too long in a long game, reset the game by declaring a jail break.

Teaching points

Competitive tag games like this can lend themselves to disagreements about being tagged. Best as the leader to be watching to mediate any disputes.

The Heart of Play

MOONBALL

(8 - 40 Players)

As simple and fun as it gets—essentially, cooperative volleyball.

Set Up
1. Blow up a beach ball. 16 inch or 20 inch beach balls are the best.
2. Gather your group together and ask them to cooperatively see how many times they can hit the ball up in the air without it hitting the ground.
3. The simple rule is no one can hit the beach ball twice in a row.

Game Play

Its great to set goal that is doable for your group. Set a goal say 37 times and see how long it takes the group to reach that goal. If there are more than a dozen or so people in your group, add another ball and break into two or more groups and have the groups work on their own goal. If they reach it, have them try to set their own personal record.

Have the group work within a certain amount of time to reach the set goal or their own personal record.

Variations

Rather than use numbers, use the alphabet A through Z. Another variation is after they have mastered this cooperative experience, have them challenge themselves to hit the ball with vigorous energy. This can be fun with an athletic group as beach balls fly off in weird angles when struck with force.

Teaching Points

Remind the players to be aware to not jump into each other. Also, stop after a few attempts and have the group problem solve how they can work together more efficiently to accomplish their goal. Putting someone in the middle often helps, and hitting the ball more gently will create more success.

Active Games

MULTIPLE STEAL THE BACON

15 - 40)

This is an example of creating a great MAP for a game. The standard version of Steal the Bacon can be fun, however only two players are playing at a time. In this version, everyone plays at once.

Set Up
1. Take about one third of your group and give them three soft play items to guard (fleece balls are ideal).
2. The guards can squat by their "pieces of bacon," however they can't be touching them with their body in anyway.
3. The guards spread out around the play space and place their "pieces of bacon" on the ground.

Game Play
The other players now must try to steal the "pieces of bacon" from the guards. If a player steals one they hold onto it. When they get three they now become guards and they choose a place in the play area to guard "their bacon." If a guard tags a player, the tagged player must leave that area, and go to another guard and not return for another try for a while. If the player has just taken a piece of bacon from that guard, and they are tagged, they must drop the ball and move on. If player steals a "piece of bacon," the guard could go after them, however that would mean they have abandoned their other pieces of bacon, which would be stolen very quickly.

Teaching points
This game has the danger of being overly aggressive with the guards tagging too hard, or the players lunging too wildly to get a ball. However, when played with some measure of self control and daring, it is an exciting and full-of-energy game. There will be a time in the game where a number of players have successfully stolen two balls. At that point the facilitator could either hand them a ball and now they have three, or you could encourage players who have just one ball to give their one ball to the person who has two thus creating a new guard. Success in acquiring pieces of bacon usually comes from two or more people ganging up on a guard. Another very successful strategy is a little dive and knocking one of the "pieces of bacon" away for someone else to retrieve. You may make this strategy illegal as it lends to wildness, however it is fun.

The Heart of Play

MULTIPLE PERSON KEEP AWAY
(11 - 22 Players)

I created this one day when I was a PE teacher at a private school. It takes just the right number of players to create the dynamics of this game. If you have ever played Monkey in the Middle, this is essentially a multi-player version. Also works well if you can play this in one end of a gym or room where you have a few walls for backstops.

Set up
1. Set up eight gym spots on which the players, the catchers, stand.
2. Set the spots up in two rows about 10 – 15 feet apart between spots.
3. The catchers must keep at least one foot on a spot when they are playing toss and catch with any of the other players on the spots.
4. Then there are three free players who are trying to intercept any passes between the 8 players.

Game Play
Put two or three balls in play and the action begins. If a ball is intercepted, the player who intercepted the ball can go up to anyone of the 8 players and replace them, thus making one of those players a "player in the middle." It is fun for the players to say, "Hey get off my spot." They replace them and they have to the count of three to toss the ball. In other words there are no immediate tag-backs when exchanging places. Any player who is on a spot and has possession of the ball, because a ball has been tossed to them, can be tagged by a player in the middle and thus they exchange positions. It takes communication among the tossers to evade the middle players from intercepting, as welll as accurate and timely tosses to avoid being tagged by the players in the middle. If a balls is tossed poorly and goes out of the play area one of the players in the middle can run and get it and then they choose a player to gently push off their spot and take their place.

Variations
You can add a third or fourth row and have five or more players be the "player in the middle." And they can go between the rows trying to steal a ball.

Teaching Points
Once players get comfortable passing, this game works well. Shouting out the person's name you are passing to helps tremendously.

Active Games

SCREAM RUN

(Any number of Players)

Similar to the Creation Game, but this one is simply to see how far you can run with only one full breath. A nice addition to any mindfulness games you might be teaching.

Set up
1. Pick a large outdoor area that the players can run in.
2. Demonstrate they will be running as far as they can in one breath.
3. You prove it is one breath by taking a deep breath, and then screaming as you run until you are out or one breath.

Game Play

Great to start everyone off together from one set starting line. Hearing everyone screaming is so fun. See how far everyone goes on one breath. Remind the players they do not have to scream loudly, which might even be a good strategy.

Variation

Choose one set word to repeat loudly as you run, "Yes, Yes, Yes" or "Blue, Blue, Blue."

Teaching points

Great for some kids who may not be the fastest and yet if they have good breath control they may go quite far. It is all about the honor system. There is a tendency for students to naturally try to sneak in a little breath to go further. Really emphasize the fun of doing it on just one full breath—and the fun of screaming too.

The Heart of Play

SILENT JAIL-BALL

(10 - 30 Players)

This is a very simple game of dodgeball that can actually works well in a small indoor setting. It lends itself nicely to creating a certain level of self control because in this game you must be silent. (from Jacquie Adain a dear friend and colleague from ECRS - see resource section)

Set Up
1. Place five chairs at one end of the play space with just enough room to stand behind them.
2. These five chairs represent the jail.
3. Choose one bouncy yet safe throwing ball. Either a foam dodgeball or a common, lightweight plastic, air-filled ball is good.
4. When a person has possession of the ball they cannot move.
5. A player must who is hit by the ball below the waist is immediately sent to jail.
6. Any player who speaks during the game is also sent to jail

Game Play
Place this one ball in play. If that ball strikes a person below the waist that person goes into jail. As each person arrives in jail they are bumped down one chair until a sixth person arrives and that bumps that person standing behind the fifth chair back out into play.

Since their is the basic rule is that if anyone talks during the game they are also sent to jail it is good to have a referee to remind anyone who has spoken to go into jail.

Variations
You can add the rule that since your arms are above your waist you can use your arms to guard your legs. If there are a large number of players add a second ball into play.

Teaching Points
Since there is the rule that silence must be maintained and also that a person can't move when in possession of the ball this can be played indoors in a rather small space easily. You might also add the rule no running, only walking fast.

Active Games

STAR WARS DODGEBALL

(12 - 30 Players)

One of the original New Games I learned and to this day it is a winner in terms of engagement, fun, and fantasy. Traditional Dodgeball has a bad name for itself, and rightfully so. Those red rubber playground balls can hurt, and traditional dodgeball is a game of elimination. Here with Star Wars Dodgeball the idea is for more continuous play.

Set up
1. You need to have two foam swords (see resource section for Epic Toys) or pool noodles could work that represent the light sabers that the Jedi Knights hold.
2. Make two sides divided in the middle as if it were a standard game of dodgeball.
3. There are two teams one is lead by Darth Vader, the other by Luke Skywalker.
4. Just behind the end line is the home planet base for Luke Skywalker, and the death star for Darth Vader. (Gym spots). If the Jedi Knights are standing on this spot they are safe.
5. On the center line place a dozen or so soft play balls that will be used to throw at the players on each side as in a standard game of dodgeball.

Game Play

At the start of the game everyone runs from their back line up to the center line, grabs the balls and the game begins. (You can also start with everyone having balls in their possession in their own territory, eliminating that rush to the center line). If a player is hit by a ball thrown by any player on the other team, they are frozen. If a player catches a thrown ball then the player who threw the ball is frozen—works best if they put a hand up to indicate when they are frozen, or place a hand on their head. They can get unfrozen by a Jedi coming forward putting their light sabre around the person and pulling them back to the back line. They can now reenter the game. The Jedi Knights can use their sword to block thrown balls.

If a Jedi Knight gets hit by a ball when during an attempt to rescue they are frozen and thus the Jedi is out of play because no one can unfreeze them. (Or you can play it such that the Jedi tosses their sword out of the game and they get one more life and can start throwing balls like a regular player). Eventually one team will be the winners.

The Heart of Play

Variations

With a lot of players on each side, have two Jedi knights. Or try doctor dodgeball. Each team has a doctor who heals players by bringing up a scooter and transporting the "patient" back to the end line.

Teaching Points

It may be best to have someone who acts as a referee to make sure players know when they are hit by a ball.

> from, *A report from the Alliance for Childhood* by Edward Miller and Joan Almon
>
> "The importance of play to young children's healthy development and learning has been documented beyond question by research. Yet play is rapidly disappearing from kindergarten and early education as a whole. We believe that the stifling of play has dire consequences—not only for children but for the future of our nation."

Howard Moody

Tag Games

Tag Games are a core aspect of play for children. They love to chase and to flee. This really is not a competition. It is just pure play, primal and deeply unifying, and it occurs throughout nature. This can take the form of playing hide and go seek, or chasing your kids around the house while acting like a monster, or playing a full-on game of capture the flag. Eventually it can become complex sports, such as football or soccer, which is really just a lot of chasing and fleeing with various kinds of balls and sticks and other props with different rules thrown in.

As I have been writing these books on play, I came across a story of a school that banned tag. Their reasoning was that kid's self-esteem would be hurt because only the fastest kids had success, and kids would push each other and get hurt physically as well. Banning Dodgeball is one thing, but tag? Tag is fun. I understand that they were responding to children's feelings getting hurt. However, this choice to ban tag was made from a place of over-protectiveness, not understanding what happens in play, not knowing how to support children in dealing with conflicts. Please visit the resource section on programs and organization that deal specifically with bullying and conflict. For now, we are talking about optimal game design and play leadership, where sometimes there is just a natural expression of hurt feelings and disappointment during play. It's okay.

Working with emotions and helping students resolve conflicts is what helps them learn resiliency, and emotional regulation. It also supports developing empathy. In this situation, it's a clear example of adults over-reacting to a need that is being expressed. First of all, there are so many tag games that have better fun-to-safety ratios than just a standard game of tag, where only the fastest kids succeed. Also, when I learned New Games, the simple idea of giving someone a soft ball in their hand to tag with created a much safer way of playing, or flags can be used that are pulled off a player's waist, to indicate a tag. Finally, there is the concept of the Maximum Activity Plan, discussed earlier. Tag games can be structured to be fun for everyone playing. Use your imagination. Get creative. Give kids choices. Make up new versions of this classic game.

One reason I wanted to include active games and tag games into this manual is the simple fact that kids need to move—and they need to learn how to move amongst each other safely. Active games are the best way to help them

The Heart of Play

learn how to do this. A recent study came to the conclusion that a majority of the young children entering school did not have the basic core strength, flexibility, and vestibular development necessary to engage fully and "safely" in play as in sports. So it is paramount that kids are given the opportunities to run around and play, to climb things, to crawl over things, and generally challenge themselves in every reasonable way. Play offers a diversity of opportunities to strengthen those very muscles.

This book is in no way meant as a curriculum manual for PE teachers, however I hope it can add some truly great games to any PE teacher's repertoire. Nor am I am expert in dance or movement-based activities. When I was a PE teacher, one of my first lessons for my kindergartner and first graders, was having them hold a hula hoop and move throughout the space of the room. I would then talk to them about moving around in the space, making sure that their hula hoops would not touch any others. I would then talk to them about personal space and being aware of each other. Then I would add in other lessons of movement to music, and basic cooperative games, like using parachutes, and then get kids outside to just run and climb.

When it come to playground activities, tag can help kids learn healthy boundaries better than any other game. The reason you give someone a soft ball to play with is that they haven't yet learned the physical skill, body awareness, and control to tag gently. Teach them how to do soft "butterfly tags" and then every other active game you play will be safer and more fun.

Tag Games

BACK HAND TAG

(15 – 40) (From Jacquie Adain)

A very simple, fun and active game of tag that can played in small space. Having everyone relatively close will create more action and make the game more fun.

Set Up
1. Inform the group that you are going to play a fast moving tag game in a relatively small amount of space.
2. Each person places one hand behind their back.
3. Everyone is it.
4. The object is to tag the person's hand that is placed behind their back.
5. If you are tagged on your back hand you are frozen. You place your hand on your head, count to ten, and then resume play.

Game Play

Everyone spread out a little bit. "Ready set go." The game is fast paced. In a very short amount of time there is lots of action. Stop take a few breaths and play again.

Variations

Vary the amount of time they are frozen.

Or try Heads and tails tag. Half the group has their hands on their head and the other half has their hands on their tails (i.e., their hip pocket). The objective is to seek out someone different from you and if you tag them they immediately change to your side, meaning they switch where there hand is. Eventually there will be only one group left.

Teaching Points

One key reminder to demonstrate. You cannot use your free hand to try and block a person from tagging your other hand. Also point out that it is tempting to spin around or jump back to avoid being tagged. Remind the players to be aware of who and what is around them.

The Heart of Play

BLOB TAG

(20 - 50+)

One of the original games I learned in my first New Game trainings. A very simple game of tag and as the name suggest everyone becomes one big blob by the end. The more players the better.

Set Up
1. Pick a large play area. This game is great with twenty or more people.
2. One person starts out as It. All the rest of the players scatter and try to stay away from the It.
3. Demonstrate that if a person is tagged by the It, they join that player by holding hands. When they tag another player, that player joins the growing blob.
4. Once the blob becomes four people it can split into groups of two.

Game Play
Give everyone a chance to run free. After about ten seconds the It chases and tags a player, making the blob grow. Groups of four or more can split into groups of at least two so you now have multiple pieces of the blob. Then it is exciting for the pieces of the blob to come together and make one big blob moving across the play area toward the remaining free people. Maybe chanting, "Blob, blob, blob." Eventually everyone is caught. Time to dissolve the blob and play again.

Variations
If you have a large group start with two or three Its.

Teaching points
It is very helpful if the first It that is chosen is a fast runner. Also it helps if the first It knows to capture another fast player first, as it is quite a bit harder to chase people when holding hands with another person.

When playing with somewhat younger children, remind them not to pull on each other's arms when paired up and chasing free players. Remind them to communicate and work together.

Tag Games

ELBOW TAG

(8 - 20+)

Although this is an active tag game it can be played in a relatively small space and with relatively small number, with about 10 - 14 players being ideal.

Set Up
1. Start the group off with everyone having a partner.
2. The partners link up by hooking their arms at the elbow joint.
3. One pair is not joined. One person is the It and the other is the not-It.
4. It is great to have a safe tagging item that the It carries and tags with, such as a soft foam ball.
5. Demonstrate how the It runs after the not-It, and tries to tag this free person and when a tag occurs they change roles. No immediate tag-backs.
6. As the not-It is pursued they can hook onto someone's elbow, joining with that person—safely. Now there are three and there can only be two hooked up so the person on the other side of this hook-up has to run free.
7. This released person is now the not-It, and the It chases them, and on it goes.

Game Play
Have the hooked up pairs separate a few feet from each other but not too spread out. Give the not it a few seconds to get way from the 'It' and then begin with the chase. Ready, go! As link-ups occur the It chases after whoever is free. After a short while add the rule that the pairs are free to walk around the space. They cannot run. After a little more play tell the pairs they can let go of each other and hook up with whomever and whenever they want. At this point it feels like a dance but watch out for the It.

Variations
Try a little science scenario. You are all atoms and are bonded with one other atom. However there is a runaway atom and when they hook up with the paired atoms it shoots the other one of you out to become the next free radical.

Teaching Points
It is helpful to demonstrate that the game is more fun when there are more hook ups. The players do not have to run fast to be successful. You may want to make a rule that the players have to hook up with someone within ten seconds.

The Heart of Play

ELVES & WIZARDS TAG

(15 - 40+)

A wonderful tag game that involves cooperation and a nice fantasy scenario.

Set up
1. In this magic kingdom there are two creatures: wizards and elves. Wizard don't particularly like the playful silly elves so the wizards are always chasing them and trying to freeze them.
2. When a wizard touches (tags) an elf with their magic orb (a soft ball), the elf is frozen by the wizard's spell, feet frozen to the ground.
3. The elves hands and voices are not frozen so they cry out for help by putting their left palm out and striking their right fist on it quickly, shouting in their high pitched voice, "Help me, help me, help me…"
4. Fortunately, free elves have a little bit of their own magic, so if two free elves can put their arms around an elf crying out for help and clasp their two pairs of hands together and shout "You are free little elfling, you are free!"
5. Be careful, if a wizard tags an elf while they are trying to free another little elf– then they are frozen also.
6. Set up boundaries with cones and create the right sized area for the number of players.

Game Play
The wizard goes in the middle of the playing area. The game is started by the wizard(s) shouting "Were going to get you little elves, were going to get you." Play for a few minutes or until all the Elves are frozen, then choose a new wizard and play again. If there are more than about 15 elves, add an extra wizard.

Variations
Star Wars Tag: Have the Its be from the Empire and when a player is frozen they take the pose of Han Solo being frozen in carbonite. Two free rebels must come and put their arms around him and say, "Long live the force."

Teaching Points
There is lots of action in this game, so it is important that students know how to move with agility and awareness of their bodies.

After the first time playing remind the elves that the more they work together the more they can avoid being all frozen.

Tag Games

EVERYBODY'S IT

(15 -40+)

A fast moving game to be played in a large area.

Set Up
1. Tell the players that this is the fastest game there is, and that everyone is It, and that everyone is compelled to try and tag everyone else.
2. Demonstrate that when a player is tagged by the hand of another player they are eliminated and must kneel down, sit down (or just squat) to indicate their tagged status.
3. You may wish to delineate where players can be tagged and where they cannot. If two people tag each other at the same time, both players are out. If there is any argument about who was tagged first– both players are also automatically out.

Game Play

The group spreads out within a marked-off area, and at the signal to start the game each person attempts to tag someone else. This fast action continues until only one player remains.

If there are only a few players left, let them know they are compelled to come toward each other and attempt to tag each other. Then, just as the victor begins to congratulate themselves, shout, "Everyone is free, let's play again. Ready 1,2,3, Go!" And the action begins anew.

Variations

Follow up with Hospital Tag. Or try Perpetual Tag: When the player that tagged you gets tagged, you are back up and free!

Teaching Points

This is fun fast moving game. Be sure the players are able to tag safely with their hands. Otherwise you can play the game with players having tails that must be pulled off. A great game to emphasize that if two players tag each other at the same time that they can instantly agree to either both be down, or one player can defer to the other and tell them to go be free rather than start arguing (which is a rule that means you are automatically out).

Also, educators often do not play tag games where children tag with their hands, they use pull-bands or flags that are available thru PE suppliers.

The Heart of Play

ELVES / GIANTS / WIZARDS
(8-20 Players)

A great game that has ritual, fantasy and running.

Set up
1. This game is played as if in a kingdom inhabited by three very different types of beings: the giants who stand on their toes, stretch their bodies as tall as possible, who look fierce and shout, "GIANTS."
2. The elves who squat down and pull in their shoulders and generally look very, very, tiny as they barely peep their name, "elves."
3. The wizards who stand hunched over with their hands thrust forward in the best spell-casting fashion, intoning their name, "Wizards…" in as magical a way as possible.
4. As in the traditional game of Rocks/Paper/Scissors, each character defeats the other. Elves defeat wizards because they are tricky so they can make the wizards cast the wrong spells. Wizards defeat giants because traditionally giants are a little stupid so the wizards spells easily affect them. And giants defeat elves because they step on them and crush the little buggers.

Game Play

Form two teams, each with a goal line about fifteen yards apart. Each team gets into a huddle and decides which of the three characters its members will portray. The teams then face off in the center between the goals. With hands placed on knees, and facing the other team almost nose to nose, players chant, "Giants and Wizards and Elves," and then jump back and do their team's symbol. If your symbol defeats theirs you chase them and try to tag them before they cross their end line. And vice versa.

Any tagged players become a part of the other team. To deal with the possibility of both teams choosing the same character, and if this happens everyone high fives, each team should choose an alternate for each round so that there can be a new face-off without going back to a new huddle.

Variations

Do rock/paper/scissors as your symbols. Create your own new symbols. Or do a game of Crows and Cranes. One team is crows and one is cranes. Bring them to the center line and when the leader calls out your name you chase the other team, and vice versa. "Ready? Crackers, crony, cranberries, CRANES—the cranes then chase the crows, etc.

Tag Games

Teaching Points

For safety, it is important to emphasize gentle tagging. Also emphasize that when you turn around to run to be aware of others. Make sure the lines are not too packed. It's fun to play it to conclusion where there are 20 players on one side and 4 on the other and maybe one sides wins. The beauty is the constant changing of players on a side.

> Play has a tendency to be beautiful. Play casts a spell over us; it is "enchanting," "captivating." It is invested with the noblest qualities we are capable of perceiving in things: rhythm and harmony.
>
> Huzinga, Johan

The Heart of Play

HOSPITAL TAG

(15 - 40+)

A fun tag game that is a great follow up to Everybody's It Tag

Set Up
1. Demonstrate a standard tag with a hand. The person that just got tagged now places one of their free hands on that spot as a "band aid," and they can continue on to tag other players with their free hand.
2. Obviously, if the tag is in a difficult to reach spot the player just does the best they can to place their band aid there.
3. Everyone gets two band aids to use, one by each hand.
4. When players have been tagged twice, thus using both hands as band-aids they only have one tag left, and that is tagging with one of their feet. They can only tag another player on their toes with their free foot. And never a kicking motion.
5. Get tagged a third time and you kneel or sit down, indicating you are out of play.

Game Play
Everyone spreads out to start the game. I have often done something fun that helps kids listen. When I say the word "Surprise," we start. Ready? "Summertime... super... "Surprise!" And everyone starts running around trying to tag each other.

If you see that many players have been tagged three times, be willing to start another round rather than wait for the last few players to be tagged three times.

Variations
Add a healer in the game who can go around and heal one of their band-aid spots. Playing a healer can be a great role for certain players, those who aren't fast or as eager to run. Healers can be exempt from being tagged. Perhaps have them wear a headband, or carry a ball that designates their healer status.

Teaching Points
Obviously, tagging with a foot can be a bit dangerous. Be sure the players understand not to stomp on other people's feet. More like a little gentle tap dancing tap.

Tag Games

HUG TAG

(12 -40+)

In many tag games there is a safe space, a way in which you can be safe and take a breather. In Hug Tag players are safe if they are hugging another person.

Set Up
1. Demonstrate to the players that a hug can simply be an arm around another players shoulders. Or a full hug if you want.
2. Give one or two players a soft ball or something that indicates they are It, and serves as something soft to use in tagging.
3. Set up boundaries. The game works best in an area not too large. Half the size of a basketball court would work well for 20 – 30 players.
4. Add more than one it if more that 15 players.

Game Play

The Its try and tag any other players. When a player is tagged, he or she becomes It and is given the tagging item. Make a rule of no "tag-backs". If players are hugging someone they are safe. Obviously, if everyone were hugging someone then there would be no game. So the final rule is: an It can go up to two players who are hugging and count loudly to five. These two players must split up by the count of five.

Variations

A good way to start this game is to have the players in groups of two or three hugging already. Give a signal to switch groups, and in the scramble the It will probably find someone to tag. Call out "Switch" again. After a few switches, regular Hug Tag is ready to go.

Change the number of people who have to be hugging for you to be safe. "Only safe in groups of three!"

Up the ante. Tell the players they are only safe if hugging in groups of four. Or, how about four or five? How about seven?

Teaching Points

The teacher may wish to be the first It and chase players just fast enough to encourage them to hug other players to avoid being tagged. After a while, change the number of players that must be hugging to be safe.

Perhaps at the start of the game ask if everyone is okay being hugged.

The Heart of Play

PAIRS TAG

(16 - 40 Players)

A good game to teach the following of rules and developing body awareness.

Set Up
1. Set up boundaries to define a relatively small confined area.
2. Everyone gets a partner. Look at your partner and shout, "Not it."
3. Who said it first? You are it, and the other person is not it. Really doesn't matter, it's just a lot of fun to shout "not it."
4. You are going to play tag only with your partner.
5. This game is played only walking, so be sure to demonstrate what fast walking looks like and when it turns into running.
6. Walking is with both feet touching the ground at all times. Kind of fun to demonstrate that funny walk that race walkers do.

Game Play
When the game begins the Its make a 360 degree turn and at the same time the not-Its start walking. (Remember, walking only). The Its are trying to catch their partner and tag them.

When tagged the not-Its become It and vice versa. The tagged person does a 360 degree turn and begins walking after their partner. Back and forth they go. Be sure to carefully avoid the other pairs who are playing at the same time in the same space. Ready set go!

Variations
Have the Its turn around twice. Or play the game Pairs Squared. Get in groups of four and divide into pairs and then the pairs link their arms together. The Its are a partnership with their arms linked, and these two pairs play Pairs Tag.

Teaching Points
This game has the potential for collisions, so really emphasize that everyone must walk, since everyone other than your partner is being an obstacle that you must carefully and gently avoid.

Tag Games

SNOWBALL HUG TAG

(15+ Players)

This game is a creation of my friend Jacquie Adain that was created during the winter retreat held each year at ECRS (See resource section). It's delightful combination of the game Hug Tag and Asteroids.

Set Up
1. Gather the group and tell them they are going to play a big game of tag.
2. Pass out a few soft fleece balls or foam balls to a few Its. Even those round soft plushy shower sponges work well in a pinch.
3. Tell people to stay close together for more action. Or set boundaries that create this dynamic.

Game Play
The Its throw the balls at the other players. Anyone hit with a ball is frozen, indicated by being arms in an expressive pose, frozen like a statue carved out of ice. Any free person can now hug a frozen person and that unfreezes them. And on it goes...

Variations
Two people have to be hugging you to set you free.

Teaching Points
As with any game that involves touching, it is great to discuss what feels good to people and what doesn't. Be sure to demonstrate that if you are running and dive into people and hug them too vigorously it could become unsafe or feel too rough. Demonstrate gentle hugs... It is delightful to discover that you can freeze someone with a ball, and then go up and hug them and unfreeze them.

The Heart of Play

TRIANGLE TAG
(4+ Players)

A full-on game that could easily go into the Wildness section.

Set Up
1. Divide the players into groups of four.
2. One player is designated as the tagger, the It.
3. The other three players join hands and form a kind of triangle.
4. The top of the triangle is the taggee, the not-It. This is the target person.
5. The other two players of the triangle are the "Blockers."

Game Play
At the start the tagger does their best to tag the designated taggee anywhere on the body. The two non designated taggee's do their best to block the taggee from touching the taggee. If the tagger does touch the "not it" then rotate the players into new roles and play another round.

The tagger cannot jump into blocker or try to plow through them to tag the "not it." The best strategies are to try reaching over to tag the taggee on the arms, or to run around in one direction then perhaps quickly changing directions to try and do and end run around the blockers.

Teaching Points
Remind all the players to stay safe in their bodies. No jumping over the joined arms. They can, however, try to go under, around, or reach over to tag the not-It.

This game is great for teaching the concept of "boxing out" in basketball. Just as in basketball, what would be appropriate contact on the court would not be a foul here either.

Howard Moody

Games of Wildness

There is an important movement within parenting and education to create living and learning environments that are inclusive, and that are physically and emotionally safe—which is at the core of Social Emotional Learning. I value safety on all levels. At the same time, so much can be learned through risk, challenge, adversity, and striving toward difficult goals. So there is this unique balances that needs to be maintained between these two ends of the play spectrum.

Through my years as a wrestling coach I loved the challenge, the hard work and discipline it took to reach for your goals, and the camaraderie of being part of a team. Then when I learned about New Games I could clearly see the pitfalls and dangers of an overly competitive culture where winning at all costs becomes the mantra, but not one that is developmentally appropriate for all ages—or for anyone all the time. But, since many children will participate in sports programming, let's do our best to ensure that they are also learning all the positive qualities that can be taught during noncompetitive group play, even alongside the competitive fervor, things like teamwork, perseverance, resiliency, fair play, sportsmanship, as well as strategic thinking.

Children need challenge. Even more fundamentally, they need at least a little wildness! Ideally this would be in nature, climbing, running, chasing, building things out of wood, mud and sticks, or wrestling with friends for fun, making up their own games... eventually this full engagement will reach the natural expression in the teen years through rites of passage, and expeditionary programming. (See ReTribe in the Resources.)

Some of the games in this section were originally called soft war games, back in the day of my early New Games training, with their motto—and accompanying philosophy—"Play hard. Play fair. Nobody hurt." These are wildly vigorous games requiring a certain degree of physical awareness, trust, and mindfulness to play safely. Wildness can be controlled and balanced by a playful sensitivity and become an elevated form of human expression.

Wildness is a cornerstone concept in the Heart of Play, along with Engagement, Cooperation, and Connection.

The Heart of Play

ANNIHILATION
(10 - 40)

Lots of full-on contact.

Set up
1. You need a soft area to play on. Either wrestling mats, gymnastic mats, a very plush carpet or a soft grassy area.
2. Divide the boundaries of an area about 20 x 20. (It needs to be a rather contained space depending on the size of the group.)
3. Everyone gets on their hands and knees and must maintain this contact at all times.
4. The objective of the game is to push the opposing team players off the playing area.

Game Play
Each team faces off on opposite sides of the playing area. Allow a bit of time for teams to plan their strategies. At the start command, players crawl forward and attempt to push the opposing team players off the mat or playing area. For this reason it is important to have very distinct boundary edges so it is very clear when someone touches outside of the boundaries. Also create a stop word. This word can be used if play is too rough or something is hurting—anyone can shout the word and then everyone shouts it back. And then everyone stops. Best to have a referee or two to make sure everyone is playing fairly, safely, and following the rules. The referees can be very clear, if someone lifts their hand off the mat to push someone they are out. Or if anyone touches outside the boundaries they are eliminated. Play until one team wins, or play for a certain time-limit and see which team has the most players left.

Teaching points
Obviously, this is a game where bigger people have an advantag. However if players work together smaller people can push bigger players off. Strategies in the game include lying down so it is harder to push someone. You could make the rule that no lying down is allowed. It's very important to keep the game playfully safe so things like really aggressive pushing or crawling very fast and ramming someone is not likely to happen. Remind players not to push with their head. Just shoulders, hips, side of their bodies, etc.

Games of Wildness

BRITISH BULLDOG

(10 - 30 Players)

One of the most fun games with full-on contact that I know.

Set Up
1. Make a place to play that is about the size of half a basketball court.
2. Best to play on soft grass.
3. All the players stand on one end line.
4. One fast player stands in the center and is the first Bulldog, and calls out the phrase, "British Bulldog 1,2,3."

Game Play
When the center player call out, "British Bulldog 1,2,3," the players try and run across the playing area to the other side. The bulldog runs after and tries to capture players. The only way to do this successfully is to grab a player and then lift them up so their feet are off the ground and then say the phrase, "British Bulldog 1,2,3." Now this player becomes a bulldog too. When the players reach the other side they wait for the next call of the bulldogs. Now that there are two bulldogs they can team up and gang up to help capture certain players. The game continues with the now ever increasing bulldog group going to the middle calling for the group to cross the play space again. And the game continues on until everyone is captured. Maybe the last person captured becomes the first Bulldog in the next game.

Variation
Play the game where the bulldog just has to capture someone and count to three. They don't have to pick them up.

Teaching Points
When I first played this game I had been a wrestling coach and I could capture just about anyone and lift them up, so I was always the first Bulldog. The players must understand not to struggle and flail their arms to get away nor should they try to run through people as if they were playing tackle football. It is a game of attrition and eventually you want to allow yourself to be caught. When playing with a fun loving group who are really safe in their bodies this can be delightful way to allow full-on body contact in a fun engaging manner.

The Heart of Play

FOAM SWORD FENCING

(Any number of Players)

The Boffer sword goes way back in the history of New Games and co-operative play. It is used as a prop in a number of games in this collection. But straight-up sparring with playful contact should be mentioned here. The wildness factor can go high with this activity.

Like in stage combat choreography, a great deal of control is needed to keep the risk of injury as low as possible. Foam Sword Fencing is like an improvisational form of stage combat that requires moment-by-moment awareness. This fun activity is the cornerstone of the LARPing movement that is growing rapidly. From the beginning of kids picking up sticks to pretend to sword play many LARPing organizations have taken this imaginative play into exciting areas. Using foam swards was the cornerstone of the creation of the Adventure Game Theater, which led to the creation of the Wayfinder Experience and also is a key component of the wonderful Rites of Passage organization ReTribe.

The vigorous aspect of this process can also yield fitness benefits.

A great resource for the swords that are the safest for children to play with can be purchased through Epic Toys. See the resource section.

> The expression of wildness in children is very important in the recipe of a complete play-program soup. When I studied alternative recreation at Goddard College, one unique movement that got my attention was adventure playgrounds. These were sometimes as simple as providing a closed-in, fenced-in space where kids could build things and tear them down. They were given, wood, tools, water, dirt, space, and an adult mentor to help them, to make sure they stayed safe, and then given the freedom to build and tear down whatever they wanted. The benefits and engagement were phenomenal.
>
> This didn't catch on in the United States because these playgrounds were often messy and cluttered, so the ones that did try to open were shut down fairly quickly. This was a missed opportunity by the U.S. to help kids learn important skills and grow in their own resourcefulness. A great example of this adventure playground play can now be found in Anji Play in China.

Games of Wildness

SMAUG'S JEWELS

(Best for 6 – 12 Players)

One of the original games I learned from the New Games Foundation.

Set Up
1. One person is the guard and takes a frisbee (or some other kind of object) and turns it upside down and that is the object the players must steal from its guardian.
2. There is the great dragon named Smaug, and he has stolen all the gold and treasure from the neighboring kingdoms.
3. You have all come to Smaug's lair to take back your treasure.
4. The player who is guarding the treasure (Smaug) can kneel or squat closely to the frisbee but not be touching it.

Game Play

With the players about 10 to 15 feet away from Smaug, he roars loudly to start the game. Anyone can try to steal Smaug's Jewels, but if a player is touched or tagged by Smaug, they are frozen for eternity—or until the game is over. The players try to sneak in from different direction and distract Smaug so a player can reach in and grab the frisbee and get away with it. The player who can grab the treasure without getting tagged becomes the next Smaug.

Teaching Points

The fun of activity is for Smaug to start the game with great energy and a big roar. The players need to exercise good control to make this a well played game. The first Smaug should be played by teacher / play leader, to demonstrate the playful form that makes it fun for everyone.

Especially if there are more players. Kids playing the dragon might not have the best control. Hard tagging by Smaug can make this game feel unsafe. When young kids play this game they tend to all charge Smaug, and that can be unsafe too.

The Heart of Play

SWAT TAG
(10 - 30 Players)

A full-on vigorous game.

Set Up
1. Have everyone get in a big circle with a few feet of space between each player.
2. Have each player stand on a gym spot.
3. Place an upside down frisbee in the center of the circle.
4. One person is in the middle of the circle, holding a foam sword (or a pool noodle can work too.)

Game Play

The person in the middle with the sword walks around on the inside of the circle and then tags a person on the legs (swatting them gently) with the sword. The tagger hustles back to the center, with the tagged person immediately chasing after them. The tagger places the sword upon the frisbee. The tagged player tries to quickly pick up the sword and swat the tagger before they get back to the spot the tagged player has vacated. If this happens, the originally tagged player places the sword down on the frisbee and tries to get back to their spot. Of course the original tagger who has now been tagged back, tries to pick up the sword and swat that person and this exchange could go back and forth many times.

Of course, if the original tagger gets back to the spot safely the person with the sword now goes around and chooses someone else in the circle. If the tagger places the sword down and it rolls off the frisbee, the tagged player points this out and calls them back in to place the sword correctly upon the frisbee. The tagged player can only point this out before actually picking up the sword.

This prevents the tagger form just throwing the sword into the center of the circle. After everyone gets the swing of this the players around the circle can exchange spots, filling up that spot that was vacated thus making the empty spot be somewhere else in the circle.

Variations

This game can be done indoors, with players seated in chairs, or standing on spots using a rolled up newspaper and placing this upon an upside down trash can or another chair.

Games of Wildness

Teaching Points

This is such a fun game, however, that transition point where the tagger places the sword down and heads back to the vacated spot is challenging because the tagged player may be heading in while that tagger is heading back to their vacated spot. Demonstrate how a collision is highly possible unless everyone is aware. Show the players how the tagger can place the sword down and look and move in circular way back to the spot and not by heading straight back.

> A school district in New Zealand was having problems with bullying, particularly on the playground. The various teachers and administrators decided to go back to having recess the way it was years ago, before more stringent safety policies, such as letting the kids bring their scooters in and build small ramps for them to jump off from, letting them play in mud at the end of the day, and sending them home dirty. During recess, they allowed the game Bullrush to be brought back, a game that was banned for being too rough. It's a game that might be called "get the carrier," where one player just tries to run through the whole field of other players and make it to the other side without getting caught and tackled. Most of the kids wanted to play. A few students knew it was too rough for them, so they opted out and did other stuff on the playground instead.
>
> The adults were amazed that the kids basically self-refereed themselves and there were no injuries, and only needed a few meetings with the students to discuss how to ensure that everyone played safely. The educators discovered that virtually all incidents of bullying disappeared.
>
> This is a perfect example of letting kids monitor and take responsibility for their play and to give space for their wildness to be expressed.

The Heart of Play

VAMPIRE HUNT
(15 - 40 Players)

This was a creation of my friend David Eaton and myself back in 2010 for the staff at Omega Institute. It is one of my favorite variations of Hide and Seek I have ever played.

Set Up
1. It is designed to be played after dark.
2. You need a large area to play in and it helps to have some ambient lighting, just enough to have lots of places to hid in some darkness but enough light to see to move around in. You could use flashlights. Nice to play in a neighborhood of houses or at a summer camp.
3. Also you need a place where it is okay to scream and not disturb anyone.
4. You need glow sticks for each person. Red is the best color. (I am not a fan of the ones you throw away. There are nice ones now that are LED glowsticks and you can use them again and again.)

Game Play

The game begins with everyone as villagers, except one or two people who will start out as vampires. The vampires are wearing their glow sticks. The villagers, who have put their glow stick in a pocket, are given a two minute head start to go out and hide. The vampires then start hunting the villagers. If a vampire catches you, by tagging you, you now also become a vampire, taking your glow stick turning it on and putting it around your neck and you are now a vampire and you will hunt the villagers. The vampires also have a horn, or a whistle (those stadium horns, Vavuzalas are perfect), and they get a certain number of horn blasts per round, such as three. When the horn is blown the villagers must scream for one full breath. Explain that the horn blast is a mind controlling energy being sent out and it hurts the villagers brains intensely. Play until everyone is caught or for a certain time limit and see if anyone has survived. One other rule that helps the game is to tell the villagers they can't hide in any one place for more than five minutes.

Play again and add in Vampire slayers. This makes the game very intense and a truly dynamic tag game. Vampire Slayers wear a green glow stick and can tag a lone Vampire and turn them back into a villager. However, if two vampires are holding hands they are safe from being tagged by a slayer. In fact, if two holding hand vampires can chase after a slayer and tag them, the slayer is frozen for ten seconds. If two more for a total of four vampires can join hands and make a circle

Games of Wildness

around the slayer, that slayer has now lost their powers and has to run away. The vampires must give the slayers thirty seconds to run away and try to hide. Slayers should not enter the game until about four or five minutes after a round starts to give the vampires a chance to catch a few players.

Variation

This is an adaptation of the game I learned known as Manhunt. Manhunt is played during the day. Choose a suitably large area to play in like some nicely cleared woods or around buildings on campus. Everyone runs and hides and one person is the It. If the It finds someone and can tag them, that person then joins them as the hunters. There can also be a home base, the goal where the players are trying to get back to, to beat the hunters. Once a person is tagged they could either put on a head band or always answer the question truthfully, "Are you a hunter."

Teaching Points

Games that involve running in the natural world or at night and sneaking around can be wonderfully fun and yet can also be risky. Remind the players to know their own limits and to know the terrain. Don't jump over bushes if you don't know what is on the other side.

The Heart of Play

WINK
(15 - 30 Players)

This is the full on version of wink. Best to played on mats, Soft grass or a very soft carpet.

Set Up
1. Everyone gets a partner and sits in a circle with one player sitting in front of their partner, so you have one inner circle and one outer circle.
2. The players in the back must look at their partners backs.
3. One player does not have a partner. That person is the winker.

Game Play
With everyone seated in the circles, the winker looks around at the inner circle and gets eye contact with one of the players and winks at them. That person has been chosen and they must scoot away from their partner by crawling across the circle on their hand and knees and must reach the winking person and tag them. The person in the back of that chosen person sees that person trying to escape and they now can grab them and prevent them from getting to the winker. If they hold onto to them for ten seconds then they have succeeded and they switch places with the winked at person now behind that person. The winker now chooses someone else. If the winked at person escapes and gets to the winker then their partner obviously does not have a partner so they immediately can begin winking.

Variations
This game can be played sitting in chairs, which is a safer version. There is one circle of chairs with a person seated in each chair except one. Now each seated person has a person standing behind them. There is one person standing behind an empty chair. They are the winker and they are winking at any other seated person and that person winked at must try to escape from their seated chair without the person behind them tagging them before they get to the empty chair. The players standing behind the seated partners must look only at the back of their partner and not at the person winking.

Teaching Points
A full-on contact game. Remind players to not try to kick out of a grab or swing their arms wildly. Make sure everyone plays within their limits.

Games of Wildness

YOGI TAG – DHO, DHO, DHO

(10 - 30 Players)

Maybe my favorite game when I first learned New Games. This a very vigorous game so be sure the players are ready to play safely.

Set Up
1. There are two teams each on their own designated side. About 6 – 10 players on a side is a good balance. Mark off an area about the size of a volleyball court about 30 x 30, with a center line separating the two sides.
2. It is best played on some soft grass.
3. Tell the fantasy story that there are two distinct universes and each species cannot breath the air of the other species in their universe, but they want to capture each other.
4. So a player can enter into the other universe by proving that they are not breathing the air in the other world.
5. So once they cross the line they prove that by uttering the phrase repeatedly and continuously, "Dho-dho-dho-dho-dho..." If they were to stop uttering that phrase, it would mean they have taken a breath in the other universe, so now they would have to belong in that universe.
6. Have everyone practice do their "Dho-dho-dhos" before the game begins.

Game Play
Each team takes a turn sending a player into the other teams territory. If they are able to tag another person or more than one person and get back to their own territory without taking a breath, then the tagged players must now join the other team.

Here is where the fun begins. Once the invading player who is "Dho-dho-dhoing" tags someone, he can now be grabbed by the players on that side. This is where the game can get aggressive and is on the borderline of being safe. If the grabbed player runs out of air they now must stay on that team.

Variations
When I first played this game, the moment the person crossed the line they could be grabbed, which is an even more intense version.

Or try Zombie Tag, where everyone moves like a zombie in chasing and fleeing in a wonderfully distorted slow motion. This can be more fun than you might think.

The Heart of Play

Teaching Points
   Be sure to remind everyone to play fairly and to grab safely... This is not a game for overly wild and unsafe players. It is incredibly fun when played well. Once everyone knows the game the moment the invading players return to their side then the other team immediately sends a player across.

> Back in the early days of my New Games training there was a category of play called "soft war" games that always appealed to me. Between that and my love of athletic challenge, I went on to co-create a whole fantasy role-playing extravaganza, with foam swords for the warriors, and with wizards and healers, monsters and deities—all playing out around wonderfully complex science-fiction narratives. But we always taught players how to make the elaborate role-playing system work with basic Capture the Flag, and adding in our game-system's conventions. These practice sessions were sometimes as much fun as enacting the full story line—and much more easily managed.
>
> Some of our Adventure Game Theater staff grew into their own group called The Wayfinder Exerience, who now play our fantasy version of Capture the Flag in Central park in New York City, and in parks in Philadelphia, which is really something to behold.

Howard Moody

Trust Games & Activities

Trust is an inherent part of connection and belonging. Trust is something that is gained and earned, ongoing, day in and day out. In the realm of play, trust can be earned by being someone who plays fairly, who is kind and supportive, and who is a good loser. This category of activities helps us learn how to put our trust in another human being—which is a wonderful phenomenon, when you think about it.

Throughout this manual there are lot of games that foster cooperation and therefore build trust, games like Human Spring, Human Statues, and other games that take lots of teamwork, like Knots, or Count Ten. However, this section will specifically entail a great deal of trust, since many activities involve a player being blindfolded or having their eyes closed. As a leader, it is vitally important to create safety during the teaching of the activity and while observing the game, ensuring that everyone is being trustworthy and safe. Be willing to stop the game to clarify what safety and trust feels like, so everyone is learning how to be a safe and trustworthy player.

It takes time to build trust. If a challenging trust activity is shared and the students haven't gotten to that place yet, then a trust exercise can have the opposite effect from the one you want. So choose the simplest exercises first. An assortment of values are learned through example and immersion in an experience. If we want our children to be trustworthy, kind, and compassionate, then we have to provide experiences for them that embody these values.

Over the years in learning from many seasoned experiential educators, I have relied on these trust games and activities for creating the integrative-social-play experience.

The Heart of Play

BLIND RUN
(10 - 30)

This is a fun and exhilarating activity, providing a first hand experience of facing the primal fear of falling and possibly getting hurt. Great to reflect afterwards on the feeling of depending on the support of the friends to be there for you.

Set Up
1. Have your group form two lines about twenty feet apart and spread out so they cover about thirty or forty yards of expanse. Imagine a big hallway.
2. One person then volunteers to be the runner.
3. Demonstrate how they are to run between the set of two lines of people—and they are to run with their eyes closed the whole time.
4. The players in the two lines are to make sure the runner does not go off course. If they start going off course the people in the line very gently, with their hands and voices, guide the runner back on course.

Game Play
Ask the runner if they would like to have cheering, silence, or something positive yelled as they run down the "gauntlet." Empower all the players to yell stop if the person seems to be going wildly off course. The lines of people are there to keep the person safe and to support the runner's experience, not to jar them back onto the course if they start drifting.

Have someone who knows how to spot in fitness or gymnastics be at the end to gently bring the runner to a stop by moving backward with them, touching them and telling them they are at the end. It is vitally important that this spotting be safe and supportive for the person running.

Variations
Have people partner up and run the Blind Run, paired and holding hands.

Teaching Points
Ask the participants to reflect on the intensity of the experience. Almost everyone hits a wall of fear, as their body is telling them they must be getting near the end. A good opportunity to discuss fear and how to work with it.

Trust Games & Activities

BLIND WALK

(Partners)

A wonderful way to learn how to be supportive and how to support. Sometimes it is useful to provide blindfolds. Best to be played outside.

Set Up
1. Each person gets a partner.
2. One person will choose to be the leader and the other player will have one of their eyes closed. Demonstrate how to gently guide a person, sometimes best with one hand on the small of their back and the other one holding their lower arm or hand.
3. For certain players having a blindfold or scarf to put over their eyes can make it a more immersive experience.
4. Be sure to demonstrate that little changes in terrain can be surprising for the blinded person. Let them know a slight hill is coming, or that there is some gravel that they are about to step on.

Game Play

Have the players lead their partner in experiencing the world through their other senses. Perhaps have them gently touch a tree, or smell a flower.

Variations

Set up a very simple trust obstacle course with simple objects you might have to crawl over and under. Another challenge could be all the un-sighted players must stay in physical contact as they traverse the course with their sighted partners just giving them verbal directions.

Or expand the nature part of the experience perhaps by touching a dandelion, putting a pine cone in their hand, have them touch some moss by a tree.

Teaching Points

Have the players reflect on what they experienced perhaps even going back over the same terrain now with their eyes open. As with any trust game be sure the players are feeling safe enough to do the activity. As with any trust activity there is the wonderful opportunity to discuss what engenders trust and what trust feels like.

The Heart of Play

CAR AND DRIVER
(4 - 40+ Players)

A fun way to play with trust.

Set Up
1. Each person gets a partner.
2. One player will be the driver and stand behind their partner who will be the car. The driver will be guiding their "car" by placing their hands on their shoulders and gently guiding them around the space.
3. The other "car" will have their eyes closed once the game starts.
4. Demonstrate that the cars can put their hands up in front of them as bumpers.

Game Play
"Ready drivers? Put your hands on your cars' shoulders. Oh wait, you have to ask your care what kind of car they want to be and how fast they feel like going. Start up your cars and around the space. Remember to drive safely and no collisions. Drivers start driving your cars...

"Okay everyone stop! Exchange places with your partner, so now whoever was the driver is now the car and vice versa. Cars share what kind of car you want to be and the new driver, drive safely. Go!"

Variations
Play the game a few times with the cars having their eyes open. Still remind the cars to let their driver lead them. This will lead to everyone feeling safe.

Teaching points
It is vitally important that the car trust their drivers. Before the game begins have the players talk about what will make them feel safe. At any point a car can ask the driver to slow down and they will comply. Also it is tempting for players to make little collisions. Players bumpers are up to mitigate any possible collisions, however, remind the players the object of the game is to not have any contact. Make sure that everyone, when they are a driver, that they are leading their partner safely.

Trust Games & Activities

CIRCLE CROSSING

(20 -40)

This is a fun auditory experience that can be played with people of all ages.

Set Up
1. Have everyone get in a big circle
2. Explain to the group that they will be walking across this circle, and they will be doing it three times.
3. The object of this game is to not touch anyone during each time walking across the circle.
4. If someone does touch you by accident, you must make a silly sound.

Game Play
"For this first crossing, let's all walk leisurely to the other side of the circle trying not touch anyone. Ready go!"

Did anyone get touched as they crossed? For this next crossing, do it in a fast walk, as if you are hurrying to catch a plane. Ready go!

"Okay how did we do, any touches?"

"For this last crossing we are going to do it with our eyes closed." The group will be hesitant. To make this work safely we are going to do it in slow motion. Have all the players practice moving in slow motion to be sure they are moving slow enough to be safe. Also, instruct them to move with their bumpers up—which is their hands up palms facing out in front of them at chest level to insure safe contact. The sound of all the players making silly noises when they reach the center and almost invariably touch someone is lots of fun.

Variations
With younger children just play with eyes open adding different forms of locomotion for each crossing: skipping, walking backward, etc. The closed eyes version would only be added later when everyone leans how to move carefully with eyes closed.

Teaching Points
This game only works if people can move carefully and slowly with bumpers up.

The Heart of Play

GUIDE AND EXCHANGE
(8 - 40 Players)

A whole group activity designed to build trust and support.

Set Up
1. Divide the group up in two equal sized groups.
2. Make sure it is an exact even number.
3. Before you start demonstrate that this will be an experience where one person will guide another to walk around the space with their eyes closed, but they won't know who is leading them.
4. Demonstrate how to guide someone gently by holding their hand and perhaps a hand on the small of their back.

Game Play

Group 1 then takes their place out on the space and they close their eyes and are still. As the leader narrates the first part of the experience, everyone in group 2 then walks over to a free person and gently touches them, and then leads them around the space. The leader then coaches everyone to bring their partner to a stop. It is important now to tell the players who have their eyes closed to keep them closed. Group 2 people let go of that person and move to another person and begin leading them around.

After 4 or 5 exchanges, call the group to a stop and have group 2 leave the space so that the lead group doesn't know who last lead them. Then have the groups switch roles. At the end of each round or at the end of both rounds, you can have the players go around and try to guess who was leading them.

Variation

Have only one person lead them and then switch roles so then the lead person only has to make one guess as the who it was.

Teaching Points

This exercise really helps players let go of the feeling of being in control. Have the group discuss at the end what their experience was. It is a lot of fun trying to guess who the people were that lead them around.

Trust Games & Activities

HUMAN CAMERA

(Partners)

A really fun trust activity.

Set Up
1. Everyone get a partner. In this dyad one person will be the camera, the other person the picture taker.
2. The camera will have their eyes closed during this variation of a blind trust walk. So be sure to go over how to gently and safely lead a person who has their eyes closed. You can demonstrate how to hold the persons hand with one hand, and have the other hand gently on the lower part of the person's back.
3. The person who has their eyes open is the picture taker. The players agree upon what is the physical way in which they will trigger the shutter of the camera. It could be gently pulling the persons ear lobes, or tapping their cheek bone. This signals the person to open their eyes quickly, then close them just getting a snapshot of whatever the person has lead them too.
4. Letting the person know if it is close-up or a distance picture will be helpful.
5. Do a demonstration so the players can see what it looks like.

Game Play
Gently lead your camera and begin taking pictures. Move around the space taking pictures of the landscapes, flowers, trees and maybe even each other. After a determined amount of pictures, say 6, switch roles and then when done share what you saw.

Teaching Points
It's really important during trust exercises that people feel that they are in good hands. Be sure to observe that the players are leading each other safely. This is a great game to reflect on how we see the world constantly through our eyes, however when just taking a quick snapshot of something it changes our perspective and allows us to see in new ways.

The Heart of Play

HUNTER / HUNTED

(10 - 30 Players)

A great game that teaches listening and awareness.

Set Up
1. Everyone sits in a big circle.
2. Two players are chosen and both are to be blindfolded.
3. One will be the hunter and the other the hunted.
4. Very simply the hunter is trying to tag the hunted.

Game Play
Have two volunteers spin the hunter and hunted around and guide them to a place within the circle to start. All the players seated in the circle have a very important role. When either the hunter or the hunted moves close to the edge of the boundary where the players are sitting, the players in the circle slap their hands on the ground like a drum role signaling that a hunter or hunted is getting too close and must move out into the circle. Obviously, very good auditory information for either the hunter or the hunted.

Variations
Give the hunted an object that makes a sound. Matches in a box, a rattle or a bell, anything that makes a sound when you shake it. Every ten seconds or so or upon the command of the hunter, the hunted must shake their object for a second. (Marco-Polo style.)

Teaching Points
For safety it is very important for both the hunter and hunter to move slowly and stealthily, and for the dynamic play of the game the players in the circle must be absolutely quiet, except when they are giving their proximity warnings. If the players are moving too quickly or unsafely, call out for them to stop.

Trust Games & Activities

PRUI

(10 - 30+ Players)

One the very first New Games I ever learned, an original classic.

Set Up
1. What makes this game fun is the story. Everyone is unaware, always seeking enlightenment. Being unaware they are walking around "in the dark" which means they will have their eyes closed to start the game. They are all seeking enlightenment. Enlightenment comes in the form of "Prui."
3. One player meanwhile has been chosen secretly chosen as the Prui and they have their eyes open to start the game because they are enlightened.

Game Play
The players with their eyes closed wander around and reach out with their hands out looking for other hands and when they find a hand they shake that hand and ask the question, "Prui?" Well, if this other player is also seeking the Prui, they will respond with the same question, "Prui?" If a questioning player seeking Prui, get's a response of, "Prui," they know they haven't found the Prui, so they let go of that hand and continue on seeking other hands. Now if they shake a hand and there is no response. Aah! They have found the Prui. They open their eyes. They have found enlightenment. They now become part of the Prui, holding on to that hand they just shook and now they don't respond if someone shakes their free hand.

So, if someone shakes that free hand, and get silence in response to their question of "Prui' they now join hands and the Prui grows. If a player comes upon two joined hands they know they have found part of the Prui, and they now go down the line feeling the joined hands, looking for the end of the line to find the free hand so they can now join the Prui until eventually everyone becomes part of the Prui.

Variations
With a large group play crystalline Prui. When someone comes upon joined hands they have found the Prui and they just hold on.

Teaching Points
With any game with eyes closed, demonstrate how to reach out with softly and gently and not stumble around. Move slowly with mindfulness and the game is lots fun and feel safe. One person keeps their eyes open and helps lost players.

The Heart of Play

RAIN

(10 - 40+ Players)

This game is an excellent auditory experience that has been an outdoor education favorite for years. If you have a quiet area and the group cooperates and performs their individual role well, the group will be able to experience the sounds of a summer rain storm approaching and leaving an area.

Set Up
1. Have the players form a circle and turn right or left and side step in toward the center of the circle so they can easily touch the person's back in front of them.
2. Tell the group that they are about to experience, through sound and touch, the sounds of a summer rainstorm—and that you need their complete cooperation.
3. Using the person in front of you, demonstrate the movements that will be necessary to create this experience.
4. The first movement is a gentle rubbing on the person's back in front of you, rotating your hands in a circular movement which will make a nice swishing sound.
5. The second motion is a tapping motion gently with your finger tips on the person's shoulder (like light rain).
6. The third motion is a heavier finger tapping with all of your fingers slapping on the persons back (like heavy rain).
7. Then reverse the order to the second motion, then the first, and finally stop.

Game Play

When the exercise begins, you as the teacher will start the first motion, and the next person passes it along to the next person, and on around the circle. When that motion finally reaches you, start the next one. This exercise is best done with eyes closed.

Variations

If the group cannot handle the touching that is necessary for this experience, then here is an alternative method: Stand in the center of the circle and tell the group to do the motion that you do as you turn and are facing them in the circle. The motions are as follows. Rubbing palms together. Snapping a finger on each hand alternately and slowly. The snap of multiple fingers faster. Then slap-

Trust Games & Activities

ping thighs. Then pounding your chest. And then reverse the order. Not as good as the first method, but this way is still very effective in creating the sounds of a summer rain storm.

Teaching Points

Great to discuss how your hearing is heightened when you close your eyes. Also fun to talk about how the sounds of nature are very comforting and relaxing.

---

continued from, *A report from the Alliance for Childhood...*

"Play Builds Competence in Many Domains. Young children work hard at play. They invent scenes and stories, solve problems, and negotiate their way through social roadblocks. They know what they want to do and work diligently to do it. Because their motivation comes from within, they learn the powerful lesson of pursuing their own ideas to a successful conclusion..."

The Heart of Play

SPECIAL OBJECT SCAVENGER HUNT
(15 – 40)

Another fun observation game.

Set up
1. Divide the group up into equal size teams (5 - 8 players will be ideal) making up 4 – 6 teams.
2. Have the teams choose someone to be the scribe.
3. Align the players equidistant from you as the facilitator.
4. You will already have gathered together as many distinct smallish items as possible, and placed them in a container that has a lid. A tin box is ideal (or you could cover the items with a cloth). Items such as a small screwdriver, a little toy duck, an eraser, a paper clip, a flag pin. The more unique and unusual the better. Ideally, 25 or more items is what you want.

Game Play

Each team sends their first player up to you as the facilitator. Remove the lid of the container for approximately four seconds and then close it again quickly. The players then hustle back to their group and quietly share what they saw, and the scribe writes it down.

Give each player a chance to come up and observe. Then, at the end of the round, pull out each object and the teams check off all the items they described correctly.

Teaching Points

Make sure everyone has space to see inside the container. This is not a race, so do give time for the players to list the items they saw, but don't give them too much time. The key here is to give the players just enough short observation time to gaze at what is in the container, but not too much time that they could identify 15 items in one viewing. Make the later viewing rounds a couple of seconds longer because at that point the observing players are looking for the 7 or 8 items that have not been listed yet but they will be still be viewing the whole collection, and will have to try their best to spot the ones that others didn't.

Variations

Perhaps put in slips of papers with various numbers. Or try it with lots of unique items from nature.

Another variation that I have done is a human scavenger hunt, and this

Trust Games & Activities

one is a race. Have the players come up and the leader says, go back and bring me one credit card, a pencil, a one-dollar bill and a quarter. The players run back, tell the group what they need, and the group must give them those correct items and then they run back and tag the leader. A new player comes up. I want three shoes, a belt, and a comb. Obviously, this is a game that will work great when people have a lot of their personal stuff available in their purses, wallets backpacks, etc.

The Heart of Play

SUPPORT A FRIEND
(10 - 40 Players)

I learned this activity from my dear friends Sophia Hoffer-Perkins and Julia Martin. This can be an emotional experience so be sure the group is prepared to be in that space.

Set Up
1. Have someone volunteer to go into the center of the circle and take a position that represents a difficult emotion they have experienced recently.
2. Maybe their head is in their hands and they are covering their face, or they are all scrunched up in a ball.
3. Ask a few volunteers to go in one at a time and support this person in the middle.

Game Play
There are two ways this exercise can be experienced. One way is for the supporters to go into the circle and gently move the person slowly into a position that is more open rather than closed. Or the supporters can go in and just touch, or hold them or anything they feel supports the person in the middle to just feel the feeling. Remind the players to go in one at a time. The person in the center can signal the end of the experience by looking up and taking a moment to see the people who came into to support them.

Variations
The person who wishes to be supported goes in to the center and lies on their back or stomach. The players coming in just offer supportive touch.

Teaching Points
This activity is all about caring. The group needs to have a sense of community and empathy already built in. A great opportunity for people to feel the struggles that all human being go through. Also a good example to show that a simple act of gentle touch can allow a person to feel supported. Surprisingly, just this basic act of supporting someone helps the emotions to immediately shift.

Trust Games & Activities

WILLOW IN THE WIND

(8 -12 Players)

Many outdoor experiential education programs would use the traditional Trust Fall. A truly dynamic experience, however many programs stopped using this because of the fear of a group not being totally prepared and dropping someone. The Willow in the Wind experience creates a similar feeling but is a much safer way to create that feeling of letting go and being supported.

Set Up
1. The set up for this activity is crucial for its success. Great for about 8 to 12 people in a circle.
2. Make a really tight circle shoulder to shoulder.
3. One brave person steps into the center of the circle.
4. All the people around the outside take an athletic stance with one foot forward and the other one back so they have a strong base.
5. They put their palms up in front of their chest, in the bumpers up position. The person in the middle now places their feet together and crosses their arms across their chest.

Game Play

To make sure everyone is prepared, the person in the center asks the question, "Ready?" The whole group responds together with the statement, "Ready!" Then the person in the center says, "Falling" and the whole group responds with "Fall!" This then is the command for the center person to close their eyes and since their feet are together they let themselves fall. The group then gently moves them back and forth across the circle.

Basically, two to three people's pairs of hands are to be on the person at all times. Two important keys here. It is not the distance falling that makes the experience rewarding for the person in the middle. It is the letting go that makes it fun. If they fall too far then one person is left to support that person and it could be too much weight. The person in the center only has to fall a little bit. Also, make sure the supporting players are not pushing the person vigorously across the circle. This is about trust, support, and letting go.

Teaching Points

Take the time before and after to discuss what creates trust.

The Heart of Play

Games of Mindfulness

Social Emotional Learning and Mindfulness in Education are two associated and relatively new, movements happening in education. SEL teaches the skills of emotional regulation, empathy, cooperation, and social awareness. In other words, how to deal with emotions and social interactions in healthy and responsible ways. The Mindfulness in Education movement is adding to these skills by showing that focus, attention, and compassion can be learned, and practiced with simple everyday exercises of mindfulness. To sum it up, we can all benefit from noticing and becoming more aware of our own inner world and how it operates. I feel passionately that Integrative Social Play can enhance both movements.

Mindfulness has been growing for many years. People of all ages are learning how to pay attention more fully, mange their emotions effectively and reduce stress, just to name a few of the benefits. I was first introduced to some of these concepts by attending the Mindfulness in Education conference held at Omega Institute in 2009, and then by being on staff at a teen mindfulness retreat led by iBme (inward Bound mindfulness education). I am now on the staff of ReTribe which comprehensively teaches mindfulness and trust as part of its rites of passage programming for teens. I have also assisted one of the leaders in the field, Daniel Rechtschaffen, for a number of summers at his week-long Mindfulness in Education training at Omega.

In learning and deepening my own practice of mindfulness I have become more and more aware that part of what I have been sharing through play all these years is a mindful way of being. When Daniel teaches mindfulness he lets people know that he is "playing mindfulness." Mindfulness is all about curiosity, presence, inner awareness, openness, inquiry, imagination, listening, and being kind—even loving. Mindfulness is also about cultivating empathy for oneself and for others. Many of the energizers, theater games, etc., in this book can be used to support anyone sharing mindfulness with their students.

Play is, itself, a very present moment experience. Again and again in my adult playshops I hear people share, "Wow I noticed while we were playing that I wasn't thinking about other things, I was just in the flow of the game—in the moment."

By bringing attention and practice to cultivating present moment awareness into play, children can learn mindfulness naturally through their innate ex-

Games of Mindfulness

pression of playing.

Many thanks to Daniel Recthschaffen and Jenifer Cohen Harper, who helped me explore how simply and effectively play can enhance any mindfulness curriculum.

> My hope is this book will inspire a wider inquiry about all aspects of play. If there is a spectrum of play possibilities, with very complex rules, like professional sports and chess on one end of the scale, to a basic and primal form of interactive movement, like puppies and kittens in Original Play, on the other, an ideal play program would include elements from all different kinds of play that are age-appropriate throughout development.

The Heart of Play

COUNTDOWN: SHAKE IT UP

(Any number)

A really fun energizer to wake up the body. Great for those after lunch blues.

Set Up
1. Have everyone stand up and find their own space.
2. Demonstrate to the group that we will take our right hand and raise it above our head and shake it ten times. As soon as that is done we take our left hand and raise it above our head and shake that 10 times. Then stick your right foot out, shake that ten times and then your left foot...
3. Then the second time through you shake each part of your body nine times, then the next time through 8 times all the way down to one.

Game Play
"Ready, here we go. Right hand 1, 2, 3, 4, 5, 6, 7, 8, 9, 10. Left hand 1, 2, 3, 4, 5, 6, 7, 8, 9, 10 and all the way down to 1, 2, 1, 2, 1, 2... 1, 1, 1, 1.

The fun is the speed it is done and when you get down to one it is really funny and crazy.

Variations
Start at eight or lower number.

Teaching Points
When the players are done have them take a few breaths and feel the energy and excitement in their body. Talk about how close excitement is to fear and anxiousness. For example when a basketball player has been playing really hard and they get fouled and approach the foul line, how do they insure they can do their best to make that free throw. They take a couple of deep breaths before they take that foul shot. They reset themselves to the calmest they can be in that moment. Connecting to their breath helps them to do that.

Games of Mindfulness

DISTRACTION GAME

(10 - 30 Players)

(from Daniel Recthschaffen) A great activity to teach staying present and focused when distractions occur.

Set Up
1. Pick one person to be the object person.
2. Have them sit in a chair.
3. Ask them if they think they can sit still and not be distracted by anything that goes on around them.

Game Play

The object person closes their eyes. One person is now the distractor and they do whatever they can to distract that person without touching them in any way. Clap, bang around the room, ask them questions, rustle paper, anything to try and distract them. Do this for about 30 seconds. Do not make any loud noises near their ears, nor any unsafe near-miss swipes.

Ask for another volunteer to come up and sit still. Choose a new person to be the distractor. Take time for reflection after a few times playing.

Variaitons

Have everyone sitting quietly focused and present. Pick two or three volunteers to move around the room trying to distract those that are sitting.

Teaching Points

When first playing the game, you as the teacher/leader should be the first distractor, thus demonstrating how it can be done within the given rules. This is a great activity for reflection on what strategies can be used to deal with distractions in life. What to do with noisy siblings while studying or how it feels when other students are doing distracting behaviors in a classroom when you are trying to learn. What is distracting to one person may not be as distracting to another. How loud sounds can be startling or disturbing and what may surprise you and scare you.

Obviously a great opportunity to share how important it is to focus on breathing.

The Heart of Play

ENEMY / ALLY

(10 - 40)

A fun exploration in movement game. Feel free to change the names. Hannah Fox in her wonderful book, *Zoomy Zoomy*, calls this game Angel and Nemesis.

Set Up
1. Have everyone spread about the space.
2. Have each person choose secretly one person who will be their ally, and one who will be their enemy.
3. They can indicate when they have chosen their ally by placing their hand on their hip and when they have chosen their enemy place their other hand on their other hip.
4. Do your best to keep your ally between you, and your enemy.
5. Remind the players to move safely as this can get quite chaotic.

Game Play

You can either have everyone start by standing still, and/or you can have them start walking and count down "3, 2, 1, Begin," and then move to where their ally is between themselves and their enemy.

The fun comes when everyone is moving because they have all picked different people.

Do this for 20 to 30 seconds.

Have the players reveal to each other who was their ally was and give them a high five and who was their enemy. Then try it again with new allies and enemies chosen.

Teaching Points

It's important to remind everyone to move safely. This game is essentially an energizer/theater game. I list it here as an example of how most any movement activity can be integrated into mindfulness lesson. Moving with grace and awareness can help to support fun play and engenders trust and connection.

Games of Mindfulness

FOUR CHANGES
(2 + Players)

A very simple observation game.

Set Up
1. Each person gets a partner.
2. Demonstrate the game first.
3. One person who is the observer looks at their partner for 15 seconds observing every detail they can about their appearance.
4. Then they turn around.
5. Now the observed person change four things about their appearance.
6. They could untie a shoe lace, move a bracelet from one wrist to the other, take one ear ring off, unbutton a button on their shirt.

Game Play
Each partner takes turns being the observer (the guesser) and the observed. Try playing again and make the changes super obvious.

Variations
There are all kinds of ways you can use this concept. One such game is make a line of eight or more people. Have one person go out of the room and change the position of one, two or more people, and have the person come back in the room and try to guess the change that were made.

Another variation of an observing game that kids love is called, In Plain Sight. Have one person take a common object such as a tennis ball, everyone closes their eyes, and then the ball is placed somewhere in the room, "In plain sight." Everyone opens their eyes and when they see the object they can raise their hand or they could sit down if everyone started standing.

Teaching Points
A great game for players to practice skills of observation. A fun way to remind them how keen their observing mind truly is. Also, the mind becomes easily comfortable at times and doesn't notice changes, which is also good to notice.

The Heart of Play

FREEZE DANCE

(Any number)

This is a fun way to initiate movement and exercise, and to focus on stillness.

Set Up
1. Have everyone spread out in the room and be in their own space.
2. Put on some great boogeying music.

Game Play

"Everyone start dancing." After 20 seconds or so stop the music, and this is the cue for everyone to freeze. After a few seconds start the music and the dancing again. Do this a few times then challenge the players to see how long they can hold their poses during each succeeding stop.

"Wow that's great, everyone held still for six seconds. Let's go for ten seconds this time."

Variations:

Once the music stops you have three seconds to join another person and make a partner statue. This next time join a partner and make a statue using negative space. There is a concept in dance called negative space or empty spaces. When one person makes a shape there are empty spaces. Place a hand or an arm or a foot into that space and make an interesting statue without touching. If the group has learned to respect each other well you can add that the statues can be touching. Then perhaps there are three person statues or four person statues.

Teaching Points

This can be a great opportunity to talk about personal space, and practice the rule that everyone is to stay in their own space while resecting and appreciating the personal space of others. Also vary the length of time you stop the music.

Games of Mindfulness

MOVE TO OPEN SPACES / FOLLOW YOUR LEADER
(Players)

A good basic warm up you can build on with many theatrical elements.

Set Up
1. Explain that you will all be walking in the space together, and the object is to always move towards where there is open space. Demonstrate this.
2. Remind people to also move through the middle of the space. There is a tendency to just move around the outside of the space.
3. Explain that you will be calling out various modes of feeling and for them to walk while expressing that feeling.

Game Play
Have everyone start walking in the space. "Continually move to open spaces, so wherever you see open space walk toward it." Then you can add in various modes and qualities of movement. "Walk aimlessly... walk with intention... walk like you are trying to catch a plane... Feel that people are magnets and that you get repelled from them... Walk angrily, happily, suspiciously...

Then to make it a game add the element of "Follow Your leader." While still walking ask them to look across the play area and pick out one person, secretly that is their leader. They must keep this leader as far away from them as possible while still moving into open spaces. After 20 seconds or so of this ask each player to "now try to get directly behind their leader" and stay behind them and follow them wherever they go. Do this safely pleas without bumping into anyone.

This will be quite interesting to see who is following who particularly if two players have chosen each other.

Variations
Also you can use this to explore various emotions. Or have everyone walk and lead with a particular body part. Feel what it is like to walk leading with your knees, or you shoulder, or your stomach, or your head. A great lead in to improv theater as it help the players remember that often a character has their own unique way of moving.

Teaching Points
Adding in simple emotions to movement is fun and a great way to refer to how much we are a being of feeling and movement.

The Heart of Play

MIRRORING

(Partners)

Probably the most basic, simple and fun game there is.

Set Up
1. Have everyone choose a partner. One person is "A" and one person is "B".
2. Demonstrate to everyone how each person will take turns being the leader and the follower. First begin with yourself as an "A" by demonstrating with just the palms of the hands and arms, moving as if looking in a mirror and seeing the other person mirror your movements.
3. Then switch to "B" as the leader.
4. Remind people "You are responsible for your partner's success," which means moving slowly enough. And that, "Eye contact is home base."
5. Also demonstrate that as the activity progresses they can add more movement with other parts of their body, moving thru space, adding sounds, facial expressions etc.

Game Play

" A is the first leader. "Have the players begin and call out the change of leaders every ten to twenty seconds. " And now change."

Do this through about four or five leadership changes. Remind them while they are playing that eye contact is home base and that they are responsible for their partners success. Then instruct the pairs to continue playing and moving, but now they are to continue moving without either person being the leader, however there is still leading and following happening. Have them mirror each other without anyone being specifically a leader or follower for about thirty seconds and then ask them to find an elegant end to their play.

Have the pairs talk about how connected they felt during the exercise.

Variations

Have them switch leadership only a couple of times and have them quickly begin again with a new partner. Do it in a circle where one person is the leader and everyone follows them. Follow the leader!

Teaching Points

Share with the players that this essentially is the essence of play. Leading and following. Also share with your partner something positive about having played together.

Games of Mindfulness

MUSICAL HUGS

(15+ Players)

A great counterbalance to the competitive nature of a game such as musical chairs where someone is eliminated each round. Great for a large group.

Set Up
1. In this game everyone is to dance when the music is playing.
2. When the music stops everyone must hug another player.
3. Introduce that you as the leader will determine the number of players that are hugging.
4. 2 means you and one other. 3 people would mean 3 people in a little group hug.

Game Play
Start the music and everyone starts dancing. Stop the music and call out the number. Hug in fours. Vary the numbers you call throughout the song. Really fun when you call out 7 or 8. Perhaps at the end of the song say one and they have to hug themselves.

Variations
Musical Statues. When the music stops, players must get together and make a statue with the number of people you call out.

Teaching Points
Demonstrate that hugs can be as simple as an arm around the other persons shoulder. Also with larger numbers tell the players to do the best they can. Only let them stay hugging for 2 or 3 seconds at most and start the music up again.

The Heart of Play

ONE BREATH RUN
(8 - 40 Players)

A fun experience that can teach students about their breath.

Set Up
1. Pick a large outdoor area where you can run and make noise:
2. Have everyone take one big breath and let it out all the while making a sound until they cannot let anymore breath out which will be signified by the inability to make any sound.
3. Now explain they are going to do this while trying to run as far as they can on just one breath.

Game Play
Ready set go. Run as far you can. When everyone has stopped see who has travelled the furthest. Have them come back and try it again perhaps trying to run a little slower.

Variation
Try holding your breath and running just as long as you can hold that breath. Was it different when you were exhaling and making a sound.

Teaching Points
It is important for the players to understand it is not about who really goes the furthest as much as it is exploring your own capacity of breathing. Some students when first doing this will not know that they stop making sound and take another breath as it is quite automatic to want to take a breath when running. So their is the honor system in place here. Suggest to the students to experiment with making louder noises. Explaining how different people have different breathing capacities and that we can develop our lung capacity with training and through exercise.

Games of Mindfulness

OVERLOAD

(4+ Players)

This game is guaranteed to create stress and frustrations for some so be sure to let people know that the object of this game is to see how easy it is for any of us to become overloaded and then how we respond to this stress.

Set Up
1. Have everyone get into groups of four and then number themselves 1 through 4.
2. Number 1 will be the first person the exercise will be focused on.
3. Number 2 stands to their left.
4. Number 3 stands in front of them, and number 4 stands to the right.

Game Play

Number 1 is the "overloaded" player who will be answering questions and mirroring movements.

Number 2 asks simple questions and perhaps making them personal to that person. The questions are asked slowly at first and faster as the game progresses. (What color is the sky? What street do you live on? What is your favorite flavor of ice cream? Etc.)

Number 3 is standing in front of the "overloaded" person and makes simple movements that Number 1 must mirror.

Number 4 asks simple math questions: 2 plus 8 equals; 5 times 6 equals, etc. The two questioners alternate the asking of the questions.

At the start of the game, questioners ask questions slowly, but as the game goes on they speed up. If an answer is not correct or forthcoming, or if the mirroring is not being followed, then that person repeats the question. The overloaded player can stop when they feel sufficiently overloaded.

Teaching Points

This is a great exercise to emphasize how easy it is when we attempt to multi-task to become stressed. Have the players reflect where in their bodies did they feel the stress, and how do they tend to react in life when they get overloaded.

The Heart of Play

PASS THE PULSE
(10 – 30)

A fun way to observe energy and for the group to feel connected.

Set Up
1. Have the players form a circle and hold hands.
2. Explain that a pulse will be sent around the circle by the squeezing of a hand.

Game Play
The leader starts a pulse by squeezing the person's hand to his or her right (or left). The players pass this pulse all the way around the circle until it reaches the beginning. Try passing pulses in both directions. It will be an interesting experience for the person who receives both pulses at the same time. Now make it a race and tell them that you will start a pulse in each direction and let see which direction wins. Finally for a different energetic experience, try passing the pulse around with eyes closed.

Variations
Time the passing of the pulse. Ask an individual in the circle who starts and stops the pulse to simultaneously say, "Go," and eventually, "Stop," when the impulse returns. Repeat the attempt a number of times to see how much the group can improve it's speed, utilizing cooperation, physical reaction, anticipation, and efficiency. Try passing pulses in both directions for speed. Or try adding in a double squeeze sends the pulse back the way it came.

Teaching Points
This is simple game that focuses on the sense of touch. The group will need some patience and let themselves feel into waiting in surprise for the pulse to get to them. Add in moments of breath awareness.

Games of Mindfulness

SHAKE AND BLITHER

(10 - 40+ Players)

(From Daniel Rechtschaffen.) This is a great warm up before teaching some theater games, particularly speaking gibberish, which is blithering in an attempt to communicate in your own unique language.

Set Up
1. Tell the group: "Okay everyone, let's stand up and put our feet firmly on the ground. Imagine your feet are frozen in place like someone has poured concrete over them, or your feet are like giant suction cups that are firmly stuck right where they are."

Game Play
"Now start shaking your whole body. Shake your arms; shake your torso; shake your hips; shake your head. Imagine you're a big bowl of jelly, or you're a rag doll, and a giant has picked you up and is shaking you." Now add some sounds, when in doubt—just babble away like a baby.

Teaching Points
A great warm up before teaching some theater games, particularly speaking gibberish, which is blathering with accent and inflection but without comprehensible words.

> Play is the exultation of the possible.
>
> Martin Buber

The Heart of Play

SHAKE AND STOP

(10 -40+ Players)

(From Daniel Recthshaffen.) This game is especially good if your students are having a hard time sitting still or paying attention.

Set Up
1. Acknowledge the pent up energy first, "Wow I can tell everyone right now has a lot of energy in their bodies. Let's play with that feeling."

Game Play
"So right now, while sitting in your chairs, go ahead and shake your whole body. When I say stop, let's see how still we can be for three seconds. Then have them shake again, and instruct, "Now this time let's be still for 5 seconds." Then say, "What's the record we can set for today? Can we be still for 10 seconds, 15, 20?"

Variations
Shake and Freeze. Instruct, "Stand up and shake and move your body while moving around the space. When I say freeze, stop immediately in whatever shape or pose your body is in at the exact moment. Ready, everyone shake, shake, shake, and FREEZE! Now, look around and see all the interesting shapes and statues. Let's do it again, ready, shake..."

Teaching Points
Any active experience like this is a great opportunity to reflect on what happens with our body when it moves. It sparks more movement. It energizes us. Sometimes it tires us and yet we can still be "hyped" up. A great opportunity to do some relaxation exercises. Or, have the students check their pulse, and then check it again 5 minutes later. Or, do a relaxing stretch, or yoga pose, or breath focus, etc.

This is also a great opportunity to praise them with some positive recognitions.

Games of Mindfulness

WALK, STOP, WIGGLE, SIT

(10 - 30 Players)

(From Jennifer Cohen Harper of Little Flower Yoga.) This is a playful way to help students learn to listen well and follow directions.

Set Up
1. First introduce the two basic movement patterns of Walk and Stop. "When I say walk you walk, and when I say stop, you stop."
2. Have them do this for a couple minutes. "Ready walk... and stop...walk, etc."

Game Play
Now tell the students, "When I say stop you walk and when I say walk you stop. Got it? You are going to do the opposite." The students really have to focus and listen to respond correctly. Then introduce the commands of Wiggle and Sit. "When I say wiggle you wiggle and when I say sit you sit."

Then add in the reverse of Wiggle and Sit. When I say, "Wiggle you sit and when I say sit, you wiggle."

Teaching Points
Of course, it can be very challenging to listen to one direction and do the opposite. However, this is a great way to teach skills of listening and focusing. Remind them that even adults can have a hard time with this.

The Heart of Play

Team-Building Exercises

Most of the time, human beings need to be able to function within the context of a group, tribe, band, unit, team, or organization of some kind. We are interacting parts within the whole of society—which, ideally, would be one big team. As an athletic coach, I realized how much being a part of team was something I enjoyed and was good at. However, I also realized I had a lot to learn about accepting other people's leadership styles, understanding differences, and listening effectively. The team-building concepts I learned from Project Adventure have been instrumental in my coaching, and in all that I continue to offer to the world. From the creation of the Adventure Game Theater, to teaching P.E., to my offering a variety of workshops for organizations to enliven businesses, the team-building activities principles are still at the core of what I do.

All the games in this book are a team-building influence, helping to mend the fabric of society by bringing people together in this way. And the benefits of social bonding are right there to be experienced, along with long-term effects. For example, when managers and owners of businesses and corporations say qualities they are looking for in applicants, they want people who know how to work in groups, how to communicate effectively, are able to solve problems. They want employees who think creatively, and manage their emotions healthfully, i.e., being a good team player.

The games in this section are like a practice of embodying the charter traits necessary to be that kind of person. These are some of my favorites that take little or no equipment. There are many other team-building activities that can involve more elaborate equipment, such as ropes courses, trapezes and even fire pits, but I chose these games because they are playful, fun and relatively simple to teach. No doubt, high ropes course elements are a very powerful aspect of this category. I have always felt that every middle school and high school in this country should have a comprehensive adventure-based program.

One of the key components in these activities is that there is a problem that must be solved. Sometimes it seems quite easy, but then when you try it becomes quite apparent that the group must work together. This will involve sharing ideas, making plans, listening to each other (or not), making attempts, and having some minor successes and some failures before truly successful methods arise. Many corporations still bring their staff together and use these team-building

Team-Building Exercises

activities to gain insight into how their teams function and communicate. In the little microcosm of a team-building game, the group's internal dynamics are revealed, and interpersonal bonds can be strengthened.

This is especially true during the debriefing afterwards, which should also be conducted a little playfully.

> I remember as an athlete I was never the best at anything. I never had the opportunity to go to sports camps. I spent a lot of time playing baseball, not knowing that my eye condition was a true inhibitor to me being successful. I would have been better off playing soccer, or doing gymnastics, or started wrestling at a younger age. Growing up as an athlete you hear statements from coaches, and other such as, "Nice guys finish last. Winners never quit and quitters never win..."
>
> Hmm, I thought I was a nice guy and I finished 2nd in my conference and 3rd in the state wrestling tournament in only my second year of wrestling. I have also learned as I have grown that sometimes a great gift you can give yourself is knowing when it is time to stop. I tried out for tackle football and quit after one week. Was I a quitter? No. I just wasn't strong enough at that time to compete in that sport, at that level. I later went on to win three championships in adult league flag football.
>
> Then, there is the famous quote about winning from Vince Lombardi that is repeated quite often. "Winning isn't the most important thing, It's the only thing."
>
> Well here is what Vince Lombardi had to say near the end of his life about that quote: "I wish I'd never said the thing... I meant the effort. I meant having a goal. I sure didn't mean for people to crush human values and morality."
>
> Ultimately, the popular wisdom in the adage which says it's not whether you win or lose but how you play the game, is the truer statement.

The Heart of Play

ACROSS THE GREAT DIVIDE

(Good for 8 – 20 Players)

Simple and full of lots of laughter and contact.

Set Up
1. Set up an area of the field, about the size of half a basketball court or a good size room, to cross bounded by two lines as if it were the rim of a great canyon.
2. Tell your group, "Before you, you see the Great Divide."
3. To cross it everyone must be in contact with everyone else
4. If anyone breaks the connection then the group must return to the beginning. So please work together in order to cross the Great Divide."

Game Play
The first time the group must do it just by holding hands. Very simple. Next they do it keeping their shoulders touching. Takes a little more focus and teamwork.

Then on the next crossing to stay in contact by their hips. On this journey there will probably be a break, so be sure to send them back. They will have to start coordinating their movements.

On the final crossing the group must be in contact by their feet. What originally seems like an easy task is really quite difficult. There are a couple of elegant solutions.

Debrief with the group asking how they felt working together as a team.

A good framework is asking, "What did the group do well?", "How did you feel being a a part of the group,?" and "What could the group have been done better."

Variations
With ten players or more make two groups facing each other about forty feet apart. They are the transcontinental railroad and they must both get across their Great Divide to meet the other group half way there by following the rules. The first few steps have them meet each other high five and go back and do the next step.

Teaching Points
Surprising how difficult this last attempt is. As the facilitator, watch closely and let them know when there are breaks and send them back and continually

Team-Building Exercises

encourage them. Some easier solutions for the group are moving sideways with one person out front and the rest behind them in a line and the group shuffles slowly sideways or also sitting or kneeling on the ground and shuffling along and keeping your feet together that way.

> continued from, *A report from the Alliance for Childhood*
>
> Research shows that children who engage in complex forms of socio-dramatic play have greater language skills than nonplayers, better social skills, more empathy, more imagination, and more of the subtle capacity to know what others mean. They are less aggressive and show more self-control and higher levels of thinking."

The Heart of Play

AIRPORT

(10 - 30 Players)

A fun game that focuses on listening carefully and giving clear directions.

Set Up
1. You need a large room or an outdoor area a little bit smaller than half the size of a basketball court.
2. Mark out side and end boundaries.
3. Take all the spare toys, fun objects, balls etc. and spread them out in the space.
4. Divide the group into pairs. One person is the air traffic controller, the other the pilot.
5. Create a story that there is an airport landing field that has all kinds of debris on it. A cargo plane accidentally dumped their cargo during a very bumpy landing so there is debris spread out on the runway. You are running low on fuel and it is a foggy night. As the air traffic controller, you must guide the pilot in safely.
6. The pilot of the plane will have their eyes closed or wear a blindfold.

Game Play

Position the pilots at one end of the landing field. The air traffic controllers now stand on one side of the landing strip and gives clear commands in an attempt to guide the airplane safely thru the "debris" on the landing strip. "Ready take two little steps forward. Slide one foot to your right, Shuffle about one foot forward. Take one big step, etc..."

If a pilot steps on or touches an object they will have essentially crashed. Keep on going and keep track of the number of crashes it takes to get to the end of the runway. Switch roles and try again.

Variations

Have only one pair go at a time so the group can observe. Or you can also play it so that the air traffic controller can go stand right next to their partner. In other words, their air traffic controller is right in their ear.

This works well with larger numbers going at the same time, and is good for players that don't have big voices.

Team-Building Exercises

Teaching Points

For the debrief, you can focus on what are the obstacles that are often unseen. How often do we interpret the directions that someone has given us differently than they intended? One of the challenges of this game is having multiple people going at the same time and trying to hear your controllers directions while others are being given at the same time. Also, what did you learn after one attempt and then switching roles?

---

continued from, *A report from the Alliance for Childhood*

"China and Japan are envied in the U.S. for their success in teaching science, math, and technology. But one rarely hears about their approach to schooling before second grade, which is playful and experiential rather than didactic. Finland's children, too, go to playful kindergartens, and they enter first grade at age seven rather than six. They enjoy a lengthy, playful early childhood. Yet Finland consistently gets the highest scores on the respected international PISA exam for 15-year-olds."

The Heart of Play

BALLOON FRANTIC
(10 - 30 Players)

From Project Adventure, this is a truly fun and exciting team building game.

Set Up
1. Give each player a blown up balloon.
2. Have an extra eight or so blown up balloons on hand.
3. The object in this game is for the players to keep the balloons aloft by striking them up in the air with their hands, or really any part of their body.
4. They cannot hold the balloon in their hand—they have to keep bopping it up into the air.
5. One player is the timekeeper/facilitator and one or two other players be the referees. If more than 20 people are playing, two referees will be needed.

Game Play
Tell the players that every fifteen seconds an extra balloon will be added into the game (which will be performed by you). You can also double as the timekeeper if need be, but a player could have fun multitasking that. At any point during the game if a balloon falls to the ground the referee ceremoniously goes to that balloon and screams quite fully. This is called a "beserk" which lets everyone know that a balloon has fallen and the players have six seconds to get that balloon up into the air before it becomes another "beserk" and the referee screams again. The play continues until there are 6 "beserks." See what time has transpired and that is the base line time and now the group tries to beat that time in subsequent rounds.

Ask the group to discuss ways to be more successful and try again. A good time for a group is about one minute. With a couple of rounds of practice the time should be improved upon.

Teaching Points
Usually the groups attempt will improve quite dramatically in their second or third round. This game is just hysterically fun and doesn't necessarily lend itself to complex solutions, but a basic strategy that works is having designated people who are responsible for keeping two balloons up at a time. So just one or two extra attempts will be enough for the group to feel some successful.

Team-Building Exercises

BIG WORDS
(Any Size)

A simple problem-solving game involving scrambled words.

Set Up
1. Take some 4 x 6 notecards and write out one letter of the word per card of the various big words.
2. Divide your group into teams of 3 to 5 people.
3. Take each word, scramble it up and lay out all the letters of that one word on the floor or on a table. Some good Big Words to use are those that would fit into a theme around working as a team, such as: Teamwork, Cooperation, Camaraderie, Communication, Enthusiasm, Collaboration. Or how about a nature theme: Sustainability, Environmental, Symbiosis, Interdisciplinary, Ubiquitous, etc. Or a theme around joy: Playfulness, Laughter, Lightheartedness, Heartwarming, Magnanimous…

Game Play
Assign each team a word and give them a certain amount of time (say two minutes) to put the word together. After two minutes, the teams rotate to a new word. See how many words the team can unscramble and put together correctly.

Teaching Points
This game sounds easy, however, when all the letters are scrambled up it takes some thought and experimentation physically rearranging them in different orders. Certain people have a good sense of language and patterns, and might solve it quickly. It's quite fun when someone sees it and says, "Oh, I got it!"

Good to debrief and talk about who took leadership and how each team worked together on the problems. Who found it easy to do and who didn't?

As a facilitator, the prompt with a group might be think of common prefixes and suffixes to help with the rearranging process.

Variations
You could layout many more words than teams, and each team can run to the next free word that no one is working on, once they have completed one. Then see how many words they can put together in a certain amount of time.

The Heart of Play

DON'T TOUCH ME
(12 - 30 Players)

A simple and yet very clever problem solving game.

Set Up
1. Have the group make a fairly large circle.
2. Place a hula hoop in the middle of the circle.
3. Have the players look across the circle and pick a person across from them that is their partner on the opposite side of the circle such that everyone has a partner.
4. This is kind of fun for people to point and figure it out however you could start the game by everyone choosing partners and then making a circle with their partner being on the opposite side.

Game Play
Tell the group the problem is for each pair to touch the inside of the hoop at the same time and then arrive to the other side of the circle. The simple rule is any touching of another person during the activity is accompanied by a five second penalty. They must first make an attempt with no pre-planning to get a base line time.

"Ready? Time starts now—Go! Great, it took you twenty five seconds."

"Okay, being honest how many touches were there? Four that adds twenty more seconds to your time so your first attempt took 40 seconds. Great now take the time to discuss how you can do this faster and then make another attempt."

Add into the game that it is really fun to make the statement playfully, "Don't touch me!".... as you cross. "Ready for another attempt? Go!"

Repeat the attempts.

Teaching points
You can either set a time limit let say 10 or 15 minutes to make a series of attempts with suitable planning time, or tell them they can make four attempts. The simple solution is for the group to move in a way as to essentially make two lines as they cross in an ordered fashion.

Team-Building Exercises

ELECTRIC FENCE

(8 - 20 Players)

This was originally an activity where there was a seven to eight foot high rope and a plank was provided where the group had to get everyone from one side to the other side going over the rope without anyone touching it. (The story being that there is a full barrier, an electric fence of some kind in the way). Very challenging and on the edge of safety. This simpler version is lots of fun and a lot safer.

Set Up
1. Take a string or a rope and tie it to something, a chair works fine, and then the facilitator, or another volunteer, can hold the other end (or have two players hold it and extend it over a certain distance).
2. The height that the string is placed is important for the safety of the problem and for the appropriate challenge level.
3. It should be just high enough so that a person of average height cannot just step over it. (Probably about waist height for an most players.)

Game Play

Explain to your group that they are trapped inside a force field. To get to safety they must traverse this electric fence and they cannot touch the fence or the force field that extends invisibly down to the floor. Also, once the attempt begins, everyone must remain in contact with each other, such that if an electrical currents was sent through their bodies it would reach everyone maintaining a constant electrical contact among themselves—and they cannot touch the string or break the plane below the string from either side of the force field. If anyone touches the string, or breaks the plane, or loses the contact with the other players, then everyone must return to the original side for another attempt. To be successful all members must get over the fence.

Be sure the players do not attempt any unsafe lifts.

Teaching points

This problem solving activity is simple yet it keeps everyone involved since they all must stay in contact. Just challenging enough, and it will require teamwork to get everyone over "The Electric Fence," as one.

The Heart of Play

HOOP THE CIRCLE

(Great for circles of 8 to 30+ Players)

A simple cooperative game that is fun and challenging at the same time.

Set Up
1. Everyone holds hands in a circle.
2. Take a hula hoop and ask two players to separate their hands and put the hula hoop between them, and now they rejoin hands such that the hula hoop is now resting on their joined hands.

Game Play

Now they must lift their hands and tilt the hula hoop in one direction and the direction that the hula hoop is leaning that person steps or crawls thru the hoop thus passing it on to the next person in the circle and on it goes around the circle. The group challenges themselves to see how efficiently and how quickly they can pass the hoop around the circle.

Time this first attempt for a baseline time and now ask for suggestions as to how they can do it faster and more efficiently and have them make another attempt.

The players are not to use the fingers on their hands to help them in the challenge.

Now for another layer of the challenge. Start another hoop in the other direction and when the hoops meet the group must pass the two hoops thru each other to continue on their respective journeys around the circle. Yes it can be done. It is great to have two different colored hoops so you can see which one is going in which direction.

Variations

Have two circles of the same size do a race to see who can complete the challenge of passing one or two hoops in opposite directions around the circle.

Teaching Points

Encourage the group to support each other and remind them to do their best to not use the fingers of their hands to aid in the passing. Younger children will not be patient holding hands for a long time and waiting a long time so either make smaller circles or add more hoops into the mix.

Team-Building Exercises

LAP SIT

(20 – 4,000 Players)

This is a wonderful challenge for a group, and surprises everyone when it is accomplished. (The world record is some amazing number of 4,000+ people.) In the original New Games Festivals this was the stand out piece. I don't use this very often, however with a very aware group it is a simple but visually stunning accomplishment. It is important for safety reasons to teach this challenge properly.

Set Up
1. Have all the players form a circle and arrange it so that people are standing close to someone of their own height, to the shortest and smallest at the other end. I have actually done it from tallest to the shortest and I stand right behind the tallest person because having been a wrestler and having done this before, I can have someone very tall and large sit on my lap.
2. Once this is done, tell the group, "We are all going to sit in chairs—only, without the chairs!"
3. Next, tell everyone to turn a quarter turn, so their left arm is facing inside the circle.
4. "Now everyone take one side step toward the center. Reach out and gently rest your hands on the person's waist in front of you. You should be able to touch your elbows onto your own waist while touching the waist of the person in front of you. If not, take another little step toward the center of the circle. To check if we are all at the right spacing, there should be about 3 inches between your toes and the person's heels in front of you.
5. Okay, we are all going to sit on each others knees. If we all do it together, everyone will be a chair for everyone else. First we need a practice round. On a count of one, we will start sitting back; on two we will be almost there; and on three there will be direct contact of our bums on the person's knees behind us. As soon as you make contact, pop right back up and we will check for any weak links.
6. Explain that the commands will be: "1, Part way down. 2, Almost There. 3, Direct Contact—and then we will pop back up. Ready, 1 Part way down, 2 Almost There, and 3 Direct Contact. Everyone back Up! Any weak links? (Meaning did people feel they were going to fall, or that they couldn't sit down completely). If there are any, it is probably because the players are not standing close enough.

7. Also, remind the players that they have to commit and sit back, otherwise the person in front of them does not have a lap to sit on. Also, keep your knees together! Now each person has a lap to sit on."

Game Play

"Okay, this is the real one. On three we will be sitting on each others knees. Ready, 1 Part way down, 2 Almost There, 3 Direct Contact."

Once the group is sitting and solid, everyone can give everyone else a neck rub. Or, if it is a small group, ask the group to try and walk around in a circle. Left foot, right foot, etc. It can be done for quite a few steps, but generally the group will end up in a heap on the ground.

Teaching Points

This activity take an incredible amount of focus. There is the potential of falling down so it must be with a group that will listen well, and if anyone starts falling tell people to immediately stand back up. Younger children will actually enjoy falling down however adults will not land as safely as smaller children.

> In the early formative years, play is almost synonymous with life. It is second only to being nourished, protected and loved. It is a basic ingredient of physical, intellectual, social, and emotional growth.
>
> Ashley Montague

Team-Building Exercises

OGRE'S TREASURE

(10 - 20 Players)

This game is an adaptation of the young kids game Red light/Green Light.

Set Up
1. The story is a fun and important part of the process.
2. There is powerful Ogre who has stolen the town's sacred treasures. This can be represented by a rubber chicken, a frisbee, or foam ball.
3. The townspeople are at one end of the play area, the Ogre at the other, guarding the sacred treasure.
4. The Ogre has a playful heart so challenges the townspeople that if they can get the treasure without being seen moving they can have it back, but the Ogre has great visual powers and of course a threatening nature too, so if he sees someone moving he can make them go back to beginning.

Game Play

The Ogre turns his back to the group and says, "Green light, 1,2,3 Red light!" When the Ogre's back is turned, the townspeople move forward. When the Ogre says, "Red light," he turns around and if sees anyone moving they are sent back to the beginning. "Okay, green light, 1,2,3... Red light."

When the players get close enough to the treasure they can pick it up and try to get back to the start line while still playing the game Red light, Green light. Now that the treasure has been taken the Ogre still turns around after saying Red Light and can now can point to one or two players (depending on the size of the group) and ask them if they have the chicken. If correct, the Ogre gets the treasure back and the townspeople have to start all over and try again. Have the group discuss successful strategies to defeat the Ogre.

Teaching Points

It takes a couple of times for the group to realize whoever gets there first can't just pick up the treasure. They have to work together to distract the Ogre, being sneaky, passing the treasure from person to person. Tossing the treasure is okay and may be a good strategy. Red light is fun movement challenge game, but it is easy for players to get upset because leaders can obviously abuse their power. Therefore, the concept of "Total It Power," is in play here.

This takes some teamwork and problem solving for the group to figure out how to get the treasure without being seen by the Ogre.

The Heart of Play

SPEED JUGGLE
(8+ Players)

(From Mitch Ditkoff and Idea Champions.) This is my go-to favorite team builder because of the simplicity, fun, and predictable responses it creates.

Set Up
After having played the game group juggle, the group is now ready for a team-building version of the group juggling experience. Have them choose four different colored balls.
1. Have them pick an initiator (leader) and set the repeating pattern.
2. If you have just done group juggle then it could be that person who started the cycle. Have them repeat that same pattern they have set up in group juggle.
3. Have someone be a timekeeper, preferably with a stop watch.
4. Have the group set a baseline time of how long it takes to pass the four balls through the complete cycle ending back with the initiator.
5. It might take a group of ten people about 15 to 20 seconds or so.

Game Play
Now that you set up a base line time your group must see how much faster you can do it. Here are the rules, and it can be done much faster following these. Have these rule printed out for the group to refer to.
- The balls must pass in the same person to person sequence
- The balls must touch each person in the same color to color sequence.
- The balls must touch each person one at a time.
- The rules do not apply to the initiator.
- If you have done this before please don't share the solutions.

Give them time for numerous tries. Constantly asking them after a try, how can you do it faster. Now that you have the base line time ask the group to see how they can do it faster. Staying true to the rules, it can be done in less than a second! Debrief how the group worked on this problem.

Variations
It can be done with just one ball, but then eliminate the rule that the rules don't apply to the initiator. Slightly different problem but a ramp method, with one finger of each person touching the ball in sequence will result in an under one second solution.

Team-Building Exercises

Teaching Points

Almost every group goes through a process of learning they can reorder themselves. Then they try different touching patterns. Then they usually try a ramp or funnel often improving their times. If a group is getting stuck remind them of the rule that the rules do not apply to the initiator. The fastest solution is the initiator holds the four balls in one or two hands and swipes them across one outstretched finger of each person in the correct order. Voila a half a second!

If you have large numbers you can do this with multiple groups and then ending after a couple of groups have solved the problem. Just because a group didn't get to the final solution does not mean they didn't have success. The success is in the process of being a part of well functioning group.

> I was playing when I invented the aqualung. I'm still playing. I think play is the most important thing in the world.
>
> Jacque Costeau

The Heart of Play

THE CLOCK
(15 - 30 Players)

Another problem solving activity that doesn't really need any equipment and is best with a medium size group.

Set Up
1. Your group is sitting in a circle on the ground such that they can reach out and hold hands with the persons next to them.
2. Explain that the circle represents the face of a clock.
3. At two points just inside the seated players place cones or something that indicates what would be 12 o'clock and 6 o'clock positions on a clock.
4. Designate which person is sitting right at the 12 o'clock position.

Game Play
Tell the group the challenge is to hold hands, getting up without breaking hands, start walking (for the first attempt just have them walk) turn one complete rotation of the circle with every person going around the 12 and 6 o'clock markers. So whomever is at the 12 o'clock position must get around to that position going clockwise and then stop and return to the original starting position by going counterclockwise, and everyone must sit down and do this without breaking hands.

Do this once to get the base line time then ask the group to brainstorm ideas on how they can do it faster and then give them a few attempts to see how much more quickly they can do it. Set a goal of improvement. If it took them 20 seconds the first time then maybe 14 seconds is their goal.

Variations
Feel free to make adaptations for people who may not be able to sit and get up easily. Perhaps they kneel or perhaps you allow a couple of people to be standing to start and they can help others to get up.

Teaching Points
Remind them they have to start seated on their bottoms. Have them discuss what would work best to get people standing up. Also remind everyone to be safe and not pull peoples hands.

The key in this activity is that if they try to go faster by running faster, centrifugal force will cause breaks in hands. It will work better with support to get everyone up, staying close together, coordinating the transition point of stop-

Team-Building Exercises

ping and going the other way, and by actually staying close to the two points of the clock. So staying bunched up actually works better as they just have to get the one person who has to be at 12 o'clock to that point and then turning around and returning and then everyone sits down... but let the group discover these points on their own.

There is no rule that states they have to be sitting in the same spot when they return. It is more just about fun, holding hands, working together then it is a deep thinking problem solving activity.

---

continued from, *A report from the Alliance for Childhood*

How Kindergarten Has Changed. The traditional kindergarten classroom that most adults remember from childhood— with plenty of space and time for unstructured play and discovery, art and music, practicing social skills, and learning to enjoy learning— has largely disappeared. The results of three new studies, supported by the Alliance for Childhood and described in this report, suggest that time for play in most public kindergartens has dwindled to the vanishing point, replaced by lengthy lessons and standardized testing.

The Heart of Play

Communication & Sharing Exercises

Play is, at it's heart, a form of communication that is understood on a primal level. One of my favorite quotes is from Julio Olalla, who said, "More suffering is caused by miscommunication than anything else in life."

I fell in love with a body of work known as Non Violent Communication, NVC, which was foundational in my understanding the importance of Social Emotional Learning. Created by Marshal Rosenberg, this method helped people learn how to listen with empathy, which is more of a skill than most people realize, but as a result, speaking with empathic kindness has been found to resolve conflicts very effectively. Then I trained extensively in Conscious Communication (an offshoot of NVC), sometimes called the language of connection. In this capacity, I am on the training staff of the Social Harmony Institute, which is a powerful whole-systems approach for dealing with conflict in schools and helping develop healthy cultures through understanding the importance of connection at all levels.

I have included a handful of communication exercises that I use regularly to deepen the interpersonal potentials within groups. They can be interspersed within games and play to foster connection and practice listening skills. They go nicely with Trust games and Mindfulness activities. Emphasizing reflection and debriefing as a regular part of sharing-games and play will help in developing the deep listening skills that are the basis for real communication.

This chapter is divided into two sections. The first part are basic games that can be used as easy stand-alone exercises in a variety of settings, helping people to be present with each other. The second section is group sharing exercises that build upon each other to facilitate even deeper connection within small groups or a whole group. The first two exercises, Lightning Rounds, and If You Really Knew Me, can be used to facilitate deep sharing in a group. In my work with Re-Tribe, a rites-of-passage leadership organization, these two exercises lead in to an process we call "Hot Seats," which requires competent training and the support of licensed counselors or therapists. Even when leading an exercise such as, "If you Really Knew Me," be prepared for some raw honesty and vulnerability. Be sure to have the appropriate support systems in place such as the access to counselors, etc.

The Council Process model can be surprisingly powerful.

Communication & Sharing Exercises

GRATITUDE BALL

(5- 30+)

This exercise is a simple way to express thankfulness in your life.

Set up:
1. Take a soft foam ball or plush toy. This is the gratitude ball and it has been used by many groups and is collecting lots of positive energy.
2. This can be done in a circle or just popcorn style in your classroom or at home.
3. Please share something you are grateful for in this moment, such as, "I am grateful for my mom," or, "I am grateful that the flowers are blooming," or, "I really appreciate how kind everyone has been today."

Game Play

The first person shares an appreciation and then hands the ball to the next person in the circle. Or do it in popcorn style and toss it to the next person who has their hand up wanting their turn next and on it goes. If doing it in a circle remind the players they can always pass and then check in with them again after the circle is completed and ask them if they want to now take a turn.

Variations

Or you can notch this up into a greatness ball toss, by lobbing the ball to another person and giving directed appreciations to that person. For example, Joe tosses the ball to Sue and says,

"Sue, what I noticed today was how nice you were to James. That tells me you were showing the greatness of thoughtfulness and caring."

The good folks at Life is Good Playmakers teach a similar activity called News Ball. Rather than sharing gratitude, they share something briefly about what is happening in their life. Great for younger children to share about what is new for them. "I just got a new puppy," and then roll the ball to another person.

Teaching Points

The tossing of the ball keeps the exercise light and fun, although the sharing of gratitude can be very touching too. A great way to reflect on what is going well and how important it is for our brains to focus on positivity.

The Heart of Play

I COULD TELL YOU ABOUT...

(10- 40+)

(From InterPlay) A simple and fun communication exercise.

Set Up
1. Create small groups of 4 to 6 players.
2. Talk about how often people love to go into long stories about who they are and what they have done. However that takes time.
3. In this exercise it is all about sharing what you could talk about if you had the time, so in this activity the idea is to share a brief statement about something that if you did have the time, you could share in great depth about so in other word, "I could tell you about..."

Game Play
Go around the circle two or three times with each person using the stem and saying one thing. "I could tell you about..." and they fill in the blank. "I could tell you about my trip to China." Then the next person might say, "I could tell you about quantum physics." Then the next person, "I could tell you about how to knit a sweater," and the next, "I could tell you about the new kitten we just got..."

Variations
Choose a different stem. "If I had more time I would love to talk about..." Or maybe do some slightly longer shares but keep them concise. "If I could change one thing in my school it would be..."

"If I could learn one new skill, it would be..."

Teaching Points
This exercise is good for people who may be hesitant in a group to talk a lot. It gives everyone just a moment to say something about themselves but not have to go into a long story. Remind everyone that at another time you can go up to a person and say, "Hey tell me about your trip to China."

Communication & Sharing Exercises

IN THE PRESENT MOMENT I AM AWARE OF...

(2 - 30+)

A simple mindfulness exercise.

Set Up
1. Break into partners.
2. Ask for a volunteer and demonstrate the activity.

Game Play

The speaker just says what they are aware of in each moment. "In the present moment I am aware of... the birds singing outside."

"In the present moment I am aware of my belly telling me it better be lunch soon."

"In the present moment I am noticing your blue eyes..."

"In the present moment I am noticing I am thinking about the test I have to take next period and I am feeling anxious about it."

You can either alternate back and forth, or one person says what they are aware of for thirty seconds or a minute, and then change to the other person speaking.

Variations

You can do this is in a circle with each person taking a turn, turning to the person next to them and declaring what they are aware of in that moment that they are noticing about that person, and keeping the observation very concrete. "In the present moment I am aware of the blue color of your shirt," and then that person turn to the next person and might say, "I notice that your glasses are purple. This can also be very specific which is great for younger children to get used to just naming things without judgement "I notice that your eyes look brown" and each person speaks the same basic stem. "I notice your eyes look hazel to me."

Teaching Points

This exercise is great opportunity for people to notice their own thoughts and see how their mind is constantly noticing things virtually all the time. This practice of noticing our thoughts, sensations and feelings is a key component of mindfulness.

The Heart of Play

SPEAK ABOUT ONE THING

Players

When a conversation is happening our mind is usually spending its time thinking of what we are going to say in response to what we are hearing the other person say. This is a great exercise to emphasize the skill of just listening, since when it is your turn you will be given a different subject to talk about, the person can just listen.

Set Up
1. Divide into partners.
2. Tell the two players to pick one person who will be the first speaker and the other the listener.
3. Each player will be given a subject to talk about for 30 seconds.
4. Let them know that when they switch that the second speaker will be given a different subject to talk about so the first listener should do the best they can to just listen and not think of what they will be saying in response.

Game Play
Person number one will speak uninterrupted, about how they feel, or tell a story, or offer insights, or a stream of consciousness about the given topic. "Okay, the first person will talk about... chocolate, go!

"Okay stop! Now the second person will talk about... cats!"

Variations
Experiment with different time lengths. It is interesting to give a person a full uninterrupted minute to speak. That in and of itself is an interesting exercise as for many people that is long time to speak with someone without any interjections or interruptions.

Teaching Points
So often in conversation our minds are always thinking about what to say in response to what someone else is saying. This is an exercise where it is structured that the listener only listens. When it is their turn they will not be speaking on the same subject so they are to do their best to let go of whatever their mind is thinking about in response to what that person is saying. Have the players share whet it felt like to just listen and to just talk.

Communication & Sharing Exercises

Concerns and Appreciations, If you really Knew Me, and Council Process

Whenever possible it is great to have opening and closing circles in classes or group settings. This can be as simple as a one word check-in or asking everyone to share how they are feeling and getting the pulse of the group. Other formats for check-ins are a high and a low, or a rose and a thorn, or share your feelings in a like it is a weather report. Today I am feeling cloudy, or sunny, stormy or fair...

Concerns and Appreciations is one way to help students begin to learn how to speak and share their feeling and express their needs in a simple format. As in any good communication it is helpful to speak in "I" statements, trying our best to refer to our own experience. In the Conscious Communication trainings I teach it is all about learning to share feelings and needs without judgements and blame taking full responsibility for sharing our feelings and needs with compassion. This is not something that can be taught to children easily. It is a developmental process that is best learned by observing adults do it well. What can be initially taught is for them to learn to speak in "I" statements, and then have adults help them to solve their problems by the adults modeling and coaching healthy compassionate communication. The activity Concerns and Appreciations is a simple and yet effective tool to model how by sharing our concerns, we can let others know we have had our feelings hurt and that hopefully then our needs can be met through making clear requests and through healthy conflict negotiation.

To go deeper and facilitate conversation among older kids or adults breaking people up into small groups is always helpful. In our ReTribe program we use a model that we learned from iBme. It is comprised of the exercises called Lightning Rounds, If You really knew Me, and the third exercise are called Hot Seats. I have not included Hot Seats here as it takes a bit of training to know how to hold a safe container to facilitate these opportunities. What I have shared is the council process model which can accomplish the same depth. For more information about working deeply with teens, contact ReTribe (see resources). The council process is also a great way to create safety and open sharing in a whole group.

Offering gratitude and appreciations at the end is a great way to conclude a group process.

The Heart of Play

CONCERNS AND APPRECIATIONS

This was shared with me by Curtis Brock a retired principal for the Oakland City school system. This is a process he would use everyday with his students.

Set Up

4. Get your group in a circle, or if the groups is larger or you are in a classroom-set-up, just have them sit at their desks.
5. Ask who has any concerns they want to bring up. First, just list their names on the board or a flip chart. Just get the names of people who have concerns.
6. Then go back and ask each person what there concern is. Encourage them to keep it brief and concise. If there is not enough time you still have the list and when there is time later it could be addresses.
7. Remind people to keep their concerns concise and as factual as possible.

Enactment

For example, Sue may say, "I was upset when Jim took the jump rope away for us. I knew he just joking but he interrupted our game and it wasn't funny to us."

"Okay Jim, did you hear that Sue was upset?" Jim says yes. "Sue what request would you like to make of Jim. Jim please don't take our jump rope when we are using it. Jim can you agree to that."

Or Tim says. "I went and asked Joe if I could join the game and he said they had already picked teams. I was mad that I didn't get to play and I felt excluded." Joe could you repeat back what Tim said so we can be sure you heard it and that it is correct information.

After concerns are shared the magic sauce so to speak is offering appreciations. After a while of doing this concerns will start to diminish and students will want more time to give appreciations.

In my previous book, *Nurtured Heart Play* the cornerstone of the Nurtured Heart Approach is offering timely, specific acknowledgment for the greatness that each person is exhibiting.

Ask the students to be specific with the appreciations and point out the exact behaviors. So not, "Bob your such a good friend," or "Molly, you were nice to me today." Make it specific. "Bob, I was struggling with my homework and you took the time to show me how to solve those problems. Thanks... Molly you sat down with me at lunch and shared your cupcake with me. That was really nice."

Communication & Sharing Exercises

Teaching Points

Just the process of naming concerns helps people to feel safe and included. In group settings, it helps to bring concerns up in real time, and to be heard by everyone. The key is modeling concise clear communication of feelings and then helping your students make clear requests of each other. Making amends and apologies may be appropriate when necessary, but not forcing kids to apologize when they aren't ready. Often it is just enough to hear that their behavior was perhaps hurtful and being in the whole group together bring awareness to how behaviors have impact on others. Make sure to hold the container of everyone listening with respect and not mocking each other in anyway. In other words, no put downs.

---

continued from, *A report from the Alliance for Childhood*

Striking a healthy balance In a healthy kindergarten, play does not mean "anything goes." It does not deteriorate into chaos. Nor is play so tightly structured by adults that children are denied the opportunity to learn through their own initiative and exploration. Kindergartners need a balance of child-initiated play in the presence of engaged teachers and more focused experiential learning guided by teachers.

The Heart of Play

LIGHTNING ROUNDS

Players

Lightning rounds are a simple way for each person to be heard for just a moment, and to get to know their opinions, thoughts or feelings without a lot of conversation.

Set Up
1. Best to have everyone in a circle.
2. The leader explains what a Lightning Round is. You can start with something light and move into something deeper.
3. The idea is to pose questions that are one word answers to begin with and then slightly longer answers however the idea is for the sharings to be quick and concise.
4. First the leader can pose a few questions and then it can be opened up to the group to suggest questions.

Game Play

When the question is posed, the questioner answers the question first and then picks the direction to go around the circle. A person can always pass. A sampling of possible questions.

1. What is your favorite animal / color / movie?
2. If I had a super power what would it be?
3. What makes me comfortable in a group is...
4. When I daydream I think about...
5. When someone puts me down I feel...
6. I'm proud that I...
7. The qualities I value in a friend are...
8. If I could be an animal, I'd be a... because...
9. What my friends like about me is...
10. If I could have everyone in the world do something for 15 minutes every day it would be to...

Teaching Points

Remind the players to keep their answer to one word or a short concise answer. Keep the pace moving. Three to five Lightning Rounds can be done in less then ten minutes in a small group, and will lend itself to people learning fun and interesting things about each other quickly.

Communication & Sharing Exercises

IF YOU REALLY KNEW ME...

(4 – 8 Players)

This is a great follow up to lightning rounds and a format for people to share a little more deeply, especially teens, and helping people stay succinct and not tell rambling stories.

Set Up

1. Depending how open a group is pick a set number of times they will say, "If you really knew me..." For example, say three times. Or pick a designated time, say, 1 minute.
2. Let the group know that each person will use the stem: "If you really knew me," in front of each statement sharing something personal about themselves.
3. Ask the group for no cross-talk or commenting when the person is speaking.

Game Play

One person starts off with the stem of the sentence. "If you really knew me..." and then adds whatever they want to share. After that one statement they repeat the stem again... "If you really knew me you would know that I love chocolate... If you really knew me, you would know that I love to play soccer... If you really knew me, you would know that my uncle, who I was really close to, died last month... If you really knew me, you would know that I broke my leg in a bike accident when I was 12..."

And on and on till the time is up. The idea is for the person sharing to let it be a stream of consciousness, to reveal whatever they feel safe to share with the group in that moment.

Variations

With younger kids, or in general, you could just go around the circle with them just onece or twice. Or, shorten the time and do just 30 or 45 seconds for each person. Or, if working with adults, they can do two minutes of If You Really Knew Me...

Teaching Points

As the facilitator you can model this by sharing a couple of light, if you really knew me's, and then a couple of more vulnerable ones.

The Heart of Play

COUNCIL PROCESS

The council process is modeled on the Native American process (and other indigenous cultures) whereby you sit in circle together, deeply listening and holding sacred space for people to share what is in their hearts. This is not something easily done for people who are used to offering their opinions and judgments all the time, and who haven't learned to just hold space for others to share their feelings. However, learning to do this is a great tool for social-emotional excellence. Often, just being heard and having others hold space for you to share, helps emotions move and allows creative ideas and support to then come forward after people have shared in the circle. Traditionally a talking stick is passed and someone can speak only if they are holding the talking stick.

Set Up

Here are the guidelines for council process:
1. No cross talk.
2. Confidentiality. What is shared in the circle stays in the circle.
3. Listen with respect.
4. Speak with sincerity, honesty and from the heart about your own experience.
5. Be mindful of being concise, not too much or too little.
6. Only the person holding the talking stick (or object) may speak.
7. Make "I" statements about your own experience, and no judgements about other people's sharings.
8. If something that someone else said touched your heart, or caused a reaction inside of you, you can refer to that feeling, but as best as possible, not from a place of judgment. (For example: "Wow, when Joe said they were bullied on the playground I felt really sad, and I was also angry that happened. I am sorry no one stood up for you Joe..." Or, "I am really frustrated about all the violence that is happening in the world. I actually get scared when I am walking home…" Or, "I am really concerned about passing my test next week. Could someone help me study?"
9. Anyone can pass, and once the talking stick has gone around the circle if a person that has passed now wishes to speak, they will be given that choice.
10. In order to keep a respectful space while someone else is talking a person can show that they agree with what is said by either snapping their fingers or by saying, A-ho (a Native American expression).

Communication & Sharing Exercises

Enactment

You as the leader can begin the sharing, thus modeling the process or ask for who would like to go first. The person takes the talking stick and shares, then passes the talking stick to the person next to them, and the stick gets passed around the circle. If necessary, set a time limit for the sharing, i.e., 1 or 2 minutes. A timekeeper can be chosen and when time is up a chime can be rung and the person talking can take a few moments to complete their sharing. This keeps the group on time. You can also pick a subject to focus the conversation on. For example, Something, as simple as, "One thing I really like about myself..."

Or, "How is the school year going so far?"

Or, "What are a couple of stressors in your life?"

Or, "How are you feeling about the violence you see in today's media?"

Variations

Place the talking stick in the center and a person volunteers to go into the center, pick it up, and return to their spot in the circle to address the group. When they are done speaking, they return the talking object to the center, and then the next person volunteers to go next.

Teaching Points

Holding a space of non-judgment is not easy. As a facilitator, it may at times be appropriate to break in and remind someone to make I statements or remind people to speak about their own experience. It is not easy to speak about one's feelings, or to know what is in our heart unless we practice this. If working with deeper issues, a longer time length for sharing may be needed.

> There is an old Sanskrit word, lila, which means play. Richer than our word, it means divine play... It also means love.
> Stephen Nachmanovich

The Heart of Play

The Art of Saying Yes

Games of Improvisational Theater

In the Adventure Game Theater, which was our own mythic world of play, we created an improvisational role-playing experience that was as experimental as it was fun. Eventually, we even took it upon ourselves to study improv theater. One of our teachers was Martin De Maat, who was the creative director of Second City Theater for many years. He emphasized that the skills you learn in improv are skills for life. I use improv games in almost all the trainings and playshops I lead.

Improvisational theater is a big topic, so for the sake of this play manual, I am including my very favorite games that I have used over many years, beyond the role-playing camps, to stand-alone Improv workshops. By definition, Improv is very playful, which necessitates creativity, collaboration, curiosity, and imagination. These are all woven together to make the tapestry of skills that encompass SEL outcomes. Use these games as a platform for that kind of learning if you like.

Being an improviser is all about flexibility in thinking, being willing to be surprised, it is about being in connection with your fellow players and exploring the broad range of human expression.

Wouldn't it be great if when you were born you are given a manual on how to live, maybe with a special chapter on how to respond to change with grace. And one on how to communicate effectively, or how to know what our gifts are and how to live a happy life... those sorts of things. But life is a kind of improvisation. Might as well learn the skills of how to be a good improviser. At least we can have more fun on this playground called life. How much of your life can you turn into an ad hoc improv game?

Here are the the skills that make improvising easier and more fun.

#1, Say, "Yes And..."
Accept the offer and build upon it. This is the basic tenet of improv, is a kind of saying yes to life. One actor says to the other, "Hey look at that gorilla over there." The fellow actor doesn't say: "I don't see a gorilla." A better path is in saying yes to the idea, accepting it, and then building upon it: "Yeah, I see that gorilla—and you know that money I owe you? Well, that gorilla is holding my

The Art of Saying Yes

wallet. And if you want that 200 bucks back, then you better help me get that wallet..." And the scene goes on much better in that way.

Saying, "Yes and..." to life means being in acceptance of whatever is happening and finding a way to flow with it. Not only more effectively dealing with stress, but also conserving your energy, and allowing you to focus on changing the things you can and maybe even the sanity to know the difference.

#2, Make your Partner Look Good
Take responsibility for your actions and support your fellow players. This is my favorite tenet. I believe true happiness comes from being in service to others in the world around you, and sharing the burdens of life. I also believe that competition is overrated, and cooperation undervalued. In Improv, the goal is to be in absolute cooperation with your partners. This is manifested in choosing dialogue that is supportive and makes it easy for your partner to say, "Yes and..." to. Ask yourself, are you making kind and supportive offers in life, to your friends, family, and coworkers? Are you complementing them and telling them how wonderful they are? These a like little games in themselves.

"Hey, can I help you with that project..."
"Hey, let's go to a movie..."
"Wow, you look more radiant today than usual. Is that new sweatshirt?"

In a world of schadenfreude and excess ego-selfishness, this practice of shining a light on others has downright spiritual connotations.

#3, Dare to be Average
In improv, if you try too hard to be funny, you may do something really creative, but how can your partner follow up on what you just did? Rather, the simplest situations can be highly interesting and entertaining. Everyday moments in life can be full of humor, wonder, and grace. Even though we are all more average than we care to think.

In a culture addicted to stimulation and entertainment, a simple storytelling game, a simple mirroring game, or just passing the energy in a circle can be a delightful experience and full of surprises.

#4, Be in the Present Moment
Improv actors have to be in the moment, since their scenes are all being created in real time. And from a meditative standpoint, this has psychological potential and significance (along with number 2). The more we can just breath in

The Heart of Play

life, be right where we are in acceptance and love, then the easier it is to flow with the changes that are happening in each moment. Easier said than done, however well worth the effort. Again, these are skills that you work on.

The beauty of improv acting is that you learn to just trust that you will have an idea that comes to you, sometimes as if by magic, surprising even yourself—moment by moment.

I have broken the improv theater games up into three chapters. The first chapter is simple warm up exercises. These theater games are relatively easy for everyone and are done with everyone participating. The second chapter are games that are can be played in partners or in small groups, again where everyone is playing all at once. The last chapter are improv structures where you have an audience watching with a few volunteer performers up in front of the group—"on stage".

All of the theater games in this chapter were chosen based on the accessibility for the new improvisers. There are many more theater game structures that you can find on the internet (see Resources section for a few of my favorites), and elsewhere. Many people are intimidated by the thought of getting on stage and doing improv. Fortunately, theater games and improv games can be very user-friendly. They are just fun, and spark playfulness, imagination and storytelling. You don't have to perform on stage to do improv. Sure, to go up there and take suggestions from an audience and just creating in the moment can be a thrill, but usually requires practice and discipline to get really good at it.

However, the basic principles that make good improv scenes can be taught, and—as we know—they are great skills for life. Many schools are adding this into their curriculum to teach problem solving, creativity and emotional flexibility. Managers in corporations are teaching their staff improv skills or for creativity, innovative thinking, and for better social bonds among the staff—the team.

The simplest warm up theater games can be played by all ages and are fantastic at creating trust, laughter, and connection. Games such as Mirroring, Memory Loss, What are you doing?, Yes Let's, and One Word Story will teach the basic guidelines for improv. Also Games like, Whoosh, Elephant Palm Tree, and Human Machine, in the energizers and circle game sections are essentially theater games. After all, improv is about making things up in the moment, so you can make up almost any game. It is all about having fun and feeling alive.

As a Play Leader, keep creating an environment of safety and acceptance, where "mistakes" are welcomed and the creative expression of you fellow human beings can flourish.

Howard Moody

Improv Warm-Up Games

These are the games you use to warm up a group of experienced players, or to initiate a group of new players to improv. Less experienced folks should do more of these games, which are also especially great at creating trust and rapport. Many improv groups will use a game like Count Ten, or Pass the Clap to get everyone into unison, artistically connected, and really listening to each other.

There are a number of other games in this manual that are essentially theater games, such as in the Energizer or Circle Games section, that I use regularly in any playshop. See games like Elephant Palm Tree, Human Machine, Human Statues, Enemy Ally, and Whoosh. Conversely, these theater warm up games also make great energizers. Also great for any social-emotional-learning curriculum.

A number of these games are great for practicing the four guidelines of improv. For example, Yes And, Memory Loss, and Yes Let's are great to teach the concept of Say Yes And,

The games Accept and Build, and Invisible Tug of war are great to emphasize Making your Partner Look Good.

What Are you Doing? is great to teach Dare to be Average.

Empty Vessel, What's in the Box, and Mirroring are great for practicing Be in the Present Moment.

> Also, from other sections of the book:
>
> Count Ten
> Elephant Palm Tree
> Enemy Ally
> Human Machine
> Human Statues
> Whoosh

The Heart of Play

CELEBRITY

(10 -30)

More of a party game than a straight improv game, it's an easily accessible acting game for most people.

Set Up
1. Make at least four small slips of paper for each player.
2. Give the players (4 or more) slips of paper, and ask them to write down the name of one celebrity from fact or fiction on each slip of paper. Please write down names that you think most of the other players would know.
3. Put all these slips into a hat or some other suitable container.
4. Divide the group up into 2 or 3 equal-sized teams of about 4 – 6 players.
5. Choose a timekeeper.

Game Play
Round one is one minute long for each player on each team. A player for team 1 gets up and pulls a slip of paper from the hat. They begin describing this person. The rest of their team makes guesses. As soon as it is correct, the players toss that slip aside and picks another slip. Players can pass if they don't know the celebrity. Then the next team has their first person go, alternating between teams until all players on each team has gone. After all the players have taken a turn in round one take any slips of paper out of the hat that were not guessed and take all the correct guesses and place them back in the hat.

In round two you only have thirty seconds and you can only use one word to describe the celebrity. Hopefully they won't guess every name, so some are still in the hat and take the ones that were guessed and put them back in.

Round three, you can only make gestures, miming as clues, no words.

Teaching Points
It is important to emphasize that during the first round, be as demonstrative as possible when describing the celebrities, as this will be helpful in the next two rounds. Also, it is important to watch how the other teams demonstrate the celebrities since they get thrown back in the hat for the later rounds.

Variations
Change the time limits for each round. Perhaps 45 seconds for the first round, or with smaller group perhaps a longer first round so you will have plenty of celebrities to choose for the later rounds.

Improv Warm-Up Games

DICTIONARY

This is an old favorite that many families play. In the standard Oxford dictionary there are over 300,000 words and yet the average person may only know abut 20 – 40,000 so there are lot of words that most of us have no idea what they mean. This game is not specifically and theater games, however, it lends itself to lots of imagination and creativity.

Set Up
1. A standard dictionary is required and one person is chosen as the reader. This reader looks up an obscure word, and announces it. Spelling it is often a good choice too.
2. Everyone then writes down on a slip of paper what they believe the definition is of the word.
3. The reader writes down the actual definition on slip of paper.
4. All the slips of paper are passed in to the reader, who shuffles them, and then reads each one aloud.

Game Play
The reader reads each of the definitions and now all the players vote as to what they believe to be the correct definition. The reader declares at the end of the vote what the real definition is. The players definition who gets the most votes wins that round. You could keep score if you want or just make it that the player whose definition gets chosen the most gets to be the next reader.

Variations
My own personal creation is gibberish dictionary. One person makes up a gibberish word. The rest of the players take turns defining verbally defining the word and then the person who made up the word chooses which one they like the best or they could offer their own definition. So what is the definition of slaggerdymuck?

Teaching Points
This is a great way to have students explore the depth and variety of the English language.

The Heart of Play

EMPTY VESSEL

This game is from action theater that builds on the simple game of mirroring.

Set Up
1. Split people into groups of four or five.
2. Demonstrate to the group that one-person volunteers, steps forward facing the other players. This person is the empty vessel orr another way to look at it is they are a lump of clay waiting to be molded by the energy of another person.
3. The other players form a line facing the "empty vessel."

Game Play
One person steps out from the line and starts doing a physical movement. It can be accompanied by sound or simple words however it is the energy of the movement that is important. The empty vessel immediately picks up that energy and mirrors it, doing essentially the same thing. It doesn't have to be a perfect mirroring just play with that same energy.

For example, one person steps out and starts to play the drums as if they were in marching band, and the empty vessel joins in and plays their drum and they march around. Now after about seven seconds or so of this, another person steps in and starts rubbing their eyes and yawning and saying, "I am so sleepy." The empty vessel person immediately picks up on that energy, and yawns and says "me too I am so sleepy... and maybe they lie down and tuck themselves in a bed. The drumming person immediately stops and steps out when the empty vessel turned to the new energy.

And on this goes until each person has stepped out and given the empty vessel a new experience. A new empty vessel volunteers to be in the center. Someone comes in hopping like a bunny, the empty vessel joins in the hopping. The possibilities are endless.

Teaching Points
Remind the players if one person comes in with high energy the next person can help the empty vessel by making the next choice something with a softer energy. The game helps players to just trust their bodies. Just step into an improv scene and do an action with their bodies and the play will follow.

Improv Warm-Up Games

FREE ASSOCIATION

(2 - 30+)

A simple word association.

Set Up
1. Have everyone in a circle.
2. Demonstrate how it starts with one person saying a word and then the next person says whatever first comes to their mind.

Game Play
One person starts and says a word and then the person on their left says the first word that comes to their mind and then the next person and on it goes around the circle. Go around the circle two or three times.

Also, great to do this with just a partner. Have each player go back and forth freely associating on the previous word. Choose a word for all the pairs to start with. Ready start with "Monkey."

Variations
Try a two-word association. Each person says two words.

Or do it with all the players lying on the ground in a circle with their heads toward the center, and everyone begins making sounds. Eventually, you can add in phrases and words, until it becomes a symphony of sound and movement. This is best to do in groups of 6 – 12 players.

Teaching Points
Free association is a great way to emphasize how much of improv is making associations in your mind. One players offer will trigger an association in your mind. Learning to trust your first thought, your first impulse is a good skill to develop in improv. This game is good game for players to notice how their minds and imagination can always make an association. It's all a matter of relaxing and trusting there is always a choice to be made and thus you are "training your brain to trust your gut."

The Heart of Play

GIBBERISH CONVERSATION AND TRANSLATOR

This is a great way to get people laughing and exercising their creativity.

Set Up
1. First for ten seconds have everyone blather and make any strange, unusual nonsensical sounds they can.
2. Start by dividing the group up into pairs. Then demonstrate how it sounds to speak in a brand-new language. A language of gibberish. Demonstrate how when the speaker believes what they are saying, adds in body language, intonation and emotion, the gibberish sounds real.
3. Then pick an everyday subject, such as the weather, what they had for breakfast, or what they are going to do when they get home from school, and then the pairs speak to each other about it in gibberish.

Game Play
Let them talk for about 30 to 45 seconds, and then stop. Have the players divide up into groups of three. Now demonstrate that the two people speaking in gibberish can't understand each other so they have to have a translator. The translator sits between them and translates each statement in English so the gibberish speakers can understand what the other has spoken. This translator therefore determines where the conversation goes.

Variations
Have everyone standing up, mingling, and talking in gibberish. Imagine being in the famous Star Wars cantina where everyone is an alien from different planets, but they have universal translators, so they understand each other. Stop after about 30 seconds. Now tell them to get in a gibberish argument. Then tell jokes in gibberish, whereby, after a few seconds you laugh uproariously.

You can also do the gibberish translator in groups of four where each person has their own translator.

Teaching Points
During the translation part, remind the players that they have to listen to the translator. Invariably, they start responding to each other without the translation. Gibberish is a great way to free up the mind, so it is just play and creativity.

Improv Warm-Up Games

INVISIBLE TUG OF WAR

This is a very quick and simple game, yet full of learning.

Set Up
1. Have everyone get a partner.
2. They then face each other about ten feet apart.
3. Narrate the story.
4. They are two adversaries, strong and so determined. Between them is a thick, long rope, perfect for the 'Tug of War".

Game Play

Ready, pick up the rope. Feel the tension as you pull the rope taut. Say something fittingly challenging to your partner, such as, "I am stronger than you..." "Well, smell isn't everything..." Et cetera.

"Ready, on the count of three. 1,2,3 go! Pull!"

After about twenty to thirty seconds, end the game. Ask the players who won.

Teaching Points

This is a great exercise to demonstrate the concept of making your partner look good.

What usually happens is the players instantly begin to struggle with each person pulling and straining, and pulling and straining. After asking who won and often neither player has won then call someone up and demonstrate what it looks like when someone lets their partner have the victory, struggling for maybe just a few seconds then getting pulled over to their side, falling on the ground in defeat, being amazed at how strong they were, and declaring how fittingly they deserved to win, even if you are still mad and embarrassed. Then demonstrate if there are two people just straining there is not a very interesting scene, the play is rather boring.

Making you partner look good, is facilitated by giving them an improv offer that empowers them.

The Heart of Play

MIRRORING

A great partner game that is fun and connecting. Seen previously in this book I just have to replicate it again here as it is a such a great activity, and it's roots are in improv theater.

Set Up
1. Everyone chooses a partner. One person is "A" one person is "B".
2. Demonstrate to everyone how each person will take turns being the leader and the other the follower. Remind them that they are responsible for their partners success, so movements should be slow and easy to follow. Eye contact is home base.
3. First begin with yourself as an "A" by demonstrating with just the palms of the hands and arms moving as if looking in a mirror and seeing the other person mirror your movements. Then switch to "B" as the leader.
4. Also demonstrate that as the activity progresses they can add more movement with other parts of their body, moving thru space, adding sounds, facial expressions, etc.

Game Play
The facilitator calls out that "A is the leader and B follows." Change between leaders every ten to twenty seconds. Remind the leaders they are responsible for their partner's success, and that eye contact is home base.

Toward the end, tell them that now they are to continue moving without either person being specified as the leader, but a kind of following the follower. After a little while of experiencing this phenomenon, ask them to find an elegant end to their play.

Variations
Play a game of Follow the Leader where one person does a movement, and everyone else follows. Walk around the room and on person leads and everyone follows and the a new leader jumps out and takes the focus and everyone follows.

Teaching Points
Have the pairs talk about how connected they felt during the exercise. This is an excellent activity to demonstrate that much of play has a leading and following component.

Improv Warm-Up Games

MOVEMENT EXCHANGE

A simple expression of movement.

Set Up
1. Get everyone into a circle.
2. Demonstrate that one person steps into the center of the circle and begins to make a repeated movement.
3. They can play with it for a bit until they have one that is nicely repetitive.

Game Play

That person then goes over in front of another player in the circle while still doing their movement. The other player begins mirroring that movement. While still doing those movements together, these two players rotate positions, so now the new player is inside the circle and the first player has now replaced that person in the circle and this first person then stops their movement.

The new player continues with that mirrored movement as they move into the center of the circle, and now they let the movement inform them as they morph into a new movement using the energy of the previous player. This player takes 10 to 20 seconds to find their new, repetitive movement, and then they choose a player in the circle to partner in the mirroring-dance, and the process continues.

Variation

As in a dance class when someone steps into the circle and does some simple movements, everyone in the circle begins repeating these movements. The person then goes over to one person and they exchange positions while still doing the movement.

Teaching Points

The fun of this is encouraging players to feel the movement they are mirroring and allowing it to change into something new, while still allowing the previous movement to inform, and heuristically inspire, their new action.

The Heart of Play

MOVING THROUGH SPACE

A simple way to be moving and walking and exploring states of emotions and characters.

Set Up
1. Demonstrate to everyone how to walk thru the room always moving to where there is open space. They do this in a neutral energetic space and in a normal pace.
2. Then ask them to try on different feeling states.
3. Walk while being curious looking with interest in others... now back to neutral...
4. Walk with a feeling of shyness, now back to neutral...
5. Walk with determination... (Other states of being to consider, angry, joyful, scared, proud, exhilarated, etc.)

Game Play
Have them experience each state for short time 10 to 20 seconds, and then have them shift into their normal walk for 5 to 10 seconds. Continuing trying on different modes of being.

Variations
Walk and lead from different body parts. How does it feel when you are walking leading with your head, or leading with your shoulders, or leading with your chest, or chin, nose, or with your right shoulder. Ask them to notice what character may be arising in them when they walk with a certain body-part leading, or what else was different from one to the other.

Teaching Points
Remind the group to remember to walk thru the center while moving into empty space. There is a tendency to walk in circles on the outside. "Find the open space."

Also great to emphasize when entering a scene in improv and creating a character it helps to choose an emotional sate and to feel their character in their body, limping, shuffling, puffing their chest out, etc.

Improv Warm-Up Games

NAME THE WRONG THING

A great opportunity to flex and exercise the creative muscles of the brain.

Set up
1. Explain to everyone that this is an opportunity to witness how our brain is great at labeling everything.
2. Demonstrate walking around the room and pointing at things and naming them the wrong thing.
3. Point at a desk and say dog. Point at a window and say pencil and so on and on.

Game Play
Have everyone walk around the room and point to objects and name the the wrong thing for about 30 to 45 seconds. For example, point to a door and say, "Cow." Point to the floor and say, "Dishes," etc., trying to be as random and varied as possible.

Stop the play, and then tell them to try it again. This time as they walk around they will name everything form a category they have chosen, such as: animals, appliances, tools, insects, etc. So, if food were the category point to things and say, squash, pizza, ice cream, broccoli, etc.

Teaching Points
At the end, have the group discuss which was easier. People are often surprised to find that being limited to one category actual helps to generate the ideas faster.

So much of our brain development has to do with labeling and categorizing. This exercise is a great practice to expand and free up the mind. One of the goals in improv is naming things in scenes so this helps with this practice.

The Heart of Play

PASS THE IMAGINARY OBJECT

A simple game of physical embodiment and imagination.

Set Up
1. Have the group form a circle.
2. Demonstrate how by using your imagination you create a simple object.
3. For example you are fishing with a fishing pole. Play with that for a few seconds and then pass that fishing pole onto the next person.
4. That person takes the fishing plays with it for a few seconds and then transforms the fishing pole into something new.
5. Ahh, it's a paint brush, and you are painting someone's portrait.
6. The first time you play this game do it silently.

Game Play
Go around the circle with everyone taking a turn creating their object and passing it on. Really fun to watch each persons creation and witness the creativity of each player.

Variations
People can make sounds or use language in their interaction with their object. Or make it a tossing game. Once an object is made, it is then tossed across the circle to someone else, who then turns it into something new, etc.

Or the leader creates an object and tosses it to someone, however this time the players keep the object the same, they play with it for a moment then toss it to someone else. Then very quickly add three or four objects being tossed around the circle.

Could be a beach ball, a frisbee, and a chain saw etc.

Teaching Points
Encourage the players to dramatize taking the object as it is passed to them and play with it using the form of the previous object, which can often inspire the transformation into the new object.

Improv Warm-Up Games

RHYME MIME

I call this the simplest game of charades. Surprisingly basic, yet so very fun.

Set Up
1. Gather everyone in a circle.
2. One person has a secret word and they give a clue word to the group, i.e., "I have a word and it rhymes with cat."
3. Everyone else is the guesser.
4. For example, the secret word they have chosen is "rat."

Game Play
Anyone that wants to can act out, mime out, a word that rhymes with "Cat." One person jumps up and mimes out the word they are thinking of. The person who has chosen the secret word now becomes the guesser of what that person is acting out, and responds in ritualistic fashion, saying, "No, it's not bat,"… "No, it's not mat,"… "No, it is not fat,"… until someone mimes out the correct word. "Yes, it is rat." That person who guessed it correctly will now pick a new secret word and gives a clue of what it rhymes with. I have a word and it rhymes with "bear."

Variations
The game also works very nicely with two small teams of three to six people on a team. Each team huddles up and chooses a word. One team begins and when the word is guessed the other team goes. When playing in teams when they see the word being mimed is not the correct word the team tries to say in unison "No it's not hat."

Teaching Points
This is one of my all-time favorite games with small groups of people. Remind everyone that it is very strict rhyme pattern. For example, the word "sleep" in this game does not rhyme with "feet"(which is a near-rhyme). There are lots of words that are in the "near category." Fear, steer, clear. Or, how about the "ore" sound? Floor, store, bore, etc.

Or try urt, or ow…"

The Heart of Play

WAH

Great for building energy and developing a group essence. From Playback Theater.

Set Up
1. Everyone is in a circle. Best to have circles with no more than 10 to 15 people.
2. Teach everyone the expression, "WAH," said clearly and loudly with bold expression.

Game Play
The designated starting person brings their arms above their head, hands together, like a church steeple and bends forward like a giant tree falling, and says, "WAH!" with their arms outstretched, hands together and pointing like one big arrow at another person. That person who is being pointed at raises their arms up in that steeple formation, and saying "WAH," which is now the signal for the people on each side of them to act like they are great lumberjacks who take their big axes and in perfect unison make imaginary chops at the person's midsection, while saying loudly, "WAH." This initiates the felling of the tree who falls forward saying, "WAH," with a clear pointing at the next person and thus it continues.

Variations
This game is simple version of passing a distinct sound and motion. You can play a similar game by passing ninja throwing stars, or knives or an imaginary ball.

Teaching Points
The essence of this game is in the creating the rhythm and the guttural expressions such that there is a smooth rhythm and timing to the movements and sounds. WAH, WAH, WAH. This is a great game to emphasize that in improv, it is all about listening, being in the moment, being aware of the people around you, and being in rhythm with each other.

Improv Warm-Up Games

WHAT ARE YOU DOING?

A very simple and yet very engaging partner game.

Set Up
1. Have everyone choose partners.
2. Demonstrate the activity with a volunteer.

Game Play

One person, Joe, begins by acting out a simple action like, brushing his teeth. His partner, Sue, asks him the question "Joe, what are you doing?"

Joe says something totally different from what he is doing, "I am flying a kite." Sue now acts out flying a kite. Then after 5 to 10 seconds of acting out the suggestion, Joe asks, "Sue, what are you doing?" And Sue replies, "I am washing the dog..." and Joe acts out washing the dog and back and forth it goes.

Do your best to never repeat anything that has already been said.

Also you could demonstrate how adding adverbs can help the play. "I am playing basketball awkwardly, I am singing opera badly etc."

Variations

If you have a small group this a great game to do in a circle. The person to the left asks the question, "What are you doing?" And it goes around the circle.

A nice addition is to have the players concentrate on adding an adverb, (a word ending in "ly"), to their activity. For example, "I am riding a bike clumsily," or "I am brushing the dog angrily..."

Also, demonstrate how combining two activities together is fun to act out. For example, "I am skipping rope and eating an ice cream cone."

This can also be game where two players come up in front of the audience and have a few players on the side ready to come on and if one person hesitates or repeats something a new player replaces them.

Teaching Points

This is a simple activity, so you may want to remind the players of two key guiding principles in improv theater. One is, "Dare to be average." Any simple activity can be fun to act out. And the other principle is, "Make your partner look good." So if your partner might be embarrassed by suggestions such as, "picking my nose," then just choose something more basic to act out, such as, "washing the dishes," or "playing basketball..."

The Heart of Play

WHERE AM I?

A simple miming game.

Set Up

1. Have everyone in a circle and explain that this is a simple miming game.

2. Choose one person who will begin the scene.

Game Play

One person goes into the center of the circle and begins miming an action indicating where they are. For example, one person goes in and starts walking around and they seem to be pushing something. They reach up and grab something, and they place it in their imaginary cart. Ah, they are shopping.

Anyone that knows what is happening goes in whispers in that persons ear what they believe they are doing. If they nod yes then that player joins the action perhaps doing something different from the other person but approprirate to the setting.

Next scene: Maybe someone is playing baseball, or is a zookeeper feeding the animals, or they are a part of a circus or they are construction workers.

Variations

A person just joins the action without whispering into the first person's ears. At the end of the facilitator can ask that person what action they were performing. Was it what the others who joined thought it was?

Begin adding in language to the scene and eash person get to speak on line about what they are doing, why htey are there, what their expereince. "Oh I better put this sun scren on before I get burnt." "Oh let me help you with that honey"

Teaching Points

Miming games are great for beggining improvers as it teaches them to use objects and play with the objects in space and to defein their space by htier actions.

Improv Warm-Up Games

YES, AND...

A simple and effective way for people to understand the principle of saying "Yes and..."

Set Up
1. Have people in groups of four or five players.
2. This is simple game of saying, "Yes and," to each previous statement, and when possible, to build on that statement.
3. Demonstrate how that will look.

Game Play
Player number 1 starts out by saying, "I had waffles with whipped cream and strawberries for breakfast. Player 2 says, "Yes, and after I had breakfast I went to Starbucks and had a mocha latte." Player 3 says, "Yes and I went to the gym this morning and I had a fruit smoothie after my workout." And player 4 says, "Yes, and I skipped my breakfast and studied for my chemistry final..." The next player says something like, "Yes, and on my way to work this morning I witnessed a bank robbery..."

And on it goes, each person practicing the power of saying, "Yes and..."

Have the group go around more than once.

Variations
Try the stem "Yes and that means..." Have a group build a story using that stem each time. "I got up and ate a big breakfast this morning." Yes and that means I decided to walk to work today to work off some calories." "Yes and that means I stopped downtown and looked in the jewelry store window and bought my wife a new necklace..."

Then have the group repeat that same story, but now acting out each piece or part, doing the actions in present time. Then have them do it again, really exaggerating the physical actions and emphasizing being fully in their characters.

Teaching Points
Notice how often people say, "Yes, but..." which simply negates what the previous person said, instead of acknowledging it. This can be a difficult habit to break. This is the fundamental skill of improv, saying yes to ideas and then build upon them. The more improvisers can practice the skill the better.

The Heart of Play

YES, LET'S...

This game is a great opportunity for everyone to practice the concept of saying yes to any offer.

Set Up

1. Have everyone gather and tell them that anyone can make a suggestion and everyone's response will be to say, "Yes let's."
2. Once "Yes let's" is said, then everyone begins acting out that suggestion.

Game Play

Someone starts and makes a suggestion, like, "Let's fly a kite." Everyone then responds, loudly and with enthusiasm, "Yes, let's." And everyone begins acting out flying a kite. After a short bit of time, someone may suggest, "Let's rob a bank." The group replies, "Yes, let's." And everyone pretends to rob a bank. "Let's give a back massage to our friend... Yes, let's!"

Variation

For a more advanced class, you can add the direction that when anyone feels bored or not interested in doing that activity, they can sit down. End the game when a majority of people are sitting.

Teaching Points

Afterwards, debrief and ask what activities people enjoyed the most. It may have been the simplest ones, or the ones where people were doing something together. What made an activity more interesting than others?

In the advance version ask the players why they chose to sit down when they did. At what point did people lose interest? This is a good exercise for improvisers to learn about what keeps the interest of their fellow players and proably an audience.

Howard Moody

Improv Partner (or Small Group) Exercises

These are simple games where you can be in circles with people volunteering to play the group game, or they can be in small groups all playing at the same time. The focus here is on fun, participation, and players trying on some more complex expression, using more creativity and imagination.

Starting to build on the warm-up games, now that the group has more trust, and the spontaneity of improv begins to flow more freely. One of the keys is helping people to say the first thing that comes to their mind. Like Alan Ginsberg said about writing poetry, "First thought, best thought." Or another way of saying it is, "To train your brain to trust your gut." All creativity is association, and our minds are filled with these connections. It's just a matter of trusting our own imaginations.

Having said that, remember the guiding principles that help the Improv to flow: Say Yes And, Make Your Partner Look Good, Dare to be Average, and Be in the Present Moment, which then become transcended by an inner sensibility and feel for the process.

Encourage players to say yes to other player's ideas. Encourage them to keep it simple and trust their intuition, going with the first thing that comes to mind. These games will help the players build their skills and confidence before taking on the challenge of volunteering to be on stage.

Other games throughout his book that could also be in this category are: Human Statues, Human Machine, and Night in the Museum.

The Heart of Play

A TO Z

A nice partner game that takes a particular focus.

Set Up
1. Have everyone choose a partner (or it could be in groups of three).
2. Demonstrate in front of the group.
3. The simple structure of this game is each sentence must begin with the next letter of the alphabet.

Game Play
Ask the group to shout out a letter of the alphabet. "G." So the first player starts a statement with the letter G. "Gosh you look really happy."

The next player must begin the next sentence with a word that begins with the letter H. "How can you tell?"

"It's written all over your face."

"Just had a great date."

"Karen's her name, right?"

"Let me tell you about her."

"Maybe that's not such a good idea, maybe it should remain a secret."

"No, No, I have to tell you."

"Pause for a minute, take a breath before you tell me all the details."

"Etc."

End the game on the letter before the one you started with, thus having used all the letters.

Variations
Play the game in a circle with each person starting their statement with the appropriate letter as the story goes around.

Teaching Points
This game take a certain focus to remember what is the next letter to be used however it also is good because you know what the next sentence has to begin with. Get creative with x and z. X is usually challenging, but there is always x-rays, x marks the spot, Xerox, and xylophones. For Z you could say zounds or zoo or zebras.

Improv Partner (or Small Group) Exercises

I AM A TREE

This is a very simple game, like Human Statues, however, in this version, you go into the scene and declare what you are.

Set Up
1. Have the group in a circle.
2. Demonstrate that you have to be in relationship to the previous creation. So someone steps into the circle and says, "I am a tree," and they hold a pose representing a tree.
3. The next person goes in and says, "I am the cat climbing the tree", and they take a pose embodying the cat.
4. And the next person goes in and says, "I am the fireman climbing the ladder to rescue the cat stuck in the tree."
5. Then the two previous people go out and the fireman becomes the next object person.

Game Play
Once you have demonstrated this, continue with three-person scenes. So, someone would go in and say. "I am the hose that the fireman is holding." And they take a pose representing the hose. And the next person goes in and says, "I am the fire hydrant that the hose is connected to," taking a pose representing a fire hydrant.

The two people go out and then another person goes in and says, "I am the dog peeing on the fire hydrant," and the next person goes in and says, "I am the dog's owner walking the dog…"

The first two people go out. New person comes in, "I am the young boy holding my mom's hand who is walking the dog…"

Variations
No one goes out, and you build the whole tableaux with numerous people making the scene until it feels complete.

Teaching Points
When working with a group the first few times, ask for a show of hands and pick a person to go in. When a group gets better at Give & Take, let each person jump up and join spontaneously when they have an idea.

The Heart of Play

IN THE MANNER OF THE ADVERB

This is now becoming one of my favorite games to play because of its theatricality and improvisation potential.

Set Up
1. First demonstrate how the group will be acting out mini scenes or simple actions in the manner of the adverb that the group has chosen.
2. For example, let's say the chosen word is "slowly." The guesser who doesn't know the chosen word will ask perhaps two players to "dance in the manner of the adverb," so they get up and dance slowly. After ten seconds or so, the facilitator or guesser can say, "Cut," and that ends that mini action.
3. Great now that we know how to play choose someone to be the guesser, and have them leave the room so the group can choose an adverb for the group to illustrate.
4. For example, the group chooses the word, "enthusiastically."
5. Call the guesser back in.

Game Play

The guesser comes back in and begins to ask people to do actions in the manner of the adverb. "Mike, please wash the dishes in the manner of the adverb..." Or, "Everyone, eat a banana in the manner of the adverb"... "Sue and Joe, will you dance in the manner of the adverb?" The group can converse, but be careful not to give the adverb away in the dialogue.

Instruct the guesser to get at least three actions before they make a guess, and only one guess at a time.

Variations

When first playing the game making suggestions of simple actions is good. A more advanced level of play is for the guesser to offer little scenarios. "Jose, Derek, and Carol, you are in the Amazon jungle trying to capture a rare species of butterfly... in the manner of the adverb."

Or, "Everyone you are performing in the circus... in the manner of the adverb."

Or, "You and your friend are on a roller coaster ride..."

Or, "You are studying for exams...

Improv Partner (or Small Group) Exercises

Teaching Points

When I explain the game, I use the word "slowly" to show how it would be to act something out in the manner of the adverb. This game is not as easy as it first seems, because many adverbs are very similar. So, if the group chooses the word aggressively, the actions might look like the word angrily. So, if the guesser says angrily, tell them they are close.

You may want to help the group by sharing a few adverbs that are fun and maybe a bit challenging. Some suggestions are: defensively, anxiously, excitedly, compassionately, awkwardly, disgustedly, and mysteriously.

The guesser wants to be as creative and inclusive as possible, meaning include as many people as they can in their suggestions.

In 1985 Brian Allison and I created a live improvisational role-playing game that we called the Adventure Game Theater. We adapted it in 1987 as a program for teens at the Omega Institute in Rhinebeck NY. Over the past thirty years it has continued to grow and is now being run in numerous locations by various participants of our original theater camps.

In the early 90's I decided to enroll in an improv class being taught at Omega by Martin De Matt. Martin was well known for working with actors such as John Beluhsi, Dan Akroyd and many of the members of the original cast of Saturday Night Live.

Martin had taken the work of Viola Spolin and made it popular with a whole new group of actors excited about the possibilities that happen within improvisational theater. In the training I attended, Martin's focus was not on getting people to be good improvisers up on stage so much, but his emphasis was on teaching improv as Skills for Life. This concept impacted me deeply, so whenever I share improv with organizations or individuals it's all about how impov theater is a great metaphor for learning skills of interpersonal dynamics and creativity.

Thank you Martin for leaving such a rich legacy that continues to live on and inspire the best in people.

The Heart of Play

MEMORY LOSS

A very simple partner storytelling game. Could also be called fill in the blank.

Set Up
1. Divide the players into pairs.
2. Bring up a volunteer to demonstrate how the activity is done.
3. Have the group suggest a topic for a story, such as going on a vacation, or going shopping, and demonstrate by telling just a few lines of a story for the group to see how it is done.
4. The first player begins telling the story, but then has a memory loss indicated by stammering and not having any words, "Ummm, aaah, umm..." The other player now fills in the blank with a word or phrase and the story telling player continues with this new idea thrown in.

Game Play
Decide who will be the first storyteller in each pair. How about the person in the pair with the longest hair will be the first storyteller. Now that the players see how to play, take a new suggestions different from the one you just used for the demonstration. "Ah, going on a vacation." Each pair you are going to tell a story about going on a vacations. Before you start, know that after about a minute or so, I will be shouting out "You have 20 seconds to bring your story to an end..." In about ten seconds I say, "Try to find an appropriate ending to your story in ten seconds." Switch roles. Pick a new subject, and do it again.

Variations
Have the storytelling person just start telling any story. You can also do this in groups of three, with two people alternating filling in the blank of the memory-loss moment. Or bring a pair up and have them tell the story in front of an audience.

Teaching Points
After the story is done, ask the players who were filling in the blank if they did their best to support their partners with interesting and yet supportive ideas.

This is a great activity to teach the fundamental principle in Improv theater, which is to say yes to any idea and then to build upon it. In this activity, the storyteller takes what their partner has said and continues the story from that point, thus saying yes to their idea.

Improv Partner (or Small Group) Exercises

MUTANT MINGLE

A variation on the game one word story.

Set Up
1. Have everyone get a partner and link up, arm-to-arm.
2. The two of you are joined together. You have two heads but only one brain, so when you speak it comes out one word at a time with your partner.
3. Demonstrate with a partner how this would look.
"Hi…"
"My…"
"Name…"
"Is…"
"Bob…"
"I…"
"Like…"
"Dogs…"

Game Play
Everyone is with their partner and they walk around the room, taking a journey together and describing what they see. Then have them go up to another two-headed mutant and have a conversation. Continue on and have more conversations with other mutants.

Variation
Try this as one head of the mutant speaks in gibberish and the other head translates for the other mutant head.

Teaching Points
As with One Word Story, the key in the game is for the partners to really listen to each other and not be thinking ahead to what they are going to say staying in the present moment. This a great lead-in to the improv structure Three Headed Expert.

The Heart of Play

ONE WORD STORY

A simple game which helps people focus on being in the present moment.

Set Up
1. Divide players into pairs.
2. Have someone volunteer to demonstrate the activity with you.
3. We are going to tell a story that has never been told before and we are going to tell it one word at a time, alternating between each of us.
4. A simple and easy way to get a story started is with the classic, "Once upon a time…or ….Once there was."
5. The beauty of a one-word story is you have to stay in the moment and listen carefully, because where you expect the story to go is probably not what your partner is thinking.

Game Play
The players start telling their one-word story. Remind them to notice where a sentence would naturally end, and be sure to start new sentences with "then" or "suddenly" or some appropriate word to begin a new sentence. After the story is complete have them tell the moral of their story one word at a time. "The… moral… of… the… story… is… little… boys…love… chocolate… covered… ants." (Keep it to one sentence long.)

Variations
Do it with a whole group of people going around the circle. Or try a two-word story where each person can say two words at a time.

Teaching Points
Sometimes one-word stories can get stuck. Empower any player to say the word "again" and the other player(s) repeat the word "again" and start a new story. A reset, a do over! Also remind the players that if they bring in an element of the story to bring it back again. Don't keep on adding elements. If in the first sentence the little boy loves chocolate covered ants make sure that is what the story stays about.

Improv Partner (or Small Group) Exercises

PRESENT A GIFT

This game is a variation on What's in the Box?

Set Up
1. Have people choose a partner.
2. Explain that each pesrson will be presenting their friend with a gift.

Game Play

Hand your partner an imaginary gift box. Tell them how much you have wanted to give this gift to them, and how you thought very deeply about what they would want. As they begin opening it, declare what it is. "I know you have been wanting to go to the Hawaii so here are two round trip tickets for you to go."

Switch roles.

Variations

This is also fun activity to do in a small circle and the whole group watches as each person takes a turn handing the person to their left a gift box. And on it goes around the circle.

The other option is more like the game, What's in the Box?, where it is up to the person receiving the gift to declare what the present is.

Teaching Points

When appropriate, it is good to add in the instruction that after the person getting the gift has received it, they thank their giver in some way. It could be with a respectful bow, or gently touching them on the shoulder, or maybe with a big hug, thereby adding to the connection of the experience.

The Heart of Play

PROPS

A great warm up game.

Set Up
1. Find a few objects that are unique and possibly on the large side for visual purposes, and preferably light-weight. This also can be as simple as a scarf, a rope, or an empty cardboard box.
2. Place one of the objects in the center of the circle.

Game Play
Players take turns coming out and using the object in some way other than what is its normal function, and showing and sharing what it is. You can either do it silently or use dialogue. This can be a simple and quick representation of what the new object is. Or you can pass an object around the circle and play that way.

Variations
Place two (or more) objects into the center of the circle and let the players combine the props in their actions. Also, it is always good to have hats or scarves on hand for to embellish any improv scenes.

Teaching Points
One of the keys in improv is trusting your body. Encourage the players to take the object and explore using it with their bodies and in that way the movment may inform what the object now becomes.

Keep an evye out for unusual objects in your daily life. Collect a nice assortment of weird and unusual props for this purpose.

Improv Partner (or Small Group) Exercises

STORY CIRCLE

As simple as it gets, but so much fun.

Set Up
1. Everyone is seated in a circle.
2. Pick a person who starts telling the story.
3. The group can either pick the subject of the story or this first story teller can just start right in telling whatever story they choose.

Game Play

Each person in turn tells a piece of the story, perhaps two or three sentences, and then turns to the person to their left and passes the sentence on to them. This can be done by saying any appropriate connecting phrase, such as, "And..." or, "Suddenly..." Or just by ending a sentence and gesturing to the next person. For example, "The little boy walked into the forest..." And the next person says, "He saw a large tree with a door in it. He walked up to the door and knocked. Suddenly...." And the next person says, "A little elf with a plate of cookies opens the door..." And on the story goes around the circle.

Variations

The storyteller points to anyone, or has a ball and tosses it to someone in the circle to continue the story.

Teaching Points

This game works well when everyone remembers the elements of a good story. One is if you bring in something in the beginning, remember to keep that element in the story. Also, really bizarre changes in the story may be too drastic. The more everyone listens well and trusts their first instincts, the more connected it will be. If anyone in the circle wants to pass, they can just say, "And," and then pass it on with a gesture and some eye contact.

The Heart of Play

TWO OR THREE PERSON SCENES

A great way to have people practice some simple improv, by placing them in fun little set scenes.

Set Up
1. Have people get in groups of two or three, depending on the scenario. Some possible scenarios.
2. Three starfish (lying on their bellies) stranded on a beach, wondering if the tide is coming in or not.
3. Two best friends on their last day of the summer, building a sand castle at the beach, knowing they will be saying good-bye soon.
4. Two zombies trying to become vegetarians.
5. A 16 year-old teen trying to convince his dad that he needs the car to take his date to the movies.
6. Two warriors chained up in an a giant's cave, wondering when the giant is coming back and if they will be eaten.

Game Play
Have them start to role-play. Encourage them to practice good give-and-take skills, and really listen to each other. After a minute or so, you can call freeze and interject little prompts. "You both have a confession to tell the other," or, "You think you see or hear someone coming to help you…"

Variations
These could also be acted out in front of the group as an audience.

Teaching points
Encourage the players to make simple and honest choices. What is their character wanting in the scene. What is their motivation in the scene.

When working with beggining improvisers it's good to have the players do as much practice as possible before doing it fornt of an audience. Also these two or three person scenes are good options to do in front of an audience as it gives new improvisers very set scenarios to improvise.

Improv Partner (or Small Group) Exercises

WHAT'S IN THE BOX?

A great game to teach the concept that creative choice is always available.

Set Up
1. Everyone gets a partner.
2. Explain that our imaginations are endless, and that players in improv get to choose what they create.
3. Demonstrate that they will be handing a box to their partner who will open it and declare what is in it.

Game Play
Hand your partner an imaginary box. The person reaches in the box, pulls something out and as they do that they declare what it is. "Oh wow, a brand new jacket." Or, "Oh look, the mud pies your children made this morning out in the yard after the rainstorm." Or, "Wow, a weasel…"

Then the first person who received the box now returns the favor and hands a box to their partner.

Variations
The players can play with handing different sized boxes. Maybe a really big box or maybe a really small box. Also a good game to play in a circle and witness each person's creativity as a new box is handed to each player around the circle.

Teaching Points
The key of this game is to emphasize that there is always something in the box. Creativity is just the next thought that comes. Encourage the player to reach in and not know what it is until they pull it out. Be in the moment. Also, encourage the players to play with the size of the box they are handing the person. Perhaps they are bringing it in on a pallet, and thus it is really big. Or maybe they smell something before they open it or perhaps they shake it to see if it makes a sound.

The Heart of Play

Improv Performance Structures

This is where improv becomes more like a performance art, with people on stage taking suggestions from the audience and creating characters in the moment. Now the games require the players to arrange themselves as an audience with a stage or performance area. Spotlights and floodlights not required. A good game to start with is One Word Poem, where the point is for the audience to be in unconditional support of the players on stage. In an improv class, this models the role of the audience being fully entertained by the creativity happening on the stage.

Most of the games here involve taking suggestions from the audience, which can be very challenging for the players, so have some defined guidelines. It takes time for improvisers to learn all the nuances of how to create a character, embody it on the spot, and create a live scene with other players. Some people are more comfortable with this than others. For some people it is a major accomplishment just to rise to the challenge of performance.

In addition to the guiding principle mentioned earlier, another helpful guideline for getting a scene going is naming the Who, What, Why, and Where. When you enter a scene, try to name who you are, what you are doing, maybe where you are, and why you are there.

Sometimes this is set up for you, but not always. For example, in the game Name the Object, player A is on stage and moving their arms back and forth. Player B steps in and says, "Hi mom, let me help you with the sweeping..." Right away we know that one character is the mom, the other a child, they are in a house and something needs to be cleaned up. "Thanks Tommy, I just spilled the flour on the floor. I am baking a cake for you father..." Now we know the child's name is Tommy, and mom has spilled some flour on the floor. So, in two lines we know the who, what, where and why the action is happening.

Remind the players to make statements, and to avoid asking questions, which only puts others on the spot. Make supportive offers, honest choices, and make their fellow players look good. Remember the power of saying, "Yes, and..."

Improv Performance Structures

BOOM CHICAGO

A great set up that allows the players to have simple success. From my friend Lindsay Dilley, an improv performer and teacher in Asheville, NC.

Set up
1. Ask for three players to volunteer.
2. Two players will start the scene.
3. The third player stands off stage.
4. Choose the characters and their relationship, and a problem that needs to be resolved.

Game Play

The first two players start the scene. They explore the problem, but they don't have a solution. The third person enters the scene and solves the problem. When the problem is solved all the players and the audience say, "Boom Chicago!"

For example: Sue, the daughter of Carol, was supposed to be caretaking the house cat that never goes outside. Sue leaves a door open, The cat goes outside and gets stuck in up in a tree. The scene begins. They try to lure the cat down with catnip, by singing to it, etc., but nothing works. In comes the third person, who has the solution to the problem. "Hi, I am Dave. I am a certified animal communicator. Let me talk to your cat. Hmm, your cat has an issue with you Carol. The cat needs you to acknowledge her beauty more. You need to tell your cat she is beautiful."

They chime in, "Fluffy, you are the most gorgeous cat in the neighborhood." " Oh look Fluffy's climbing down." Everyone, even the audience, says together "Boom Chicago!"

Or, it could be that Bob the fireman comes with a ladder. "Boom Chicago!"

Teaching Points

Use this game as an example of the payoff of introducing a problem in a scene and then moving towards a solution.

The Heart of Play

BUS STOP

A fun structure that allows people to be rude. For this reason, it's a favorite for children.

Set Up
1. Place two chairs up in front of the audience.
2. This is a bus stop.
3. The first player sitting at the bus stop is a normal business person, mom, or whatever character might be waiting for the bus.
4. Create a line of players on the side waiting to enter the scene.

Game Play
The next player who enters the scene chooses a character whose only objective is to get this first player to leave. Obviously being gross or weird can be quite effective. For example, the entering player is coughing and sniffling and sits down next to the person at the bus stop. They turn and say hi to the person and they sneeze onto the players shoulder. Encourage the entering players to also try other subtle ways to make this happen. This can be done with interesting character choices. Maybe a punk rocker, a vampire, or an obnoxious sports fan. When the first player leaves the entering player moves over one seat and becomes the new "normal" person and a new scene starts.

Variation
Choose other places where people would be waiting. A doctor's office, the department of Motor Vehicles, waiting for an elevator, or perhaps being in an elevator.

Teaching Points
Encourage the players to think of more subtle ways to get players to leave. Also, you may have to remind the "normal" person to eventually leave, because that is the intention of the game. Perhaps discuss and set some guidelines around touch as this game lends itself to invading other people's space.

Improv Performance Structures

CELEBRITY DATING GAME
(4 or 5 Players)

A simple and fun guessing game.

Set Up
1. Set up four chairs in front of the audience.
2. These chairs represent the three chairs of the contestants on the dating game show with the other chair put off just a bit to the side for the person seeking a date.
3. The interviewer and the person seeking the date goes off stage where they can't hear.
4. Ask the audience for suggestions as to what famous celebrity, past, present, or fictional, that each of the three dating game guests will embody.
5. For example, one person is Lebron James, one Lady Gaga, and one Mickey Mouse.
6. They answer the questions in the way they feel that character would respond.

Game Play:
The interviewer now comes back in and the host of the game show introduces them. The interviewer begins asking questions of each dating contestant. Contestant number one, "On our first date, where would you take me?" Number two, "If we were both animals what animals would we be and why?" Contestant number three, "What is your favorite romantic music that you would play to get me in the mood?"

The fun for the interviewee, as they get a sense of who the characters are, is to ask questions that might further reveal who they are. The interviewer might also ask the same question for each contestant. At a certain point, end the questioning and have the interviewee guess who the characters are.

Variations
The moderator or host of the show is an optional choice to have in the game. The game can just begin with the interviewee asking questions.

Another variation is to make it a game of dating game quirks. Each prospective date rather than be a celebrity are given quirks they must act out and the interviewee must guess what their quirk is through the standard asking of dating game questions.

The Heart of Play

Teaching Points

In traditional improv the actors on stage take whatever choice the audience offers and act that out. However, when playing with beginning improvisers I like to check in with the actors to see if they know who that celebrity is that is being suggested for them, and if they have a sense of how to play that character. If not, choose a new celebrity.

> To be playful and serious at the same time is not only possible, but it defines the ideal mental condition,
>
> John Dewey

Improv Performance Structures

CHARACTER BUS

This game is simple and designed to have lots of players, so it's great for beginning improvisers.

Set Up
1. Imagine there is a bus, so set up a chair for the driver.
2. Next set up two more rows of chairs. Two sets of two chairs on each side of the aisle of the bus just behind the driver's seat.
3. Then one last row at the back of the bus with four or five chairs.
4. Start with one bus driver in the first seat.

Game Play
One player is in the driver's seat, acting like a normal bus driver. As the game begins one player comes onto the bus embodying a character. Perhaps it is a football coach, all revved up for the big game. The driver immediately picks up this energy, mirroring it and acts like a coach. Two coaches acting all amped, and the entering player now takes a seat on the bus. After ten seconds or so of these two sharing some dialogue, and embodying the physicality and emotions of that character a new character comes thru the door of a bus. Ahh, it's an old lady sputtering about her son who hasn't called in two months. Now both previous characters immediately become old people sputtering about their ungrateful children. Next it might be a cheerleader, so everyone acts like cheerleaders, then perhaps next a mother about to give birth to a baby...

Variations
See the game, Emotional Taxi.

Teaching Points
This game is all about emphasizing the physicality and emotionality of a character, and how fun it is to mirror what is happening. Encourage the players to fully express and even exaggerate the character they are portraying.

It's also an exercise in flowing from one emotion, right into another.

The Heart of Play

EMOTIONAL TAXI

A great fast-moving game that helps the players realize that it is often more the emotion that is important in a scene, rather than the dialogue.

Set Up
1. Place four chairs on the stage with two chairs behind the other two thus representing a taxi.
2. Place three people in chairs with the seat behind the driver's side in the back left empty. The first three people just act normally, maybe engaging in a bit of dialogue.
3. The fourth person (let's call her Sue) is standing off to the side of the taxi, on the side that has the empty chair.

Game Play
Sue flags the taxi, goes over, opens the car door, and enters very emotionally. Dialogue is okay, but it is the emotion that is the key. For example, she is crying hysterically. Everyone immediately picks up on that emotion and they too start becoming upset. Sue might say, "My dog died last night, and I had her cremated and her ashes are in this urn." Another player might say, "My cat is really sick…" The taxi driver might say, "I ran over a raccoon last night…" And they are all sad about it. Ding! The director ends the scene after only 20 to 30 seconds and then everyone moves one seat counterclockwise with the driver exiting the scene and a new player flags the taxi for a ride, who enters with a new emotion, perhaps really scared. "I am being followed, go, go, go. Drive!" Everyone becomes paranoid, looking around to see if they are being followed…

Variations
Allow a more involved scene to develop. Or put four people in the taxi and give them a scene. You are four clowns on your way to the circus. You are four fans of Justin Bieber on your way to his concert.

Teaching Points
It's all about the emotion. So, less dialogue, and more emotion.

Improv Performance Structures

EXPERTS

A simple structure that emphasizes making your partner look good.

Set Up
1. Pick a couple of players. One is the expert, the other the interviewer.
2. Best when first playing for the faciitator to demonstrate how to be a supportive interviewer.
3. Have the audience pick the interviewee's expertise.
4. They are an expert on belly-button lint..

Game Play
The interviewer begins, "Good afternoon I'm Timothy Smartpants, welcome to the show. Today's guest is Dr. Shirley Tummystock. Dr. Tummystock, you are the world's foremost expert on belly button lint. So glad to have you here." "Thank you for having me."

"Doctor, in reading your book, *101 Uses for Belly Button Lint*, I loved the story about when you were seven years old, and you used to take a pair of tweezers and pull the lint out of your mom's belly button and used it. Oh I'll let you share that story yourself."

"Yes I used to take my Mom's belly button lint and use it as a pillow for the dolls in my dollhouse..."

The interviewer needs to make good offers to the interviewee, to make it easy for them to respond. After a few questions and answers, open it up to the "studio audience" for more questions.

Variations
Alien Experts. The same game as experts, but now the expert is an alien and speaks only in an alien gibberish language, so it is up to the interviewer to translate what it is the extra terrestrial is speaking.

Teaching Points
The interviewer offers high status to the interviewee, They make eye contact, angling their chair, leaning in a bit thus making the interviewee the focus of attention and making offers that are easy to work with thus making the interviewee look good.

The Heart of Play

FAIRY TALE

One of my favorite improv games.

Set Up
1. Place four chairs set up side by side in the performance area, and ask for four volunteers to come up and take a seat.
2. Another person is the director and sits on the floor in front of the four chairs to direct the story that is about to be told.
3. The four players will be telling a common fairy tale that the audience chooses.
4. Make sure the four volunteers know the story suggested.
5. Now have the audience pick a character-style for each of the four volunteers to use in telling the story, such as a valley girl, an evangelical preacher, a rap artist, and a nerd. Make sure that they feel they can embody that character that the audience has chosen for them.

Game Play
To start the game, the director points to a player who begins telling the tale. After a sentence or two, by putting up a hand in a stop gesture and then points to the next character to continue the story from that point. It is best for the director to go straight across the first time, and then pick and choose which character might be best to tell the next piece of the story. Remind the characters to tell the story as the fairy tale goes, to the best of their memory, but in their unique style of diction.

Variation
Have the players make up their own fariy tale and tell it from the point of view of these unique characters. Take suggestions form the audience as to what is the fairy tale. Perhas it is "glenda the good vampire."

Teaching Points
As a director you may have to remind them to move the story along and then to bring it to an end.

Improv Performance Structures

FREEZE TAG

A very simple and yet a very advanced game.

Set up
1. Bring two players up on stage.
2. Take suggestions form the audience. Where are they, what is their relationship, what is the problem that is existing. Two farmers whose cows are not producing milk.
3. The scene starts and then any players in the audience member can yell, "Freeze."

Game play
The person that yelled freeze now enters the scene tags one person and that person leaves the scene. The tagger takes the exact pose of that person and starts a brand new scene. For example one person is kneeling down looking at the cow's udders. One player at a time yells Freeze, comes in tags the kneeling person out, and then declares who they are. For example, "Honey we have been dating for ten years and I know I have commitment issues, but will you marry me." "Yes I will, however only if you give me a piggyback ride down this mountain because I have my best shoes on and I wasn't prepared to hike all the way up this mountain. Nice place to ask me to marry you though." And just as this person is about to climb on their back someone yells freeze. Hmm, what will this scene become?

Variations
Allow players to say Freeze and just join the scene as a third person. Have them mirror or join in whatever pose is frozen and proceed to change the scene.

Teaching points
When players first play this game, if they haven't learned the skills of naming their relationship, their character and where they are, this game may not go as well as it can. Also encourage players not to ask questions. Make statements whenever possible. Also encourage players to not yell Freeze too often, meaning give the scene a minute or so seconds to develop. Also encourage players to yell freeze without even knowing what that the pose they see that made them yell freeze. They don't even know what character they are going to choose as they walk in. Just take the pose, and in that moment let the posture inform who they are, what they are doing and what is their relationship to the other players.

The Heart of Play

GIBBERISH POET

Oh what a simple and fun game. Great to play after you have led some basic gibberish games.

Set Up
1. Invite two players up to the stage.
2. One of the players is a world-famous poet, and the other is a translator.
3. The translator sets the scenario as at a cafe, a slam poetry event, or a party—being the host and translator.

Game Play

Introduce the poet with a fictional name from a far away place that speaks an obscure language. For example, "Hi, I am Scott Armstrong and welcome to the Improv Play Cafe. For tonight's poetry extravaganza, joining us from a little country between Mongolia and Russia that no one has ever heard of before, Olga Kolaska is here to share some amazing poetry."

The translator perhaps adds a little more introduction, and then directs the poet to begin. The poet makes a statement in Gibberish. "Goobasneika, Olga, commmistika, speelatka arviesh."

The translator says, "My name is Olga, the title of this poem is Darkness comes before the light." "Gishma, keena tooffa." The translator says, "I am afraid of the dark." And on it continues.

Variations

Just do it in partners or small group, each person taking a turn being the poet, the other the translator, and whoever else the small audience. You could even do it in a classroom with writing. One person speaks gibberish and the rest of the class writes down what is being said and then everyone can share their translations.

Teaching Points

Remind the players to really listen to each other. As the poet speaks, the translator wants to feel into the emotion and physical expression of the other actor. Then, in turn, as the translator translates, the poet takes that and lets it inform the next bit of gibberish. It's a wonderful exchange.

Improv Performance Structures

GUESS THE EXPERT

Fun for the audience as they are an integral part of the scene.

Set Up
1. One person is chosen to go out of the room.
2. The group then decides on this person's area of expertise. Take suggestions and decide what the guest be an expert of.
3. The more experienced the group the more obscure or bizarre the expertise can be.
4. Let's say the group decides this person is an expert on peanut butter and jelly sandwiches.

Game Play
The guesser comes in and the audience raises their hands if they have a question, and the expert chooses a person to ask a question. The fun is for the audience to slowly reveal clues. The first question could be, how did you get started in this? "Well, my dad turned me on to this when I was a boy." Next question, "I can imagine you have become really keen on the different textures people like, what kind do you prefer?" The experts just offers an answer, "I like smooth ones." Next question, "I hear that you grew up in Georgia, I am sure this impacted your becoming an expert in this field. Did you ever meet Jimmy Carter?"

"Yes, he is my dad's good friend and we would visit him often at his farm." This gets laughs and applause from the audience in confirmation that this is a good answer.

"Well when I was growing up and going to school, bullies would beat me up and take mine from me. Did that ever happen to you?"

Finally, someone may ask something more revealing. "I understand Smuckers and Jiffy are both sponsors of your work. Is that right?"

"Yes, I am an expert on peanut butter and jelly sandwiches..."

Everyone applauds wildly when the area of expertise is named.

Teaching Points
The key to this game is actually the audience being clever and then step by step being helpful with their questions.

The Heart of Play

NAME THE MOVEMENT

Great for teaching the concept of declaring your character (who you are, what you are doing, and why you are doing it).

Set Up
1. Bring four or five players up to the front and have them line up.
2. One player steps forward. They will be the first person who starts the first movement.
3. This player launches into a repetitive physical movement.

Game Play
One person in the line now steps forward and begins to mirror that same movement. This player's responsibility is to name the movement and declare the relationship of both characters. Such as, "Hey Mom, I love baking cakes with you, won't Dad be surprised with his party tonight." "Yes darling, now beat that frosting faster." "Here Mom, taste it. I think it's perfect." Then maybe she slaps it on her mom's nose. End scene.

Now the first-person steps back into the line and the player who came in second starts with a whole new motion to start a new scene. It is basically a three-line scene.

Variations
Let the scene go on longer and see what develops. Or just do it with partners as a warm-up game.

Teaching Points
This game offers a couple of simple lessons for improvisers to learn. One is trust your physical movement. Do a motion that is repetitive, and dialogue will come from that. Secondly a fundamental skill in traditonal perfomance improv is to take the responsibility for naming the action and your relationship to the other players as you enter a scene.

Improv Performance Structures

NEW CHOICE

A great opportunity for the actors to think on their feet.

Set Up
1. Pick a couple of players to come up and then the group selects a scene for them to be in.
2. Another person is chosen to be the director.

Game Play

The scene begins and at certain points the director yells out, "New Choice." Whereupon, the actor who made the last statement must make a new choice. For example, the scene begins with two friends out by the lake camping. "Wow, looks I caught a five-pound Trout—" New Choice. "Wow, I snagged my hook on a log—" New Choice. "Wow, I'm going to take off all my clothes and go skinny dipping..." and on the scene goes from there.

The director continues offering "New Choice" whenever it is deemed appropriate to increase the fun and create a pleasing rhythm.

Variations

Instead of "New Choice," use the phrase, "No, you didn't." One person begins a story monologue. Another person acts as the director. Encourage them to make it action oriented. "The alarm clock went off and I realized I was late for work. I jumped out of bed and into the shower—"

The director interrupts with, "No you didn't."

"I kissed my wife on the cheek—"

"No you didn't."

"I jumped out of bed and stepped on the cat..." and on the story goes.

Teaching Points

Even though saying "Yes and" is the guiding principle of improv and saying "New Choice" is sort of like saying "No" to that person's first impulse, it's done in a playful and constructive way as an exercise in thinking quickly on your feet. Enocurage the players to trust their next thought, as you dig deeper into the possibilities.

The Heart of Play

ONE WORD POEM

Another great example of supporting your fellow players and daring to be average.

Set Up
1. Ask for some volunteers who will line up on the side of the stage or performance area.
2. They will be walking out to center stage and delivering a one-word poem.
3. Have one person be the emcee in the role of announcing who is coming up to deliver their one-word masterpiece.
4. Audience, you have a very important role in this game. When the one word poem is offered you go crazy because you feel it is the best poem you have ever heard.

Game Play
The emcee announces the first performer, who walks out and delivers their one-word poem. For example, "We have straight from Siberia, Sergei Kolenkov." Sergei staggers to center stage looks at the audience and says, "Vodka!" The audience goes crazy. Then the next performer steps up and the emcee announces, "Joe from Green Bay Wisconsin." And Joe walks forward and says in a really proud and loud voice, "Hike!" Again, the audience goes crazy. It's up to each performer to enact their word in the way they wish to portray it.

Variations
The performers announce themselves. Or perhaps it is a two word poem.

Teaching Points
Coach the performers to step to center stage, take a good long moment and be present before they speak their one-word poem. This game is really all about the audience. No matter how simple or average the one-word poem is, the audience's job is to cheer wildly. In an improv class, it is vitally important that the audience is offering unconditional support for their fellow players. So in any improv class this a great game to play early on to emphasize this point. Everyone in the group is always offering unconditional support to each other. Mistakes are okay. There are no wrong chioces in improv.

Improv Performance Structures

PARTY QUIRKS

An old stand-by favorite on the show Whose Line is it Anyway.

Set up
1. One player is chosen as the host of the party.
2. Three or Four players are chosen as guests.
3. The host leaves the room as the guests are then given unique quirks that they will portray as they take turns ringing the doorbell and entering the party.
4. Have the quirks written on pieces of paper and the players read their quirks so the audience knows what they are.

Game Play
The host starts by acting out setting up the party scene. A table for drinks, messing with the stereo, etc. A player rings the doorbell, the host opens the door and the player enters acting out their quirk, perhaps not so blatantly at first. The host interacts with them improvisationally. Another player rings the doorbell and the scene continues with each player, one at a time, entering the party.

The host can guess what their quirk is at any appropriate moment.

Teaching Points
Choose quirks that will be fun to act out, and perhaps have a physical component. The creativity for this is endless. "You are someone who experiences more and more gravity." "You are afraid of elbows." "You are a recently graduated therapist looking for new clients." "You are a 5 year old, lost, and looking for your Mom." "You believe the world is about to end." "You only speak in three-word sentences."

Write out a number of quirks beforehand. Have the players pick one. If a player isn't sure how to act it out give them a different one. During the game, the host may need some clues to guess all the quirks.

Variation
Take suggestions from the audience at the start of the game for the actors to portray.

The Heart of Play

SOAP BOX SYMPHONY

We all have pet peeves. Here is an opportunity for players to get up on their "soap box" and speak out about them, maybe turning mayhem into music.

Set Up
1. Assign someone as the conductor.
2. Choose four volunteers to come up in front of the group.
3. Ask the audience for things that people like to get worked up about, i.e., vexations, and assign one to each player. For example, littering, tailgating, potholes, and old Tupperware.

Game Play
Player 1 having been given littering as the focus of the polemic, they take 30 seconds and pontificate loudly with enthusiastic disgust against it. Then the next person is given tailgating, or texting while driving, or anything really and they polemicize for thirty seconds until each player has been given their topic and spoken for thirty seconds. Now the conductor gets to choose who speaks when and at what volume by giving louder or softer signals and when to stop and start as a conductor would in a symphony with perhaps all speaking at one time by the end. The Soap box symphony.

Variations
Create a larger symphony, adding in extra players who in sounds like crying, laughing, cheering, etc.

Teaching Points
Best to demonstrate with yourself, the facilitator, as the first conductor, and then do the game again and choose from the players. Pet peeves lend nicely to the idea of having an emotional investment in a scene. When players have a strong opinion about something, it makes it easier for other players to react to a situation in a scene.

Improv Performance Structures

SLIDE SHOW

A game that involves fun movement.

Set Up
1. Choose two people to be the hosts of the party.
2. They have invited everyone here to their slide show, their pictures of their recent vacation, adventure or event. Take suggestions from the audience as to what kind of event it was. A safari. A trip to New York City. Their wedding anniversary...
3. Now invite four or five volunteers to be the subjects of the photo slideshow. Demonstrate that when a host says, "Click", it is time for the players to move for three or four seconds, and then come to a frozen position.

Game Play
The hosts stand to the side, or if it is a small group they can be sitting as if everyone in the audience is sitting in their living room. "Hi everyone, thanks for coming tonight. Bob and I are so excited to show you our photos from our safari."

"Okay here is our first slide. Click."

The models up front move and freeze. "Oh, look honey, that is where you tripped getting off the plane and fell on your face. Look there is the pilot laughing while the stewardess kneels beside you to see how you are."

"Click." The players move again and then freeze... "Look, this is where a monkey comes up and steals your purse."

And on it goes.

Teaching Points
Remind the movers to move and choose a pose relatively quickly. Let the hosts interpret what the collection of poses mean. Obviously, the subject material can effect the poses they make, however, best to just take positions that are in relationship to the other players.

The Heart of Play

STORY, STORY, DIE
5 Players

A storytelling game for four players with one director.

Set Up
1. The players are seated in chairs.
2. Ask for suggestions form the audience for a subject to tell a story about.
3. The director sits on the floor in front of the four players.

Game Play
The director point to a person, who then begins the story. When the director puts a hand up in a Stop signal, that player immediately stops, and the director points to another person, and that player immediately picks the story up from that exact point. No repeating of words and no hesitation. If a person doesn't immediately pick the story up, or repeats a word, then the audience and/or director will say, "Die."

Then the audience makes a suggestion on how this person must act out their death. For example, die by one thousand kisses from an elephant. So they act that out quickly, and then they leave the stage. The story picks up right where it left off. Sometimes because there is this interrruption of the dying player, the director, or the audience can remind eveyone of the last statement. The director continues directing the players to tell the story until there is only one person remaining, who brings the story to a conclusion.

Variations
Play the game without eliminating anyone. Or skip the part of dying just tell the story quickly with anyone making mistakes being eliminated.

Teaching Points
This would only be a game you play with a group that has been together and has some trust, since it involves elimination.

Improv Performance Structures

STORY STYLE REPLAY

A fun way for players to try on different ways to act out a character by replaying a scene.

Set Up
1. Pick two or three players to come up front.
2. Ask the audience to shout out movie/theater styles, such as horror, comedy, western, melodrama, soap opera, musical, etc.
3. Take suggestions from the audience as to who, what, where they are and what problem they must move toward solving. For example, you are newlyweds with a teen stepson, living in an old house that has leaks in the dining room, and it's raining outside, and guests are coming over for dinner...

Game Play
Have the players act out the scene until it reaches something like an endpoint, and the director yells cut! Now, give the players a movie style to play out, "Horror!" And they do the same scene they just did in that style. It's important for the players to capture the essence of the scene in that style. They don't have to say exactly the same things they said the first time, but should play out the same action choices in that new theater style. Then choose another movie style, perhaps "Science Fiction."

Variations
As on the show Whose Line is it Anyway, the director comes in and yells cut and has them do the same scene in another way the director is making up on the spot. Do it like you are three motorcycle gang members. Do it as if you have just escaped from prison. Or choose an emotion. Do the scene with anger, or sadness, and replay that scene fully in that emotion.

Teaching Points
This takes the skill of knowing how to be in a character. Being more challenging, it is also more fun and exhilarating and worth the effort.

The Heart of Play

STRING OF PEARLS

A great game for lot's of participation. From Martin De Maat.

Set Up
1. We are going to create a story together, one phrase at a time.
2. Ask for three volunteers to come up and stand in a line.
3. One person at the beginning, one at the end, and one in the middle, leaving enough room in between for another six or more people to come up and join the line.
4. Ask the group what a great first line of a story is. "It was a dark and stormy night," or, "Sue screamed when the door opened."
5. The first person in line will always say that line.
6. Then let's choose an ending line of a story.
7. "The sun sets as they looked deeply into each other eyes."
8. The person at the end of the line always says that line.
9. Now let's choose a line for the person in the middle.
10. "Doug looked at his watch and realized he was going to be late."
11. And that person always say that line.

Game Play

One person at a time to comes up and fills in the line wherever they feel it is appropriate. Whenever one person joins the line each person in order says their line. Let's say the first person comes up and stands right next to the middle person and says. "Doug was busy playing video games on his computer and had forgotten about the time." So then the string would look like, "Sue screamed when she opened the door." "Doug was busy playing the video game and had forgotten about the time... Doug looked at his watch and realized he was going to be late." "The sun set as they looked deeply into each other eyes."

So maybe the next person comes up and stands next to the first person and says "She thought it was going to be Doug—instead it was her mother in law whom she thought was dead." And on it goes until there is a coherent story going down the line.

Teaching Points

This game gets lots of people involved and helps players learn how to build a story. Encourage dramatic emphasis in delivering their line.

Improv Performance Structures

TEN SECOND STORY

A fun way to focus on being concise.

Set up
1. Pick three players to come up and be in the scene.
2. Ask the audience for suggestions about who are our characters, where they are, and what problem they are struggling with. For example, a couple on their honeymoon, driving in the English countryside, and they get a flat tire...
3. Start with two players on stage with the third waiting in the wings.

Game Play
As the scene unfolds and the problem is established, the third player enters to help resolve the situation. Try to reach a conclusion in about two minutes. Now explain to the players that they must do their best to replay the story in one minute. Perhaps give them a time check half way through. Time! Now tell them to do it again in 30 seconds. Then, finally, try to do it again in ten seconds.

Variations
The times are arbitrary, so play around with your own. Can the players get it done in three seconds? Pick a common fairy tale to retell in one minute, and then thirty seconds, fifteen, and do a five second challenge.

Teaching Points
After playing once, ask the players what the key memorable points and lines of that previous story were. This will inform the next time they play, as everyone reflects on what were the key lines and the key actions. It is often those simple yet clear choices that stand out and when the ten second story is told you will see which elements really stood out.

The Heart of Play

THREE HEADED EXPERT

This game is a great follow up game to One Word Story.

Set Up
1. Bring three people up and have them sit on chairs close together, joined as one three-headed expert.
2. They can only speak one word at a time.
3. As the game is explained, let the three-headed expert know that if any one of them feels that they have answered the question fully they can say, "Next question" and the other two heads immediately pick up on it so together all three of them say, "Next Question," in unison.
5. Another person can be the narrator/interviewer/host.

Game Play
"Good evening ladies and Gentlemen. Welcome to the Dandy Dana Show. I have here with me the world's foremost expert on virtually everything. Doctor please introduce yourself."

(Player 1) "Hello" (Player 2) "I" (Player 3) "Am" (Player 1) "Doctor" (Player 2) "Joseph" (Player 3) "Hightower."

"Well Dr. Hightower, so good to have you here. I know we have many questions from our studio audience... Over there, what is your question for Dr. Hightower."

Player from the audience, "Why does chocolate taste so good."

The three-headed expert. "Because..." "It..." "Has..." "Sugar...." "NEXT QUESTION..."

Teaching Points
You can add an element of fun to the game and cover the three people with a blanket and then it looks like they have one body. Or you can call it the alien or mutant expert who happens to have three heads.

Improv Performance Structures

WHY WERE YOU LATE?

A fun game that is great for miming and group participation.

Set Up
1. One player is chosen to be the guesser, and then leaves so they cannot hear what the group is deciding as to why this person is late for work.
2. One person is chosen to be the boss and will be quizzing and questioning the guesser. Behind the boss stand two other players who are the workers.
3. First thing the group decides is where do the players work. Say for example, it is a pizza parlor. The two workers are behind acting as if they are making pizzas.
4. So now the group decides why was this person late.
5. They decide that the guesser was mugged by a guerrilla and had his wallet stolen. He had to chase the guerrilla down and wrestle him to get his wallet back.
6. Also have the group choose a really unusual mode of transportation that the guesser has to take to get back to work. Perhaps riding an elephant, or riding a unicycle.

Game Play

The guesser comes in and the boss asks, "Why were you late? You know we have a big pizza order every Friday night." Meanwhile, behind the boss the two workers start acting out the scenario of the guesser being mugged by a guerrilla. The boss will periodically turn around and chastise the players for not doing their jobs, and they have to do their best not to get caught acting things out. The boss may even fire a player and a new volunteer can jump in and take their place. The guesser should just keep on guessing.

The boss can help them out by giving clues, maybe saying something like, "Hey, stop monkeying around with me. Why were you late?" The audience can let the guesser know through applause when they are getting closer, and finally when they have gotten the answer.

Variations

Have some volunteers just off stage so the boss can feel free to fire as many workers as necessary. Also, someone can phone in to the boss and make clever suggestions in the guise of a phone call. Ring, ring, "Hi, I would like to place a large order of pizzas for the circus that just arrived. How about thirty pizzas, and

The Heart of Play

could you put bananas on ten of them? We have some hungry primates over here."

Teaching points

A good idea for the first boss to be an experienced player, or you as the teacher, to model making good suggestions and helping the guesser move towards a successful conclusion.

> Play so that you may be serious.
>
> Anacharsis

Games Manual

Resources

Books on Play, Education and Parenting

Parenting for Peace, by Marcy Axness, Ph.D.; First Sentient Publications; edition 2012

Play, by Stuart Brown, M.D., with Christopher Vaughn; Avery; 2009

Playful Parenting, by Lawrence J. Cohen, Ph.D.; Random House Publishing; 2001

Spark, by John J. Ratey, M.D., with Eric Hagerman; Little Brown & Company; 2008

The Way of Mindful Education, by Daniel Rechtschaffen; W. W. Norton & Company; 2014

Whole Brain Child, by Dan J. Siegel, M.D. and Tina Payne Bryson, Ph.D.; Delacorte Press; 2011

Improv Books

Improv Wisdom, by Patrica Ryan Madson; Bell Tower of Random House; 2005

Playing Along, by Izzy Gessel; Whole Person Associates; 1997

Zoomy Zoomy, by Hannah Fox; Tusitala Publishing; 2010

Nurtured Heart Approach Books and Resources

Transforming the Difficult Child, by Howard Glasser and Jennifer Easley; Nurtured Heart Publications; 1999

Igniting Greatness, by Howard Glasser and Melissa Block; Center of the Difficult Child; 2015

The Heart of Play

Notching Up the Nurtured Heart Approach, by Howard Glasser and Melissa Lynn Block; Brigham Distributing; 2011

Play Equipment

Epic Toys — In a number of games were mentioned foam swords. The go to resource is from my friend "Shaggy" Aaaron Hoffer-Perkins www.epictoys.com

S&S worldwide — One the better catalog companies for PE equipment and much more. www.ssww.com

Play Organizations

Collaborative.org Massachusetts Educational Website — A wonderful set of standards for social emotional learning thru play http://www.collaborative.org/programs/early-childhood

Eastern Cooperative Recreation School — A recreational collaborative that provides intergenerational retreats for over seventy-five years resulting in an incredible amount of fun for everyone, www.ecrs.org

Hand in Hand Parenting — Play-oriented resource for parents, www.handinhandparenting.org (650) 322-5323

Great Activities Publishing Company — Great games for elementary educators, www.greatactivitiesonline.com, (800) 927-0682

Life is Good Playmakers — Wonderfully affordable training's for front line caretakers of young children, www.lifeisgood.com, (503) 227-0803

Playmeo — A great resource to see games that are video taped and how to lead them

Playworks — An organization helping to restructure recess in all major metropolitan areas, www.playworksinc.com, (864) 814-2230

Resources

Project Adventure — The premier experiential learning organization. Great resource for trainings and books on team-building, www.project-adventure.org, (978) 542-4800

ReTribe — Great rites of passage programs for teens, www.retribe.org, (802) 371-5027

The Wayfinder Experience — A fantasy-role-playing theater camp for teens, based on the program originated by Howard Moody and Brian Allison, www.wayfinder-experience.com, (845) 481-0776

Also I highly recommend everyone who works with children from age 3–8 to take a training with Life is Good Playmakers. Also go the web site for the Great Activities Publishing company as there is wealth of resources there for this age group.

The Heart of Play

For workshops from play specialist Howard Moody, please visit www.howardmoody.com

Howard Moody

Index of Games

Across The Great Divide	202
Airport	204
All Hands on Deck (grades 2 +)	107
Alphabet Race	46
Animal Catcher	109
Annihilation	158
Asteroids	127
A to Z	252
Back Hand Tag	145
Balloon Frantic	206
Balloon Volleyball	47
Behavior Modification	83
Big Words	207
Birthday Line-Up (& Other Line-ups)	48
Birthdays	49
Blind Run	170
Blind Walk	171
Blob Tag	146
Boom Chicago	265
Boop	50
Braak Whiff	51
British Bulldog	159
Bumpity, Bump, Bump	37
Bus Stop	266
Car and Driver	172
Car Wash	110
Celebrity	234
Celebrity Dating Game	267
Character Bus	269
Circle Crossing	173
Come Along	84

The Heart of Play

Commonalities	52
Concerns and Appreciations	224
Consensus	53
Core Group Formation	85
Council Process	228
Countdown: Shake It Up	186
Count Ten	86
Create a Tableaux	55
Creation Game	56
Dictionary	235
Distraction Game	187
Don't Touch Me	208
Dragon Dodgeball	128
Elbow Tag	147
Electric Fence	209
Elephant / Rabbit / Palm Tree	87
Elves / Giants / Wizards	150
Elves & Wizards Tag	148
Emotional Taxi	270
Empty Vessel	236
Enemy / Ally	188
Esti Run	129
Everybody's It	149
Evil Magician	57
Evolution	59
Experts	271
Fairy Tale	272
FFEACH	60
Fire On the Mountain	89
Foam Sword Fencing	160
Fooop	130
Four Changes	62
Four Changes	189
Four Corner Relay	131
Four Corners	63
Free Association	237

Index of Games

Freeze Dance	190
Freeze Tag	273
Funny Face Hot Potato Catch	111
Ga - Ga	133
Gibberish Conversation and Translator	238
Gibberish Poet	274
Gold Rush	135
Gotcha	64
Gratitude Ball	219
Groove-a-liscious	90
Group Juggle	92
Guess the Expert	275
Guide and Exchange	174
Have You Ever	93
Ho	95
Hog Call	65
Hoop the Circle	210
Hospital Tag	152
How's Yours?	66
Hug Tag	153
Human Camera	175
Human Machine	96
Human Spring	67
Human Statues	98
Hunter / Hunted	176
Hurricane	112
I am a Tree	253
I Could Tell You About…	220
If You Really Knew Me…	227
In Plain View	68
In the Manner of The Adverb	254
In the Present Moment I am Aware of…	221
Introduce A New Friend	38
Invisible Tug of War	239
Jump In, Jump Out	69
Knots	70

The Heart of Play

Lap Sit	211
Lemonade	113
Lightning Rounds	226
Magic 7 / 11	72
Many Ways to Get There	114
Memory Loss	256
Messy Backyard	115
Mirroring	192
Mirroring	240
Moonball	136
Move and Shake it up	117
Movement exchange	241
Move To Open Spaces / Follow Your Leader	191
Moving Through Space	242
Multiple Person Keep Away	138
Multiple Steal the Bacon	137
Musical Hugs	193
Mutant Mingle	257
Name and Movement and Alliteration	40
Name & Movement Replay	39
Name the Movement	276
Name the Wrong Thing	243
Name Whip	41
New Choice	277
Night at the Museum	73
No, No, No, You Mean	74
Octopus	118
Ogre's Treasure	213
One Breath Run	194
One Word Poem	278
One Word Story	258
Ooh-Aah	99
Order up	75
Overload	195
Pairs tag	154
Party Quirks	279

Index of Games

Pass A Funny Face	119
Pass the Clap	101
Pass the Imaginary Object	244
Pass The Pulse	196
Pass the Sound and Movement	102
Present a Gift	259
Props	260
Prui	177
Quick Line-Up	76
Rain	178
Rhyme Mime	245
Robots	77
Scream Circle	103
Scream Run	139
Set em Up / Knock em Down	120
Shake and Blither	197
Shake and Stop	198
Silent Jail-ball	140
Sing your name	42
Slap Pass	104
Slide Show	281
Smaug's Jewels	161
Snakes	121
Snowball Hug Tag	155
Soap Box Symphony	280
Speak About One Thing	222
Special Object Scavenger Hunt	180
Speed Juggle	214
Stand Off	78
Star Wars Dodgeball	141
Story Circle	261
Story, Story, Die	282
Story Style replay	283
String Of Pearls	284
Support a Friend	182
Swat Tag	162

The Heart of Play

Team Ro-Sham-Bo	79
Ten Second Story	285
The Clock	216
The Cool Breeze Blows for Anyone Who	122
Three Headed Expert	286
Tiger/Fireworks/Person	80
Toss a Name Game	43
Touch Blue and Freeze	81
Triangle Tag	156
Two or three person scenes	262
Vampire Hunt	164
Vegetarianism	105
WAH	246
Walk, Stop, Wiggle, Sit	199
What Are you Doing?	247
What's in the Box?	263
What Time is it Mr. Fox or Mrs. Fox	123
Where Am I?	248
Who Changed the Motion?	124
Why were you late?	287
Willow in the Wind	183
Wink	166
Yes, And…	249
Yes, Let's…	250
Yogi tag – Dho, dho, dho	167
You Are Susan!	44

Games Manual

Thanks for playing!
Please visit www.howardmoody.com
and keep the ball bouncing.

The Heart of Play

Made in the USA
Middletown, DE
05 January 2024